How to create a
JARDIN
PAYSAN

How to create a JARDIN PAYSAN
BY LOUISE RANCK

Translated from French by Paul Carslake, with additional translation by Joshua Jordan, revised and edited by Jean-Yves Gilg.
Original title: Le Jardin Paysan
Copyright November 2002 by Éditions du Rouergue, parc Saint-Joseph BP 3522, 12035 RODEZ Cedex 9 (France)

Horticultural consultant (English edition): Catherine Gamble
CNG Garden Design, www.cngdesign.co.uk

Published by Ascent Publishing Ltd
2 Sugar Brook Court
Aston Road, Bromsgrove
Worcestershire
B60 3EX

ISBN 0-9544669-5-0

First published in the United Kingdom by Ascent Publishing Limited, April 2005

Colour reproduction by Wyndeham Argent
Printed and bound in China by Hanway Press Ltd

Internet: www.renovationfrance.net
Email: renovation@centaur.co.uk

How to create a
JARDIN
PAYSAN

LOUISE RANCK

Contents

Contents

Acknowledgements

Ascent Publishing Ltd are proud to be publishing the English edition of 'Le Jardin paysan', originally published in French by Editions du Rouergue. Our warmest thanks to: Judy Sherren, Ian and Mary Roberts, Peter and Judith Harris, Laura Hudson and Penton Spring for reviewing this edition of the book and for their kind and constructive comments; to Catherine Gamble, for bringing her perspective as a qualified garden designer working both in Britain and France and for her enthusiastic commitment to the project; to Jackie Canham for her careful proof-reading; and to Estelle Kalp for creating an inspired design for the book and for her patience throughout.

Louise Ranck is most grateful to Julien Fouin, who has encouraged her and supported her through the writing of the book, and to Michel Fontaine, who suggested the idea and allowed her to take it through to completion at Maisons Paysannes de France. Many thanks also to Pierre Robert, who provided the plant drawings, for his patience and kindness and to Nathalie Locoste and Michel Fontaine for the practical diagrams; to Didier Bouillon, Patrice Gayou, Pierre Rougier, Denise Guillemot and Collette Gouvion for their careful proof-reading; to Serge and Brigitte Lapouge at the Jardins de l'Albarède, Nathalie Becq, at the Jardin de campagne, Mr and Mrs Cornet, and Odette Lapeyre, at the Jardin ethno-botanique d'Antignac, for their warm welcome; and finally to Mr and Mrs de Saint-Wandrille, Marie-France Piel and Alan Mousquey, Guy Clénet, at Maisons Paysannes de Vendée, Patrick Petit, Jean Mougin, l'Ecomusée d'Alsace, Dominique Firbal, Annick Stein, le Jardin de Sauveterre, Jean-Claude Sonnet, l'Atelier Reeb, Philippe Roussille and Denise Baccara-Louis, for kindly allowing us to use their photographs. Louise Ranck is particularly grateful to Guy Lavogez and would also like to thank Danielle Dastugue and the publishing team at Editions du Rouergue for their precious support.

Maisons Paysannes de France

For the past thirty five years, Maisons Paysannes de France (MPF) has been working for the protection of the countryside and rural heritage. Maisons Paysannes de France believes that rural gardens are just as important as buildings in terms of rural heritage and kindly sponsored the original French edition of this book. Members of Maisons Paysannes de France are a unique source of knowledge on traditional rural houses in their regions. In every département, information centres and local representatives provide surveys and reports on buildings, organise visits to discover the local heritage and training sessions on traditional building, renovation, restoration and gardening techniques, both for amateurs and professionals. For more detail on the organisation's work or to become a member, contact: Maison Paysannes de France, 8 passage des deux Soeurs, 75009 Paris; Telephone: 01 44 83 63 63; Fax: 01 44 83 63 69; Web: www.maisons-paysannes.org

Understanding rural gardens

The unassuming nature of a *paysan* garden contributes to the charm of old rural houses.

It is a beautiful day in the French countryside. Walking down a small path in a lush, green valley you suddenly come across it: there, just in front of you, a house that is so perfectly at one with its surroundings, looking so naturally part of the landscape that it feels as though it has just grown there. An old vine twists its way across the stone walls, while poppies, irises and sunflowers sway in the gentle breeze, contrasting with the faded blue paintwork of the shutters. A rickety wooden gate, slightly ajar, reveals a neat vegetable plot with dahlias and gladioli down one side.

A majestic lime tree stands proud in the courtyard, ivy is creeping up the low drystone wall along the side of the kitchen garden, reaching the eaves of the barn. Across the wall, in the small orchard, apple and pear trees are heavy with the weight of ripening fruit, their lower boughs almost touching the ground. A hedge of hawthorn, hazel and blackthorn offers protection from the wind, covered in parts with sweet-smelling honeysuckle.

This idyllic picture is now quite rare in the French countryside. Born out of necessity, the country garden which once grew around farm buildings and produced useful crops both for household and agricultural use, is no longer such an essential requirement. Vegetable plots, orchards, ponds and farmyards have been neglected or 'landscaped' away. And the disappearance of smallholdings has dramatically changed the landscape, resulting in the loss of hedges, sunken paths and terraces. Today, many French farms are converted into homes, and traditional gardens are

replaced with gardens designed to suit urban aspirations. The lack of genuine connection with rural life often means that anything that does not look neat and tidy is removed. Grass is trimmed, hedges are clipped, the ground is levelled, and paths are covered in asphalt. In short, natural gardens are being sanitised.

Around villages, architecturally bland housing estates have sprung up, gardens are hemmed in by 'walls' of evergreen thujas, and new homes seem to show little aspiration to blend in with their environment. And yet, it does not take much to achieve greater harmony between houses and their gardens, whether old and new, and the surrounding landscape. Little money is required. On the contrary, good old thriftiness and common sense are the best guides, as well as attention to detail and an awareness of the surrounding environment.

Understanding local traditions and respecting the identity of a place is all that is required to preserve its unique character and charm. Improvements that are regarded as essential for the enjoyment of the garden should endeavour to fit in with its rural character. This does not mean that restoring an old house with a derelict garden should be a constraint. It is possible to be very creative without losing the original charm of the garden.

To rekindle the spirit of these rural country gardens, you will need to reflect on their *raison d'être*. Some plants were grown for practical uses, whether it was for food or because they had medicinal properties, and others were left to grow freely for no immediate purpose; in some parts of the garden nature was tamed, and in others it was left as a wilderness. The rural garden was a combination of spontaneity and simplicity. It was maintained with care rather than obsessively manicured, and looked after with the greatest respect for the natural environment as whole. The rural garden was not a sterile exercise in decoration for its own sake but part of the surrounding landscape; a balanced eco-system which provided a habitat for small animals, insects and birds – creatures who, in turn, helped the garden to thrive without resorting to insecticides, weedkillers and other chemicals.

Anyone embarking on a garden regeneration project should think through these elementary principles. The reward will be a garden that looks after itself, is a pleasure to the eye, and produces abundant fruit and vegetables crops.

Farms, barns and rural houses all have their own identity deeply steeped in regional traditions, reflected in their gardens.

Nestling in the
greenery, this barn
is almost like a
visitor to the garden.

THE ORIGINAL RURAL GARDEN

Unlike formal gardens around chateaux and manor houses, or those of monasteries, Renaissance gardens, or even English gardens, the French rural garden has not been the object of extensive research. Gardening lore was passed on through oral tradition and has not always been recorded systematically. It is, therefore, fortunate that there are still gardeners around today who have inherited these techniques and continue to pass them on.

In the countryside, the house and the land were regarded as work tools in their own right. So was the garden, which would have to provide for a whole family, and where each section had a specific purpose: the vegetable plot, the orchard, the pond, and the farmyard - complete with its manure heap.

The various outbuildings of the farm were also part of this vibrant and productive organisation, whether they were used for keeping animals (horses, cows, rabbits, poultry), for activities relating to everyday life (baking bread, fetching water, pressing fruit), or for storage (for wood, straw, tools and equipment).

All these buildings were laid out in a fairly informal way, depending on what was most convenient at the time. Plants, except for the vegetable plot and the orchard, would be left to grow without particular constraints. Hedges would be allowed to creep up to the house, and a few trees would be planted in the courtyard. There were a few flowers too, often grown for their medicinal or religious significance.

The vegetable plot and orchard were what constituted the garden in its strictest sense. Usually located within easy reach of the kitchen, the vegetable plot was often found at the back of the house and was looked after by the women or by *les anciens* - those too old to work in the fields.

Fruit trees were often planted among vegetables, along with a few colourful flowers to attract the bees and brighten up the place, and there would probably be a beehive in the orchard too.

In villages where there was not enough space around the houses, the vegetable plots would be grouped in allotments on land just outside the village, or on terraces in mountain villages. These vegetable plots tended to be of modest size, as their purpose was mainly to liven up the basic diet of the household. Different plots a little further away would be cultivated for specific purposes.

Cliché Plantrau

150

In the Auvergne, for example, there would be several distinct gardens: a 'bee garden' just for beehives, a 'soup garden' for the vegetables (the original *potager*), a 'small garden' for the early vegetables and fruit, and a 'hemp garden' (hemp was woven to make clothes and rope).

Cereals were also grown in small quantities in areas where they were not part of the main agricultural crop. They were planted in a small field nearby, as were potatoes or beetroots. The grain was crushed into flour which was used to make bread, pancakes or gruel, while the straw was used in mattresses, to make hats, as stuffing for chairs, and for roofing.

These various areas were constantly busy, and activity reached its peak at harvest time, or when animals were being slaughtered, often culminating in a lengthy and copious outdoor feast. The grounds around the farms and houses were a zone of transition

The traditional rural farmyard was a space shared with animals and planted with fruit trees.

between nature in the raw and the house itself, a protection zone for the household and livestock against wild beasts and the extreme weather. This is also where the water supply - a well, pond or stream - would be located. A network of paths and tracks would connect it to the outside world: fields, vineyards, orchard or woods, or the nearby village or neighbouring houses.

Thrift was evident everywhere and every *centime* was counted. The only money spent on food tended to be for salt or sugar (although many used honey instead) and, later on, coffee. The production of fruit and vegetables was taken seriously, as surplus from the vegetable plot would be sold at the market, providing a small source of additional revenue.

In an environment where so much space was put to productive use, there was no room for lawns or other areas specifically dedicated to rest or leisure.

A different perspective on gardening

This book aims to demonstrate how you can bring a French rural garden back to life and maintain it using traditional techniques, and create a space which is both enjoyable, productive and in keeping with the character of the house.

This process starts with a bit of thinking about what you are aiming to achieve (Chapter 1). Consider how the house, the outbuildings and the whole plot itself fit in with the surrounding landscape. This initial phase also involves looking at the soil types and topography, at the plants and trees already in place.

Following that, the practical work starts. Chapter 2 sets out all the classic elements of a rural garden: the farmyard or courtyard, the vegetable patch, the pond, and so on, each with a selection of

The farmyard would always be buzzing with activity.

traditional plants referenced in the Plant Finder section at the back of the book.

Other essential elements of the garden are, of course, enclosures, such as fences, walls and hedges, all of which come with their regional styles and variations, and which contribute to the character of the garden. They are discussed in Chapter 3.

For best results, some basic gardening techniques are required. You will find tips on sowing, planting, pruning and watering in Chapter 4, as well as ideas for organic fertilisers, and ways of fighting plant diseases without recourse to toxic chemicals. Many of the old-fashioned techniques used by rural gardeners form the basis for modern organic methods practised today.

Chapter 5, the final chapter, looks at structural landscaping and dealing with water.

Working with nature means that your French rural garden will be a beautiful place where you will feel at one with the environment, and you will also contribute to the perpetuation of ancestral practices for future generations.

For French gardeners and weathermen, there are only two types of climate in France: north and south of the Loire valley, with regional variations including coastal and mountain climates. The information provided in this book is based on the temperate climate of central France, with specific indications relating to other regions where relevant. You may need to adjust advice relating to the timing of certain activities (sowing, planting, etc.) to suit the location and climate of your garden: as a rule of thumb, delay by two to three weeks in the north, and start two to three weeks earlier in the south. The plants mentioned in the book grow in most regions of France unless indicated otherwise.

Chapter 1

Before you start

If I were a rich man [...] I would not build myself a town in the countryside and place the Tuileries gardens outside my living quarters. On the slopes of some pleasant, well-shaded hillside, I would have a small rustic house, a white house with green shutters; and while thatch is good roofing material in all seasons, I would much prefer, not gloomy slates but tiles — they look so much cleaner and more jolly than thatch [...]. My courtyard would be more like a farmyard, and in my stables I would keep cows, for milk, which I am very fond of. I would have a vegetable plot for a garden and, instead of a park, a nice orchard [...]. I would choose my hideaway in some isolated region where there is little sign of money but an abundance of produce and which would be both bountiful and humble.

JEAN-JACQUES ROUSSEAU, EMILE OU DE L'EDUCATION, LIVRE IV

Just like Jean-Jacques Rousseau, we all dream of having our little place in the country, with a garden that creates a haven of peace where we can just sit and commune with nature. If this kind of dream is easy to imagine, putting it into practice is often a lot more difficult to achieve. Where do you start? How do you create harmony with nature? What do you keep and what do you eliminate? So, before throwing yourself into the project, step back a bit and take a close look at what's around. Useful ideas can be gleaned just by observing nature at work, which will be very helpful later on.

LOOK AROUND THE GARDEN

Any bit of land, even if it appears at first sight pretty bare, is never completely divorced from its context. It fits in with its immediate surroundings (neighbouring land) and with its broader environment (the local countryside), as well as with the history of the area, into which the garden should blend, almost unnoticed and as naturally as possible. The lighter the touch, the more the garden will feel

Harmony: look at the house, with its garden, as one of the components of the surrounding landscape.

In this traditional farmhouse in the Gâtinais region (left), the old paving stones and the pear trees trained in *espalier* style bring old-fashioned charm to the garden. This semi-open farmyard (opposite) was turned into a simple lawn with a few trees.

integrated with its environment, and understanding this environment is the first step towards creating a true French rural garden.

The way the land lies

The first thing to examine is your plot of land itself, and all its characteristics: slopes, altitude, prevailing winds, sunshine, light and shade. This will help to work out the kind of climate, or collection of microclimates, your land enjoys. The table below lists plants that typically thrive in various locations. These indications are based on the climate in a temperate region.

WHAT GOES WHERE: CHOOSING PLANTS FOR THE RIGHT SPOT IN A TEMPERA

THE SITE	TYPICAL CHARACTERISTICS
North-facing	Minimal variations in temperature; little sunlight and little warmth. More likely to be cool and damp. You may need to provide shelter from north and easterly winds.
East-facing	The main problem for east-facing plants is the rapid switch from heat to cold during the spring, when the nights are still frosty but the morning sun is warming up. Damp can be a problem too.
South-facing	Some species will not be able to stand the heat, or the summer drought, so choose carefully.
West-facing	This suits plants that can handle cooler conditions, but withstand hot afternoons in the summer.
Open and dry	Ideal place to create a meadow or an orchard.
Wet, humid	Perfect location for a pond.

Location and lay-out of the buildings

A house should always reflect the characteristics of the land on which it is built and the climate. Consider how old rural houses are designed and which way they face, and you will begin to see how the weather conditions have shaped the local architecture. Outbuildings are often positioned to protect the house from wind, rain or cold, while windows are typically on the southern façade only. These considerations apply to gardens too.

However, assessing the situation is not necessarily as easy as it seems. There are many factors to take into account: sunlight, prevailing winds, the location of the house in the general scheme of the plot and its distance from neighbours or from the road, as well as views from different points around the grounds. To familiarise yourself with your plot, wander around the garden and ask yourself a whole range of questions, however obvious they may seem: is the house at the edge of the grounds, in a village, or alongside a road or path? Is it out in the middle of the countryside, and how close are your neighbours? Which way is the best view: looking towards the house, or looking away from it? Is there something unsightly that you may want to cover up? Which bit of the garden

WHAT YOU CAN PLANT

Hedges as wind-breaks; dense climbing evergreens such as ivy, winter jasmine, or deciduous plants such as virginia creeper; flowers including hydrangea, comfrey, ferns, violets, primroses, and in summer, columbines and geranium.

Climbing plants, such as honeysuckle, clematis, winter jasmine, climbing roses, wisteria, geranium and primroses.

Climbing plants against a wall: vines, or fruit trees; wisteria, bignonia; herbs including thyme, bay, lavender, sage.

Thick-growing climbers such as virginia creeper, bignonia, wisteria, climbing roses.

Wild flowers and trees, including taller fruit trees.

Water plants or bog plants; and if the water level tends to fluctuate, marsh plants.

A productive garden
'Joindre l'utile à l'agréable'

Gardens, of course, are not necessarily just for beauty. You could derive great pleasure in creating a productive, purposeful garden, growing your own food, herbs and medicinal plants, and providing a habitat for wildlife, or even offer medicinal cures. This would give your garden a different dimension, rekindling the tradition of old rural gardens and their true *'raison d'être'*. This does not mean that you should be fishing in your pond or eating all the fruit from the orchard. But how satisfying to enjoy your own fruit and vegetables, especially if you grow varieties that are not available from market stalls: take a stroll to the orchard to pick up apples for a *tarte*, or ripe gooseberries for a *compôte*; walk to the herb garden for fresh parsley to throw in a salad; make jam with your own plums; or pick a few verbena leaves for an infusion. And neighbours will be all too happy to be given a few of your spare courgettes, and will probably share with you the produce of their own garden in return.

is the warmest, or the driest, or the most humid, or perhaps the best sheltered from the wind? Where can you get some privacy in the garden?

With old rural houses, various outbuildings may also be scattered around the grounds. These will be typical of the local architecture, and are part of the charm, but generally, their location serves a purpose – to provide additional shelter from the sun or from wind, or for storage. Try to keep as many outbuildings as possible: they are extremely useful as storage space, as a laundry room, as workshop or games room.

Learn from the plants

If you can identify the plants that are already growing on your land, you will be able to make a good guess about the kind of soil you have (see opposite page). This will not only be invaluable when you decide on new plants but it will also allow you to find out about the original structure of the garden. A rich and fertile soil will indicate that this was probably the original kitchen garden, while a damp zone could be a former pond, and a few big shrubs in a line could once have been hedge. This will be very useful when it comes to selecting the most appropriate spot for plants. This exercise is usually best carried out in the spring when flowers are beginning to bloom, or in the summer, but avoid mowing so that you can identify which wild flowers are growing in your garden or meadow.

Soil only really gives you trouble when it has an excessive amount of any one thing: too chalky, or too damp, or too much clay. In these conditions only certain plants will survive, though the soil itself will improve with cultivation (see p.124). By contrast, soils that achieve a good balance between chalk, clay, sand and humus will allow almost anything to grow.

The table opposite shows some examples of plants that typically grow in a certain type of soil (but remember that the more existing plants you have to go by the more likely your conclusion will be correct, as some plants grow in many different types of soil). However, if you prefer a more scientific method, a soil test kit (*testeur d'acidité*) will provide an easy and reliable answer. Find out, too, if the plants are deciduous or not, so that you have an idea of what your garden will look like during the different seasons. Finally, you will need to think about how quickly these plants can grow, their eventual height, and how long they will live.

SOIL ASSOCIATIONS: HOW THE PLANTS IN YOUR GARDEN WILL GIVE YOU CLUES ABOUT YOUR SOIL

Plants you might find...	...and the likely soil they are growing in
Silver birch, chestnut, sessile oak or red oak, Scots pine or maritime pine, mountain ash, heather, broom, gorse, blueberry, hypericum (St John's wort), periwinkle, scarlet pimpernel.	Dry, sandy soil which cannot hold onto water or nutrients, and tends to dry out quickly but warms up fast. Acidic.
Gorse, spruce, white birch, red-berried elder, common water pennywort, marsh violet.	Peaty soil, which is likely to be wet, dark coloured and very water retentive. Acidic.
Hawthorn, sessile oak, dog rose, holly, apple, pear, blackthorn (sloe), hazel, rowan, field maple; woodbine, common wormwood, sorrel, dandelion, milfoil, buttercup, nettle, bramble.	Clay soil, rich in potash, which is compact and sticky, often damp, and slow to warm up but hardens as it dries in the summer. Neutral.
Alder (common and grey), pin oak, ash, black poplar, apple, elm, aspen, white willow, goat willow, Guelder rose; cuckoo flower, marsh horsetail, rush, yellow iris, meadow-sweet, water forget-me-not, creeping buttercup, creeping jenny.	Damp clay soil, which tends to be marshy all year round. Neutral.
Dogwood, silver willow, goat willow, birch, hazel, elder, Guelder rose, wood garlic, nettle-leaved bellflower, autumn crocus, honesty, comfrey, bindweed, yellow iris, European dew-berry, hop, common horsetail, narrow-leaved plantain, daisy.	Cool chalky soil. Alkaline.
Hawthorn, hornbeam, privet, beech, lime, apple, mulberry, plane, field maple, bay, ash, spindle, field violet, burnet, hellebore (christmas rose), woodruff, hypericum.	Medium chalky soil, probably planted with hedges. Alkaline.
Whitebeam, juneberry, sea buckthorn, box, traveller's joy (clematis), downy (or 'white') oak, rowan, cornelian cherry, berberis, spindle, yew, hazel, wild geranium, wild strawberry, pellitory, lavender, poppy, cornflower, thistle, camomile, wild mustard, yarrow.	Dry, chalky soil, likely to be stoney too. Alkaline.
Amaranthus, mugwort, burdock, nettle, ash, maple, elm.	Soil rich in nitrates.

The surrounding landscape

The French countryside is astonishingly diverse and is also remarkable for the way in which old buildings and villages blend in with the surrounding environment. Preserving this relationship is essential to retaining the unique identity of the landscape. The French countryside has been fashioned over the centuries by agriculture, with the creation of man-made structures such as terraces on hillsides or animal farming in the *bocage*, and by the way in which the rural fabric has developed, from isolated farms to large estates, and from small farming communities to villages. In the 20th century, the arrival of newcomers with different lifestyles and ever-increasing urban expansion are also taking their toll on the countryside.

The fine balance of these harmonious landscapes can easily be damaged by uncontrolled development, even down to the level of gardens. So try to bear in mind the broad features of the landscape, as well as the little details that make it special: whether it is open or cluttered, the way trees are planted (in lines, groves, or forests), the type of hedges (growing wild or closely trimmed, and which species), the type of fences, walls and gates, and the materials used, what the paths are like (are they paved, are there any ditches or sunken paths, are they lined with trees?), and whether there are any special features like old roadside crosses, milestones, or small stone huts.

In villages and other built-up areas, the local building style contributes to the charm and character of the region, which can suffer if budget materials are being used instead of traditional materials. If you are building or renovating, try to retain the architectural features and work with the elements of the landscape that inspired you to come to this part of France in the first place: the style and stone of the walls or pavements, the colour and texture of rendering, the scale of buildings and their distance from the street, the presence or absence of flowers and other vegetation. If the dominant element of the landscape is stone, think in terms of low walls, paving and other mineral elements; vice versa, if your garden is in lush, green surroundings, hedgerows, small fruit trees and meadows are more appropriate. It is also best to live with the garden for a while before making any changes, sometimes as long as a whole year, to see how it evolves through the seasons.

The land around a farmhouse can act as a soft transition between rolling fields and a forest (top). This Périgord farm (bottom left) naturally blends into its environment, while flowers planted alongside a façade by the road (bottom right) cushion the house from the tarmac.

STARTING THE PROJECT

Drawing a plan

Once you have had a good think about all these things, it is time to get on with the design. Start with sketching out the plot, marking where everything is: all the buildings with their doors and windows,

DRAWING A PLAN

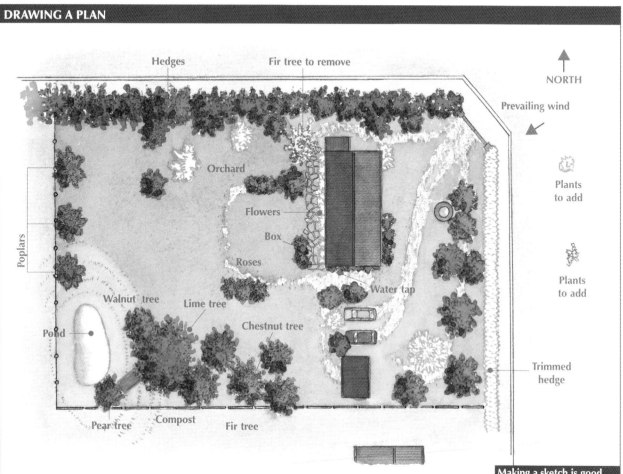

Hedges

Fir tree to remove

NORTH

Prevailing wind

Orchard

Flowers

Box

Roses

Plants to add

Plants to add

Poplars

Walnut tree

Lime tree

Chestnut tree

Water tap

Pond

Trimmed hedge

Pear tree

Compost

Fir tree

Making a sketch is good for several reasons. It forces you to really observe what your land is like. And it helps you to calculate the size of spaces that you can create, and the quantity of plants (and raw materials) that may be required.

trees, shrubs and areas of vegetation, slopes and dips in the ground, sources of water, fences, paths, areas of shade (including where the trees and buildings cast their shadows), and even elements of the neighbours' gardens too. This will give you a clearer picture of the characteristics of your plot and will allow you to decide on what to keep and what to remove. If you can, take photographs of the plot at different times of the year, this will give you a better idea of how it changes through the seasons.

The plan will also help you define exactly what you need to do, and the sequence in which the work should be done – bearing in mind the constraints of the weather in various seasons, your list of priorities, and the time and money you have available. This logical planning process will allow you to make the most of your investment in the garden (for instance, if you are hiring a mechanical dig-

Savoir-faire:

ger for a septic tank, get a pond dug at the same time).

However, at this stage, your main concern should be to think of the kind of garden you want to create, and how you will be able to give your garden its own sense of charm. Here are a few ideas.

LET NATURE TAKE ITS COURSE

Working with nature

Instead of following endless lists of instructions about pruning, sowing, mulching, and spraying, found in so many gardening books and magazines, consider this simple alternative: do nothing and let nature take its course.

After all, nature has been getting on with it on its own without any assistance from mankind in making compost or removing dead branches from trees. We have a tendency to want to step in and take control. The risk is that this can create an environment which is more vulnerable and looks artificial. On the other hand, living in a rampant jungle of weeds and thorns is not the ideal solution either.

There is a medium way where human intervention is limited to what is strictly necessary and the gardener guides nature rather than attempts to control or bridle it.

In his book 'Le jardin en mouvement', the well-know landscape gardener Gilles Clément calls this 'the moving garden'; a principle echoed by the naturalist François Terrasson in 'La peur de la nature' ('Afraid of nature'). Both extol the virtues of leaving gardens free to grow, where gardeners intervene merely to encourage or protect a plant, or curb the excesses of another (see Bibliography, p.217). This makes garden maintenance much simpler, which is an important consideration if you are often away or pressed for time.

Biodiversity begins at home

This 'back to basics' approach in favour of a wild garden is also beneficial to wildlife which thrives in this natural environment. Many animals, insects and birds that used to be a common sight in the French countryside are now becoming rare, and many are seriously endangered in some parts of France, such as badgers, hedgehogs, stoats and certain species of dragonflies and bats, not to

Take your time

You will first need to spend a little bit of time in your garden thinking about how its various components can acquire a specific role in the grand scheme of the plot. Think of where you will wash your car, for instance, park your bicycles, or kick a ball around without damaging the plants or the nerves of other people in the garden. Where do you feel you might like to sit down for a quiet afternoon nap? The more you use the garden, the more these different questions will be answered. Taking your time also means you will have time to get to know the garden through all the seasons, with the interplay of light and shade, colours, and perfumes – and notice what works and what could be improved. Above all, do not rush into anything: the different seasons can drastically alter the space, depending on the plants that are already growing in the garden and those that grow naturally, so it is always better to start by doing nothing.

planning your garden

Don't take out too much

The plants that are already there are generally those which are best suited to the garden, and are probably there thanks to the experience of the former owners. These plants form part of the garden's character, and it is often better to build on this rather than uproot everything.

Trees, in particular, are almost always worth keeping (unless they are too close or in danger of falling), as they give a sense of maturity to the garden. If you start from scratch on bare ground, it will take decades to get that 'established' feeling in a garden. The same goes for hedges and bushes. Hedges may look overgrown, but will thrive if you cut them right back down to the base, and allow them to regrow even more densely. This will also give you masses of tinder wood for your fires.

Let the garden fit in with the house

When you are creating a garden for an old rural property, it is usually better to approach it as a subtle restoration job rather than a radical style makeover. Clues about the most suitable approach can be gleaned from the architecture of the house: its style, the material it is made of, its position in relation to the overall scheme and size of the plot, and so on.

A rural cottage, for instance, carefully restored with traditional materials and in true rural style is not suited to a formal, linear garden. Rural cottages are humble buildings and what suits them best is a slightly unruly wild garden, with a vegetable plot in one corner, wild flowers, and maybe a pond.

A farmhouse, on the other hand, often organised around a central courtyard, should retain its cohesion as a group of functional buildings. The courtyard is often best left open, possibly with a fine tree planted in the middle and a few climbers on the walls.

A village house will look good with a vine, borders with flowers and a few potted plants. For walls and fences, use local materials which match the other houses in the village.

A 'maison de maitre', which is a more substantial house in a town or village, tends to be more structured architecturally. Avoid excessive planting which could interfere with the clean lines of the façade. Keep to a few neatly trimmed shrubs which will bring out the architecture of the house.

mention numerous bird species. In a few decades, air pollution, the creeping expansion of towns, new road building, and intensive farming have devastated natural habitats. There are few areas left where endangered species can survive, and your garden could become one of these precious places provided that you try to keep to indigenous species known to the insects and birds of your region. This also means avoiding many hybrid varieties, which are often short on pollen and of little interest for insects.

To entice insects and birds into your garden, you will need to avoid chemical weed-killers and pesticides, which contribute to soil and groundwater pollution. As gardening author Chris Baines puts it in his book '*Créer un jardin sauvage*': 'an environment that is safe for bugs and insects is also safe for us.' (see Bibliography, p.217). Organic gardening, which finds its inspiration in traditional gardening methods, is the solution.

A garden that is inviting for wildlife should also meet certain conditions: multiple layers of vegetation, each above the other; a variety of native species, from the trees right down to the ground-cover; and a good layer of vegetation in various stages of decomposition – dead logs and decaying tree trunks as well as fine leafmould. A natural hedgerow, for example, is ideal, with a wide variety of plants and a carpet of twigs and leaves at ground level. In a meadow or orchard, wild flowers will attract ladybirds, bees and butterflies. A wooded area will become home to insects, snails, lizards, birds and small mammals, and a hollow tree will soon be colonised by squirrels, bats, and owls, as well as all kinds of insects and fungus. Likewise, a dry stone wall can provide a great natural habitat for wildlife, and a heap of dead wood a refuge for toads, hedgehogs or slow worms. And putting up nesting boxes and bird tables for our feathered friends will bring music to your garden.

With a little thought, and simple, organically based methods, you will be able to encourage a whole range of birds, insects, and other small animals.

Make the most of the space

Think of the pleasure of discovering the garden little by little, walking past walls and along hedges, getting a glance of the landscape or of the vegetable garden, and the pond in the distance. Rather than creating a vast lawn enclosed by a fence, which will reveal the whole garden all at once, create elements of surprise by playing with perspectives, colours and textures. You should also try to conceal unsightly elements of modern life, such as satellite dishes or garages, behind a hedge. Follow nature's lead and let yourself be guided by what is already there: an orchard, a stream, or a line of trees are strong, natural features in a garden, that will provide starting points for designing the rest of the space. Let paths come to life gradually: over time, the way you move between the various parts of the garden will create a network of paths that will reflect the way your garden is lived in.

Avoid artificial adjuncts and overly decorative designs, such as winding paths for no particular reason, meticulously clipped shrubs, or exotic varieties randomly planted across a lawn. An unfenced meadow, which draws the eye far into the distance, will create an impression of openness, and for gardens on a slope, a low wall with a few shrubs will provide an ideal boundary limit while enhancing the view. Combine small, intimate spaces, such as a table under a pergola, or a bench in a secret hideaway corner, with larger open areas that can be used as a children's play area, as a visitors' car park, or just as a place to mooch around and admire the view on a warm sunny evening.

A small garden will benefit from being sub-divided into a series of sections using hedges, fences or walls as partitions and different materials as ground cover (paving, lawn, gravel, etc.). These sections might become bigger as one moves away from the house towards the open countryside.

SAVOIR FAIRE

From symmetry to wilderness

Each space within the garden has its own atmosphere. The area nearer the house will act as an extension of the house and provide outdoor living space. Paving or gravel is particularly suitable, and flowers, either in borders or planters, will help brighten up the space. As you move away from the house, the garden should gradually open up, with a grassed area or a meadow, followed by taller plants and trees filling the horizon.

In this garden (left), the eye moves gently from the well-maintained lawned courtyard to a more open orchard and further out into the forest. Opposite: the garden path prolongs the hallway of the house, creating a long perspective right through the garden, with the greenery happily invading the path.

Compare and contrast: Sharp contrast can work well, as in the case of this house in the Alsace where the pale blue-grey shutter stands out against the deep red pigment of the render and the dark timber behind a proud row of vibrant blue and yellow irises (left). Pink frilly poppies and blue shutters (opposite) work well with the softer tones of natural material like stone and sand-coloured render.

Likewise, in terms of planting scheme, one would usually move progressively from 'tamed' to 'wild': potted plants on the terrace near the house and more free-flowing designs further out, such as meadows and woodland. This is particularly relevant for grander houses, with strong architectural lines, where the courtyard should bring out the symmetry of the house: compacted sand, paving, or lawn, with clipped box or hornbeam hedges or low flowering shrubs. At the back of the house, there would usually be flowers or vegetables, a fountain or water feature in a formal, but more open, lay-out. Beyond this, wider spaces such as a park, meadow or orchard will act as a transition for the natural environment surrounding the garden.

Choosing colours

Blue and various shades of blue, ranging from grey to green and purple, are used for woodwork in many French regions. These colours work particularly well with natural building material, whether stone or rendering, as well as with the green of the garden. The bright '*charron*' blue, which softens with age, was used on agricultural tools and implements, as well as on doors, windows and shutters. Different colours are often found in Southern regions, like brown and earthy shades around the Mediterranean coast, Corsica and the Midi.

Traditionally, these colours would be made using a base such as lime, animal or vegetable waxes, or oils such as linseed or walnut, mixed with crushed natural colour pigments.

Your choice of colours for the planting scheme will need some careful thought. This involves more than simply planting a red-flowering shrub next to a yellow-flowering one. Think in terms of themes and variations, and avoid unnecessarily showy or rare species, as these may not settle particularly well or may require special care. Finally, think of the flowering cycle: select varieties which flower at different times of the year, to ensure that your garden will have colour all year round, but also enough which flower at the same time of year, for greater effect (see pp.40-45).

LANGUAGE LAB:
GARDEN PLANNING

Climber, climbing plant : une plante grimpante
Countryside : la campagne
Deciduous : à feuilles caduques
Evergreen : à feuilles persistantes
Farmyard : une cour de ferme
Fence : la clôture
Gravel : le gravier
Hedge : la haie
Landscape : le paysage
Landscape gardener : le/la paysagiste, jardinier paysagiste
Lawn : la pelouse
Marsh plant : une plante des marais
Orchard : le verger
Outbuildings : les dépendances
Path : le chemin
Paving : un dallage; paving stone: une dalle
Slope (steep) : une pente (raide)

Type of soil : le type de sol
Chalky / clay / sandy : calcaire / argileux / sableux
Acidic / alkaline / neutral : acide / alcalin / neutre
Damp / dry : humide / sec

For more gardening terms, see the Glossary p.210

Chapter 2

From planning to planting

❛ My garden has been left to its own devices. It has gone a little mad, deliberately disorganised. Everything invades the space occupied by everything else: the vegetables and the flowers, the herbs and the berries, climbers, vines and sweet peas, nasturtium, roses which climb up the walls, the tall straight sunflowers and the hollyhocks with their colourful heights. But underneath this unruly condition and the random sowing of seeds by the wind is the wish to create a garden unlike modern gardens that merely produce lawn for mowing and blue conifers, a garden like gardens of yesteryears, which will be both productive and a source of joy. ❜

ROGER BOURDONCLE

This image conjured up by author and gardener Roger Bourdoncle, describing his garden in the Quercy region, is a perfect description of the spirit of the French rural garden, of its freedom and spontaneity. In effect, this approach is simply the expression of the desire to embrace traditional rural lifestyle. In this chapter, we look at some of the different components of the garden, all of which reflect life as it used to be in the countryside when the garden was a working feature of the house.

THE FARMYARD

An open space

Surrounded by buildings or simply by walls, the farmyard was in former times the nerve centre of the farm; a scene of constant movement, with farm workers, vehicles, and animals coming and going, leaving little opportunity for plants to take root. It was also the site of many household chores, often carried out sitting on a bench in front of the house. Here, a simple paving of stones, pebbles or bricks kept the mud at bay and extended the inside into the outside. The rest of the farmyard was just compacted earth.

Climbers like this rambling rose (opposite) will bring a splash of life to an old stone wall.

Now and then (above): a courtyard left sadly barren after the discontinuation of agricultural activities (inset) was brought back to life after careful renovation and the addition of a few climbers. The courtyard of this labourer's cottage (below) has retained its character and has been enlivened by low key planting. Opposite: in this courtyard, greenery has replaced the gravel without taking away the identity of the place.

A simple trellis on the façade of the house, or a few potted plants added a bit of greenery. And sometimes a tree would be planted in the centre of the farmyard to provide a bit of shade in the summer: a fruit tree or a lime, perhaps, or an ash, more common in central France, or a plane tree in the south.

A point of transition between the road or the fields on the one hand, and the privacy of the home on the other, the courtyard was an invitation to step into the house. With an emphasis on stone and other mineral material, the yard is not quite part of the garden yet, and although it has to be welcoming, the style should remain relatively sober and bring out the surrounding buildings.

Keeping the yard clear also allows vehicles to move in and out easily and provides temporary parking for visitors. But a farmyard that is no longer part of a working farm may feel empty and soulless, and a few plants judiciously positioned in the corner will help lift the spirit of the place.

Doing up a farmyard

1 : Try to recreate or to keep the original ground material, which is often simply beaten earth, or sometimes pebbles, or paving stones (which are less common, as they were expensive). Let the grass grow, especially at the base of stone walls and buildings, , and between paving stones, to add a touch of greenery. Avoid creating gravel paths in a rural courtyard – although this may work well with more classical façades (for instance, with dressed stone or symetrical window openings).

2 : Avoid uniformity. For example, grow plants in the basin which used to be used for liquid manure (they will thrive on the rich soil beneath), instead of just filling it in with gravel or paving it over. Levelling out the farmyard could make it dull and impersonal.

3 : Keep original features: in other words, a well, an exterior staircase, drinking trough, pond, the stone bench along the wall by the entrance. All these elements contribute to the spirit of the courtyard and can also be useful – although possibly without going so far as to transform them into giant flower pots.

4 : Plant roses or grow fruit trees up the walls, without forgetting the traditional box tree close to the house. Put out flowers on window sills and walls, or on the ground right next to the house. Keep it simple, with familiar plants like geraniums, or small flowering shrubs. See pp.40-46.

Ivy league: creepers can quickly take over to delightful effect (opposite and below) but need to be kept in trim to make sure they do not grow out of control and damage the walls.

CLIMBING PLANTS

Dressing the walls

A house without greenery will almost inevitably appear unfinished and in a state of undress. But to breathe life into the walls, there are options other than resorting to geraniums (pelargoniums) – satisfying as they may otherwise be. Climbers provide a perfect choice for a natural, uncontrived effect.

Traditionally a vine would be planted against a south facing wall, and retained style and elegance even in the winter months. Alternatively, in regions where the climate was not suitable for vines, fruit trees - pear trees in particular - were trained *espalier* style, and would thrive in the shelter of a warmer wall. Other plants, such as ivy or honeysuckle, were also used.

Climbing roses appeared in the French countryside from the 19th century and rapidly became a standard adornment for old village houses. Wisteria was only introduced at the beginning of the 20th century.

With grander houses, greater restrain should perhaps be applied in the use of climbers which might mar the style of the façade, but low evergreen shrubs can be used to stunning effect.

Climbing roses

Vines and roses: a traditional combination for old stone walls, as in this delightfully unkempt courtyard (opposite).

Planting a rose at the base of a wall is not just a way of livening up a wall, it is also one of the most suitable spots for a rose. Plants will happily grow there, sheltered from the wind, and kept warm and light by the heat given off by the stones. Protection from the weather means the base of a wall is a good spot for humus to build up, and it will retain moisture when the plant needs it in the summer. All sorts of animals and insects will also choose to live there, such as earthworms, woodlice and micro-organisms which keep the ground oxygenated.

Growing next to a wall, the roots are forced to extend downwards more or less vertically, which means the plant is well protected from the heat, from drying out, and from the frost in winter. Roses are quite happy in most soils – granite, slate or clay, but you will need at least 60 cm of soil. The choice of variety will depend on the space available, the way the wall faces, and the soil type. The ideal conditions are an east or west facing wall and light soil. Pruning should take place once or twice a year depending on the variety. (See also p.173).

Putting in a climbing plant

You may need to remove a few stones near the base of the wall to allow enough space for the roots, which need to grow deep into the soil (see diagram below). The foundations should be fine if the plant is put in at least 50 cm from the wall, and you ensure the roots point away from the house. A bit of manure will help it to settle in and if the ground is particularly chalky, add some compost – preferably leafmould.

It is best to water heavily, once a week or less, to encourage roots to penetrate deeply, particularly in the south of France. Frequent light watering is not appropriate as the roots then remain too superficial.

In subsequent years, prune regularly to keep the plant under control as it grows and to prevent it from getting under the roof tiles where is could cause serious damage.

If the base of the wall has drainage running alongside it, whether natural or a pipe, plant the climber a little further out

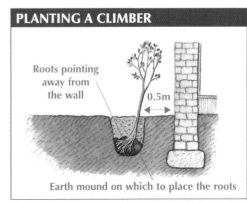

PLANTING A CLIMBER

Roots pointing away from the wall

0.5m

Earth mound on which to place the roots

Arbours and pergolas encourage plants to grow upwards and bring further structure to your garden as well as create a shaded area for those long summer lunches.

(50 – 80 cm) to avoid damage. A geotextile membrane may also be used to protect the structure from root damage or penetration.

A place in the shade: arbours and pergolas

A leafy arbour is the perfect place for a relaxed lunch in the shade or an afternoon siesta, and so much more charming than the cheap marquees that are seen in far too many gardens today. Build it next to the house, so that it seamlessly connects the building with the garden, or create a pergola out in the garden itself, which you can use as additional living space outdoors.

Building an arbour simply involves training a trellised climber outwards over a horizontal structure, away from the house, above

Building an arbour or a pergola is a simple, low-cost option to create additional space that will take a little bit of the house outside, providing you with an outdoor dining area or just a shaded spot for a table and a few chairs to see through the hot summer afternoons.

● **Slim metal sections and wire structure.** This is the most discreet option and is particularly unobtrusive in the winter. The uprights are held in place in masonry or concrete blocks, or built into a low wall around the terrace, or in concrete plinths buried in the ground. The cross pieces are simply embedded or screwed into the wall. Use strips of metal with an L or a T profile, bolted together, with a few cross-braces. You do not need to paint them; let them go rusty and they will blend in even better, but make sure that you use sufficiently strong metal, as it could otherwise rust through and break.

● **Wooden structure.** This will obviously look more chunky but can work very well with an older house, especially if you use reclaimed wooden posts. The uprights are fixed into concrete blocks or screwed onto stone. Use rot-resistant wood which will weather well and blend in with the house and garden. If using ordinary wood, make sure that it is treated (and occasionally re-treat it) to protect it from the weather.

● **Brick or stone pillars.** These can look out of scale in a rural garden, so whether they are appropriate will very much depend on the style and architecture of your house.

● **What to cover them with.** With arbours and pergolas, the choice of plants is an important consideration at the outset. Plant weight can vary considerably and a weak structure with a heavy plant growing on it will become dangerous.

All the climbing plants mentioned in this chapter would be ideal (see pp.162 et seq. for more suggestions). Some species of clematis, for instance, grow very quickly and will soon cover the arbour with flowers in the spring; ivy provides good cover for masonry pillars all year round; and annuals like climbing nasturtium bring colour around the base of the pillars. Climbers may need encouragement to start off

with, and also possibly later on as they grow, depending on the type of structure and thickness of the pillars. Ivy will readily creep up any structure, including a thick stone pillar, for instance, and wisteria will throw its twining stems around fairly thick pillars too. Clematis and vines, on the other hand, unless grown up a thin structure will need to have their stems tied to the structure, as their tentrils will not be able to grasp anything much thicker than wire on their own. In warmer parts of France, you could also use *canisses*, the woven reed panels traditionally found in Provence, over your trellis as a permanent roof to keep out the sun both in summer and in winter.

head height. In the summer, it will keep the house cool, rather like an awning, and in the winter, when the leaves have fallen off, it will let the sun in.

FLOWERS & HERBS

Flowers, latecomers in rural gardens

There was little room for flowers in the country garden before the beginning of the 20th century, and those that were allowed or encouraged to grow served some purpose or other, whether medicinal, culinary, religious or even superstitious. Nevertheless, the lady of the house would ensure that visitors felt welcome by placing a

Apart from the blossoms of fruit trees (opposite, right), the flowers that would have been seen in rural gardens were more likely to have been sown by the wind and grow wild in meadows (left), rather than be planted deliberately, unless they fulfilled a particular purpose, which could be medicinal or culinary, such as nigella (opposite main), whose seeds were used to flavour cakes.

few flowers around the house, by the front door or on a window sill, usually wild flowers picked locally. Flowers would otherwise be left to grow wild between paving stones, in odd corners of the garden or alongside paths, while others would be grown in the vegetable garden as herbs for cooking or to attract bees to help with the pollination of fruit trees. Flowers that were believed to have medicinal properties were picked wherever they grew wild in the fields, marshes and woods.

According to garden historian Michel Vivier (see Bibliography, p.217) 'ornamental flowers appeared in rural gardens in France from the mid-19th century – almost imperceptibly, but becoming more and more accepted. Curiously, the species which are the most

Vivid clumps of orange
hemerocallis cascading
into a bed of irises
(above), bright red
poppies (opposite
top), and nasturtiums
(opposite bottom), have
traditionally brightened
up French country gardens.

common today are rich in history and legend, and are renowned for various useful properties, real or imaginary. They do more than just decorate a garden: they create a joyful and yet secret space at the same time.'

Although flowers have always been a part of religious ceremonies, their role has never been as important as at the start of the 20th century. First and foremost came the rose, which has been a religious symbol since the Middle Ages: the white rose representing the purity of the Virgin Mary, the red rose the blood of Christ. Climbing roses, which first appeared at the start of the last century, and are very fast growers, quickly spread across the French countryside and were soon seen growing up the front of buildings, over garden gates, arbours and pergolas.

Later, the custom to decorate cemeteries with flowers developed after the Great War, and this too has contributed to the cultivation of more flowers in rural gardens.

Around the same time, commercial horticulture took off, providing more and more ornamental flowers which would go on to become the staples of most gardens: peonies, carnations, dahlias, gladioli, phlox, zinnias, asters, marigolds, pansies, sunflowers and helichrysum.

Chateaux with larger spaces cultivated more robust plants – brightly coloured hybrids – which today are sometimes seen as too brash for smaller country gardens, although they are part of their history and bring an unmistakable touch of cheerfulness.

Herbs

A French rural garden would not be complete without a herb garden, although, contrary to common perception, it is a comparatively modern development. Herbs, which enhance the flavour of so many regional dishes, would traditionally be planted in a spot within reach of the kitchen, sometimes on a window sill, or in the vegetable plot, in lines, or just in clumps or in borders. In fact, there was no designated area for these invaluable plants; formerly, people would just pick the required herb from the wild, wherever it was known to be growing. The current fashion for well-ordered herb gardens laid out in neat squares for decorative effect is probably inspired by the monastic gardens of the Middle Ages, and some say that it is too organised for a traditional rural garden.

Working with flowers

When it comes to selecting which flowers to plant and where, observe the same rule as with garden planning: before visiting the nursery (*pépinière*) or garden centre (*jardinerie*), step back and think through the effect you would like to achieve. Here are a few suggestions to ponder:

● **Avoid isolated borders of flowers on a lawn,** bright and clashing colours or exotic species; this is not what a country garden is all about. It does, however, form part of the garden style in chateaux and large country mansions, where parterres of flowers were partly there to display the owner's wealth and the skills of his gardeners.

● **Plant flowers at the bottom of walls,** in a slightly haphazard way. This works very well and looks natural with old stone walls. So you could, for example, put in some bushy flowers with fairly subtle and coordinated colours, with a neat edging of box, stones or bricks, or a low wooden fence. Hardy perennials, such as peonies, garden pinks, iris, asters and helianthus, will look after themselves year after year.

● **Put flowers in pots,** either plain terracotta or more colourful old ceramic ones collected over the years, and place them around the entrance to the house, on window sills, steps, or walls. This will allow you to cultivate some of the more fragile species, or position small flowers (such as pansies, petunias or carnations) in more favourable spots and move them around to suit your mood.

● **Gather woodland flowers** and plant them under trees, letting them come up in a natural, random way. Typical examples are: daffodils, violets and lily of the valley. Flowers will also look great in the vegetable garden, adding a bit of colour to the greenery, while also helping to ward off certain species of harmful insects (see pp.56 *et seq.*)

● **Give flowers time to settle in** and find their favourite spot. This allows you to determine which combinations of species work best together. Then you can start to intervene - don't be afraid of taking cuttings or transplanting elsewhere in the garden, or experimenting with seeds to see where plants are happiest.

● **Don't forget the small garden at the front, by the roadside.** If the front or side of your house is by the road, don't forget the thin strip of land that runs alongside it. A few plants will brighten up this often neglected area, particularly if the pavement has been covered in asphalt and appears quite dull. And this need not be painstaking work: throw a few hollyhock seeds in a hole dug near the wall and watch how quickly and tall they grow!

● **Window boxes** are good if you have a town or village house, but ideally choose terracotta ones and get a good mix of plants. Plant something to climb up the wall, especially in a village house, so that you can help to contribute some greenery to the street.

● **Choose decorative flowers** that are easy to look after, simple and robust, but let wild flowers take root too: meadow flowers on open ground; brightly coloured clumps of perennials for borders; and creeping or rockery flowers that can take hold between paving or stonework. However, while you should let nature express itself, you will also need to exercise some element of control or your garden could turn into a jungle.

● **If you want to nudge more of nature into your garden,** try transplanting wild flowers, but you will need to make sure that you use local specimens and that you plant them in a site where the conditions are similar to those where they would be growing in the wild. And remember that some of these are protected species. To find out which, consult your local botanical association by asking at the nearest tourist office.

Typically, there was not much variety in the types of herbs grown in rural gardens. Parsley was the most common, although it should not be grown just anywhere. Garden historian Michel Vivier writes that 'in the Bayeux region, parsley grown in the shade was said to turn into hemlock'. Legend also had it that you should never bed out parsley, or you could risk causing the death of the master of the house. It was used to encourage lactating animals to produce milk (and this included women). Tarragon and dill were used to make liqueurs, mint for invigorating infusions, and lemon balm for a good night's sleep. Lemon verbena, sage or camomile, whose scent fills the garden in the summer, are delicious as winter infusions.

Thyme, oregano, rosemary and tarragon are classic cooking ingredients in the south of France, but you should also consider lovage, sage, sorrel, Welsh onion (known in French as *oignon rocambole*), chervil, and fennel. You could also plant borage to cure coughs, and savory to prevent flatulence – old recipes for beans and pulses often included savory. Hyssop, which has become very rare in the French countryside, was used to flavour wine-based sauces and to aid digestion. It is also said to have antiseptic qualities, and to relieve bronchitis.

The delicious burnet is a salad herb which can also be added to savoury foods, such as *fromage blanc* (French cottage cheese), omelettes and sauces. Mint, chives, or basil will liven up salads and vegetables, raw and cooked, while the lovely *nigella* (love-in-a-mist), with its evanescent foliage, has delicate blue or white flowers whose fragrant seeds are often used in desserts.

Planting the right herbs

Most of these herbs grow easily almost anywhere in France, although some are better suited to the Mediterranean climate, while others prefer the slightly richer and cooler soil north of the Loire.

Herbs should preferably be planted in a sunny spot with enough room around them to grow. Perennials such as thyme, chives, lemon-balm, sorrel, and costmary (in semi-shade) should be cut back just before winter and they will grow again vigorously the following year. The evergreen sage and southernwood (a member of the artemisia family) are best clipped in the spring. Verbena is very susceptible to cold and is better grown in a pot which can be brought indoors in the winter after the branches have been cut and hung up to dry.

**LANGUAGE LAB:
KITCHEN HERBS**

Kitchen herbs are usually referred to as *fines herbes* or *herbes aromatiques*. Here are a few specimens commonly found in French gardens:

Basil : le basilic
Borage : la bourrache
Burnet : la pimprenelle
Chervil : le cerfeuil
Chives : la ciboulette
Clary : l'esclarée, toute-bonne (a member of the sage family)
Coriander : la coriandre
Creeping thyme : le serpolet
Dill : l'aneth
Fennel : le fenouil
Love-in-a-mist, nigella : la nigelle de Damas
Mint : la menthe
Oregano : l'origan
Parsley : le persil
Rosemary : le romarin
Sage : la sauge
Savory : la sarriette
Sorrel : l'oseille
Tarragon : l'estragon
Thyme : le thym
Verbena : la verveine

For more on herbs, see the Plant Finder p.176 and the Glossary p.210.

Happy cohabitants: most herbs will happily live alongside other plants and flowers, often protecting them from pests, as with chives and primulas (opposite).

Some herbs are annuals, which are best grown from seed every year, possibly in the vegetable plot. They include dill, basil, chervil, coriander, borage, savory, and clary (*salvia sclarea*, a member of the sage family) with its pretty flowers coming in various shades of purple and white. Parsley, if it liked the spot where it has been sown, should regenerate the following year.

THE VEGETABLE PLOT

A food factory

The constant battle of the farming community to get the most from the land was most evident in the vegetable plot of any rural house. Dictated by a strict sense of maximising productivity, the structure of the vegetable plot was driven by a rigorous, geometrical and linear plan, which could become something of a rural work of art. The peasant farmer, or more often his wife, took obsessive care over the vegetable plot, eradicating weeds meticulously. This was also the place where the washing was hung out, while the whole scene was watched over by a scarecrow, dipping and bobbing in the wind, kitted out according to the local traditions and superstitions.

Old favourites

Before they were grown for consumption, vegetables that are now regarded as traditional were initially gathered from the wild. Typically, these would have included cabbage, many root vegetables such as turnip and carrot, chard, sorrel, lamb's lettuce and dandelion. Cucumber, leek, onion, garlic and melon were introduced relatively early on in warmer regions, either by foreign merchants or by invading forces. Spinach, for example, was brought back by the crusaders in the 13th century. Other very early vegetables include many varieties of lettuce, peas, broad beans, parsley, dill and savory.

During the Renaissance, due to the growth in trade with Italy, new species appeared in France, such as aubergines, pumpkins, and salsifies. Melons, which were grown in the Middles Ages but somehow disappeared from gardens, made a comeback. Later, the dis-

---

**LANGUAGE LAB:
KNOW YOUR VEGETABLES**

Artichoke : un artichaut
Asparagus : une asperge
Aubergine : une aubergine
Bean : le haricot
Beetroot : la betterave
Cabbage : le chou
Carrot : la carotte
Cauliflower : le chou-fleur
Chard : la bette or blette
Courgette : la courgette
Jerusalem artichoke : le topinambour
Leek : le poireau
Marrow : la courge
Onion : un oignon
Parnisp : le panais
Pea : le pois, le petit pois
Pepper (sweet) : le poivron
Pumpkin : le potiron, la citrouille
Radish : le radis
Salsify : le salsifi
Sprouts : les choux de Bruxelles
Swede : le rutabaga
Tomato : la tomate
Turnip : le navet

For more on vegetables, see the Plant Finder p.178 and the Glossary p.210.

Tales of the
riverside: tucked
between the
woods and the
river, marrows
growing on a
traditional bed of
well-rotted manure
throw their lush
leaves over
the garden path.

LANGUAGE LAB: FROM PLOT TO PLATE

The French term for the garden vegetable, *le potager*, comes from an older name for vegetable soup, *le potage*, referring to vegetables that would be thrown into the pot. Sharing the same etymology, the word *potée* refers to a meat stew with vegetables (*potée aux choux*, *potée Lorraine*, etc.).

covery of the New World brought further new varieties: tomato and potato from Peru, beans from Mexico, giant peppers from Brazil, and Jerusalem artichoke from Canada. However, vegetables regarded as more aristocratic, such as aubergine and tomato, only began to be widespread after the Second World War.

Cabbages were probably the most common vegetables grown in France right up to the middle of the 19th century. The turnip was close behind. 'Everyone used to eat turnip and everyone used it as medicine too,' notes Michel Vivier. The arrival of the potato upset the established order, with much controversy surrounding its introduction by Parmentier, before becoming a staple food in the 1830s. The varieties known as *Belles de Fontenay, Saucisse, Rosa, Charlotte* and *BF15* are still popular across France.

It took time for the tomato to be accepted, appearing first at the start of the 19th century in northern France. It was grown mostly in the gardens of chateaux and religious orders, and under careful surveillance because it was believed to be poisonous. In 1865, the Caen agricultural society warned gardeners to wash their hands and gardening tools carefully after handling or pruning the plant.

Fruits also appeared in vegetable plots during the 19th century, during which time the varieties available skyrocketed. There were at least a dozen different types of strawberry, with the *Louis Gauthier* and *Abondance* both very popular until the middle of the 20th century. As well as apple trees and pear trees grown in *espaliers*, you would find raspberry bushes, gooseberries and blackcurrants, either in borders or running alongside a wall.

Melon used to be grown, famously, across the whole of Normandy but these days it is more often associated with southern regions. The Honfleur Melon was a regional celebrity in the 19th century, and exported to Britain. Vegetable gardens also became more colourful, as gardeners would often plant flowers like dahlias, marigold, chrysanthemum, or a line of tall flowers to finish off the side of the plot and encourage insect pollination.

Courgettes (above) need water but are otherwise easy to grow. Planting flowers in the vegetable plot brings colour and helps keep certain pests at bay (opposite).

FAMILIES OF VEGETABLES

Aizoaceae: New Zealand spinach, ice plant, etc.

Apiaceae: carrot, celery, chervil, garden chervil, parsley, dill, coriander, etc.

Asteraceae: artichoke, chard, endive, chicory, lettuces, jerusalem artichoke, etc.

Brassicaeae: cabbage, watercress, mustard, turnip, radish, rocket, etc.

Chenopodiaceae: beetroot, spinach, decorative beet (chard), orach, etc.

Cucurbitaceae: cucumber, marrow, courgette, pumpkin, melon, gherkin, etc.

Fabaceae or leguminous: broad beans, beans, lentils, lucerne (alfalfa), peas, clover, etc.

Liliaceae: garlic, asparagus, chives, onion, leek, shallot, etc.

Labiatae: Jerusalem artichoke, Chinese artichoke, etc.

Solanaceae: aubergine, chilli pepper, bell pepper, potato, etc.

All through the summer, the produce would be picked for daily consumption but also to be preserved for the winter months: fruits would be bottled or made into jams, leaves dried for infusions, and flowers packed in tight bunches to perfume wardrobes and keep insects away.

Bean pods were dried in the shade on a sheet, threaded onto string and hung up, or salted, as were onions, celery, turnips, and asparagus. Tomatoes were kept in brine, with a thin film of oil on top for extra protection. Conserving fruit in sterilised jars (*bocaux*) really took off after the Second World War, and is still practised in many rural parts of France, although it has been overtaken by freezers. As for the various fruits, these were dried out in lofts, or in the oven, or cooked with honey (up until the beginning of the 20th century, sugar was far too expensive), turned into syrup, or, for the most hardy fruits, simply kept in the cellar.

Choosing seeds and plants

In the old days most country folk in France used to buy seeds from merchants at rural fairs, but many gardeners would also simply let a few of their vegetables 'go to seed' and use those. For cabbages and salads, seeds taken from plants where the head had been removed were supposed to be of greater quality.

When buying seeds today, check the botanical name, in Latin, to make sure that you are getting the seeds you want. The French common names for plants, just as English ones, can be misleading. For example, oregano (*origan, origanum vulgare*), which has pink flowers is often sold for marjoram (*marjolaine, origanum majorana*), which has white flowers and is more fragrant, but is more delicate.

Hybrid varieties are popular for their various qualities such as early cropping, vegetables of homogenous quality, spectacular flowers, or resistance to pests, but they are harder to reproduce, and growing them from the previous year's seeds is unreliable.

The more traditional varieties are worth cultivating as they add to the biodiversity of your local area and you can have fun gathering their seeds to re-sow for the following year. Despite their interest and qualities, these rustic varieties are becoming rarer and more difficult to find even on traditional French market stalls, so it is only through people continuing to buy them that they will remain available in commercial catalogues. See the Address Book p.218 for a list of seed producers offering 'heritage' varieties.

Labour of love: neat lines of vegetables in their various shades of green with the occasional dash of colour. Watering cans are still a regular sight in many gardens as they allow for softer watering of tender seedlings and are more economical than watering with a hosepipe.

Order, order: grid planning, straight lines and paths, and v-shaped staking, lend an almost abstract quality to the vegetable garden.

Recipes from the rural garden

Soup (*potage* - see Language Lab p.50) was the usual way of cooking vegetables. Carrots, potatoes, leeks, onions, with a few sprigs of herbs and a slice of fatty meat would be cooked in water for several hours. It would be served throughout the day, even for breakfast. On Sundays and special occasions, a nicer piece of lean meat would be thrown in. This was, and still is, the *pot-au-feu*.There would be regional varia-tions. In Normandy, the *soupe à la graisse* was made with beef suet, and in the Auvergne, the *bajanat*, a soup made with dried chestnuts cooked in water and milk, was a staple diet.

Home-made liqueurs were also an essential part of a rural lifestyle. They were typically made from a base of *eau de vie* (strong, clear spirit) or white wine, with water and sugar in which flowers, herbs or other plants would be left to macerate.

La pissette (dandelion liqueur): place 1.2 kg of dandelion flowers in a jar and cover them with 4 litres of boiling water. Leave to soak for two days. Remove, squeeze and discard the flowers. Add 3 oranges, 3 lemons, 500 g of raisins and 1.75 kg of sugar to the liquid. Mix well and leave to ferment for three weeks, stirring every day. Filter through a coffee paper filter and bottle.

Cassis : clean and dry 1 kg of blackcurrants. Crush them by hand and mix them in a jar with 1 l of fruit-based *eau de vie*, and 250 g of sugar. Leave to soak for about six weeks, stirring periodically, then filter and bottle.

How to cultivate a vegetable garden

A vegetable garden will require a fair amount of work if you want it to provide you with a broad range of fruit and vegetables all through the growing season. It needs a good deal of planning and organisation to get the soil ready at the right time, sow the seeds in the right order, rotate the various crops, anticipate when to pick them, and deal with any bugs and pests.

If you are a beginner, or if you do not have a great deal of time or are not always there, then start with a few easy vegetables: tomatoes or courgettes bought as pot-grown seedlings, French beans, let-tuces and radishes, aromatics such as sorrel or fennel, or root crops like parsnip, depending on your climate. These will all grow with minimum effort from you – all you need to do is be around when they need to be picked.

For other plants it would be useful to have a cold frame where you can sow the plants from seed, allowing them to germinate earlier and more easily.

The classic country vegetable plot will bring together vegetables, herbs, and fruits, as well as flowers, planted partly for colour but also to attract insects which will feed on, or deter, bugs. This is a wonderful way to make the garden more decorative and implement sound ecological principles.

A deserving garden: set amidst a garden wholly inspired by its rural setting, this vegetable plot (above) has earned its owners a French Horticultural Society award for their observance of natural traditional methods.

● Find a good site

Choose somewhere ideally near the house, with plenty of sunshine, sheltered from the wind but with good air circulation. Do not try to create something too big. For a family of four, you will probably find that 100 sq m provides plenty. Remember you will need a water source nearby. This is essential.

● Secure the frontiers

Keep animals out by putting up a fence. A wild hedge is not ideal as it still lets in smaller animals, and its roots might infringe on the plot. More suitable alternatives include a very dense and closely cut hedge, a wire or wooden fence, or better still, a medium height wall.

● Organise the plot

Vegetable gardens are always well laid out for practical reasons. Plan a good path up the middle, wide enough to take a wheelbarrow, and smaller paths running at right angles off it, either in compacted earth or wooden boards, which will separate the various areas allocated to each type of vegetable. Alternatively, you can raise the vegetable beds behind low retaining structures such as old wooden beams.

● Companion planting

Planting flowers with vegetables is often regarded as beneficial by gardeners, with many varieties warding off pests that thrive on vegetables and vice-versa, some vegetables have a deterrent effect for other pests and protect flowers nearby. Marigolds, many varieties of camomile, and members of the compositae family are among the most effective. Nettles, chives and garlic prevent bacterial and fungal diseases. Sacrificing certain

plants will distract pests from the ones you want to protect. For instance, when thinning out and replanting seedlings, leave unused plants on the ground: slugs will feed on them rather than on the seedlings. Tobacco plants attract whiteflies and are used to protect cabbages, and nasturtium attract blackflies. Invite animals and insects that feed on pests into the vegetable plot: frogs, ladybirds, bees, birds, etc. Finally, alternate crops so that parasites do not spread.

● **Edge the beds**
Borders are not a requirement but they do help marking a clear divide between cultivated areas and other areas, and they make the vegetable garden look good. Wooden boards, half sunken into the ground, are effective at separating the vegetable plot from grass paths. Flowers are a good option too: they are a good way of implementing companion planting principles, and they bring colour and a touch of poetry to the plot. Look around old rural gardens in your area and you will often see vegetable plots lined with bright dahlias or colourful zinnias, as well as French and African marigolds whose scent wards off insects.

● **Flower borders**
If you are opting for flowers, sow annuals at the same time as you sow vegetables; they will easily be cleared out at the same time, in the autumn, when the time comes to prepare the soil for the following season. You can also sow them between the rows of vegetables. Perennials should be planted around the edge of the plot to avoid them spreading into the cultivated parts, and to provide a permanent border.

● **Mix in herbs**
Herbs make good border plants, and they are also useful to cover the scent of vegetables nearby, making them less easily detectable by insects. They help prevent weeds and they attract bees and butterflies. And do not forget strawberries, especially alongside rows of other soft fruits, as their roots are said to attract worms, which keep the soil aerated.

Getting advice: crop rotation, plant varieties, traditional methods – older gardeners will have a wealth of knowledge that you should not be afraid to tap into, and most will be more than happy to advise.

● **Deal with weeds**
Weeds and poisonous plants such as buttercup, mercury, field bindweed, petty spurge, scarlet pimpernel, dock, and knotweed, must be dug out and burned – or composted – before they reach maturity and start setting seed.

● **Combining varieties of vegetables**
Certain combinations of vegetables work particularly well. Alternate rows of peas, potatoes and corn, for instance: the former two protect the young seedlings or plants, the latter keep the soil cool. Other traditional combinations include: leeks and broad beans with carrots, celery with onion, beans with potatoes, cucumbers with strawberries, and tomatoes with garlic, asparagus, nasturtium and basil.

● **Rotate the crops**
This ensures that the soil does not become poor and contains the spread of diseases. Crop rotation consists in growing different plants every year in cycles.

Year 1: plant crops that tend to extract a lot from the soil, such as solanaceae (aubergine, peppers), cucurbitaceae (cucumber, melon), and chenopodiaceae (beetroot, chard). See p.52 for details of plant families.

Year 2: plant less greedy species, such as brassicaeae (cabbages) and liliaceae (leek, garlic, etc.).

Year 3: plant varieties that thrive in poorer soil such as leguminous plants, apiaceae (carrot, celery) and fabaceae (beans, peas)

Crop rotation is particularly beneficial for cabbages, tomatoes and potatoes, which do not like growing in the same spot two years running.

ORGANISING THE VEGETABLE PLOT

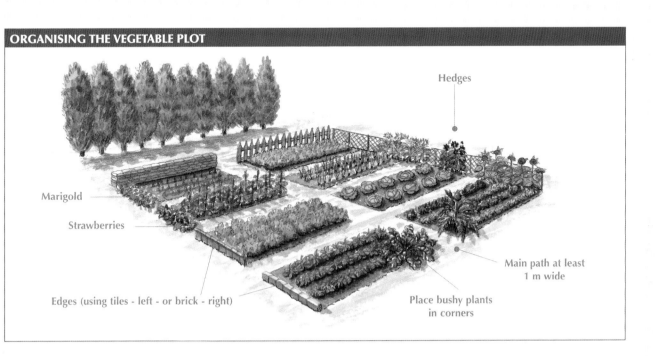

Hedges

Marigold

Strawberries

Main path at least
1 m wide

Edges (using tiles - left - or brick - right)

Place bushy plants
in corners

● **Watch the moon**
Older gardeners continue to believe that the moon has an influence on plants. Some recommend planting all vegetables that grow underground and those that must not grow to seed too quickly when the moon is waning, and fruit trees, shrubs and flowers when the moon is rising. Others take account of the phases of the moon as it crosses the constellations of the zodiac, each of which corresponds to a particular type of plant.

● **Dig in autumn and winter**
Take out roots and weeds, and put in well rotted horse manure – in principle, the only fertiliser suitable for a rural garden. You could also sow 'green manure' in the winter, which is better than leaving the soil bare. These are plants, such as lucerne, clover, and comfrey, which retain nutrients and keep the soil workable. After being cut, they are left to decompose in situ, and then dug into the soil (see Natural Fertilisers, p.128).

● **Mulch**
Mulch (a top dressing of manure, dried grass cuttings, bark, or straw - thus the French term *paillage*) contains the spread of weeds, and helps keep the ground moist. There are two schools of mulching. You can either fork the mulch gently into the top soil or leave it to insects and earth worms to break it down and carry it into the soil.

● **Use the corners**
Larger plants such as celery, fennel, artichoke, rhubarb or angelica, spread and can interfere with the growth of nearby plants. Unless your garden is large enough that you can have a dedicated row or area, these spreading plants are better planted in corners or on the outer rows, where their leaves will overhang the path but will not affect other vegetables.

THE ORCHARD

Homer described orchards as places of eternal bounty, gifts of the gods, while the literature of the Middle Ages styled them as a symbolic refuge for the rituals of courtly love. Throughout the ages, the orchard has been seen as a special place, suggestive of *douceur de vivre* and abundance.

Growing fruit trees was elevated to an art form, the high point of which was the King's garden at the palace of Versailles. However, the humble country orchard, left to its own devices, is equally enchanting.

From walled garden to open space

As we have seen, the country orchard really starts in the vegetable garden, where you will find the smaller varieties of fruit trees growing along a sunny wall: pear and apple trees, raspberry and currant bushes, or the peach tree which really took off in France at the end of the 19th century.

Full size trees such as apple, pear, quince, cherry, plum and walnut would generally be grown outside the garden walls in a separate enclosure close to the house, sometimes called a *couderc* or *courtil*, which is also where smaller animals, like pigs or geese, would be kept. A hedge would usually surround the orchard to protect the trees from the wind and keep the animals in. For this reason, the hedge needed to be strong and dense right down to the ground – typically using holly or blackthorn (sloe).

In the Perche, a region of Normandy, apple trees destined for the cider industry used to cover vast swathes of the landscape, either scattered in the fields or grown densely in orchards, but they have suffered from mechanisation. The requirements of mechanised picking have also affected the landscapes of Picardy where very few orchards now produce apples for eating (the French call these *pommes 'au couteau'*). Similar changes are taking place in the chestnut and walnut orchards in the Périgord, Corrèze and Limousin regions. Where they are not grown commercially, fruit trees may be found almost anywhere, near the house or out in the fields, alongside roads or amidst hedges.

Fruit trees would also find their way into vineyards, where it

Orchard atmosphere: orchards in bloom in the morning sunlight.

> **LANGUAGE LAB: FRUIT TREES**
>
> **Common fruit trees (tree and fruit)**
> **Apple** : le pommier (la pomme)
> **Apricot** : l'abricotier (un abricot)
> **Cherry** : le cerisier (la cerise)
> **Fig** : le figuier (la figue)
> **Hazelnut** : le noisetier (la noisette)
> **Nectarine** : le brugnon
> **Peach** : le pêcher (la pêche)
> **Pear** : le poirier (la poire)
> **Plum** : le prunier (la prune)
> **Quince** : le cognassier (le coing)
> **Walnut** : le noyer (la noix)
>
> *For more on fruit trees, see the Plant Finder p.190 and the Glossary p.210.*

Variety show: although many fruits look the same, there are hundreds of varieties for each species (currants and raspberries - opposite).

Make your own apple juice

If you have an apple or pear orchard that you want to bring back to life, you could use the services of a company called Renova, which rents out mobile cider presses. In effect, members of Renova pay an annual subscription and then take turns to borrow a mobile cider press at their own home or farm. It not only allows people to make a small quantity of juice without a big capital outlay, it also brings in a charming human dimension to the operation. Renova also offers training in orchard keeping (see Address Book, p.218). Alternatively, local growers may be willing to press your apples for you for a small fee.

would not be uncommon to see strawberries, peaches or nectarines in between the rows of vine.

In the orchard garden, it was also commonplace for people to grow fruit shrubs, or *joualles*, as they are known in the south-west of France, primarily for household consumption. And people used to go through enormous quantities of fruit in many forms: fresh, dried, preserved, in jams, in syrup, and, of course, spirits when there used to be no restriction on distillation rights and anyone could be a '*bouilleur de cru*' (home distiller).

Contrary to what could be inferred from market stalls today, France used to be home to an amazing variety of fruits. For instance, there used to be over 4,000 apple and pear varieties, each with its specific use: some for eating, others for juice, cider, cooking, preserving, etc.

There were early pears, like the *Saint Jean*, winter pears like the *poire-curé*, and bitter pears, which required cooking, like the *Pro-d'un* ('one is enough') or the *Estrangla-chen* ('dog-strangler') in the Limousin. And the same was true of apples, with some local varieties producing fruit from mid-summer right through to the end of the following spring: *pomme de Madeleine* ('Madeleine's apple'), *pomme de glace* ('ice apple'), so called because it is quite tart, or *pomme de fer* ('iron apple'), which would be picked in November and would keep until May. These have become virtual museum pieces, though some organisations still keep these species (see Address Book p.218).

Traditional varieties of pear which are still available today include *Louise Bonne d'Avranches*, *William bon Chrétien*, and *Doyenne d'hiver*. Among the apples, we can still find *Calville*, *Grand Alexandre*, and *Transparentes*.

Ground cover

Your orchard will look fresh and natural if you just let wild flowers and meadow plants cover the ground. As with the vegetable garden, these flowers will play a useful part in keeping pests and harmful insects under control. They attract ladybirds,

hoverflies and lacewings, which are all keen devourers of aphids, greenflies and blackflies.

However, for more abundant crops it is better to prevent dense grass from growing underneath the tree, as it will compete with the trees for water. This applies to younger trees especially, which require regular watering in order to get off to a good start in their early years of growth.

Wait until the end of June to mow the grass in the orchard, when grasses have seeded and enter a dormant stage. Mowing frequently before that will only make the grass more thirsty.

The most effective solution is to hoe and weed the ground around the trees in the summer and apply a mulch of straw, cut grass that has been allowed to dry first, or shredded branches. To boost growth even further, add liquid nettle manure or a bit of ordinary horse manure when watering and treat with a copper-based fungicide. As the fruit is beginning to ripen, reduce watering to increase the flavour.

Pear trees grown *espalier* style enjoy the warm, sheltered walls of this enclosed vegetable garden (above and below).

FIELDS & MEADOWS

The meadow

More than anything else in the countryside, open meadows have a very strong symbolic significance. For most of us, meadows conjure up memories or visions of picnics amidst thousands of wild flowers, afternoon naps on fresh, green grass, and games of hide-

Savoir-faire: creating an orchard

Turning a piece of spare land into an orchard can be a rewarding experience. Fruit trees bring structure to the space and will give your garden a truly rural, natural feel. Except for a little bit of work to start with, the orchard should require very little maintenance and you will be able to enjoy its peaceful atmosphere and have the immense satisfaction of picking and eating your own fruit.

● **Choosing the trees**
To plant or restore an orchard, you first need to find out which fruit trees are best suited to your region. Contact botanical conservation groups or voluntary organisations, such as the *Croqueurs de Pommes* which works to safeguard rare species of apple trees (see Address Book p.218). Another good place to start is the local market, where you will see apples grown locally, and be able to taste them. Finally, visit a local nursery. They should be able to advise on, and source, local varieties which will be suited to the climate and soil. If you buy from them, check whether they do their own propagation or buy from elsewhere in Europe as this may affect the suitability of the tree to your area.

● **Choosing the site**
The ideal plot has plenty of air but is sheltered from the wind (if nec-

essary by a strong hedge), and is also on well-drained, stony ground, slightly sloping, and facing southwest. However, these are ideal conditions only and there is no need for all to be met. It is best to plant the same species of fruit trees together as this helps with pollination.

● **If you have plenty of land, you could create an 'open space' orchard** (*verger de plein vent*) planted with taller trees (with trunks of at least 1.5 m between the ground and the lower branches). These orchards can be spectacular but the trees take approximately 15 years to mature fully and you will need a ladder to pick the fruit. No pruning is required other than occasional thinning to let light into the tree crown and stimulate fruit growth. Fruit trees need space, so count 20 sq m per tree and a minimum of 8 m in between each tree. Species particular-

ly suited for growing in the open include: apple, pear, quince, plum, cherry and walnut trees, which will happily live 50 years or more. It might be tempting to hurry nature along by planting slightly older trees but this may be more expensive and more risky. Instead, simply make sure that you choose properly grafted trees from good stock (*porte-greffe 'franc'*).

● **Alternatively, if you are short of space or time, plant shorter trees** (*fruitiers basses tiges*), with trunks between 0.8 and 1.2 m tall, which crop within three years and you will not need to climb up a ladder to gather the fruit. As with taller fruit trees, no pruning is required other than thinning the tree crown to let in air and light in order to help with fruit growth. Shorter trees must be planted 5 m apart, and feel especially at home in a walled garden, sheltered from the

wind and soaking up the heat which accumulates in the walls during the day – particularly the more vulnerable early varieties which must be protected from frost. Plant them a few centimetres away from the wall and train them either flat against the wall along a trellis or wires in espalier style to achieve a structured, linear shape, or in fan shape (*en palmette*), or simply *à la diable,* that is, letting the crown bush out and allowing the branches to grow away from the wall.

● **Ensuring healthy growth:**
There are a few precautions to take when planting and pruning fruit trees: keep the graft above ground and make sure it faces south. Pruning depends on the species and variety. Most English gardening books on pruning and grafting should provide suitable advice but if you cannot find the species you are looking for and your language skills are up to it, see the Bibliography p.217. For further information on planting trees, see pp. 110 *et seq.*

Tall grasses and wild flowers will add a touch of *insouciance* to your garden and work as a conservation area for butterflies, insects and rare flowers (above). Mowing a stretch of grass in the meadow creates a path instantly (opposite).

and-seek in fields of poppies and cornflowers. And although in many regions wild flowers have disappeared from the fields as a result of intensive farming, a lot of France is still very much true to this image.

However, these fields have a specific agricultural purpose: fields are pastures for cows, and meadows, once cut, will provide winter fodder for livestock before being used for grazing when grass starts growing again.

Originally a feature of the agricultural landscape, the meadow can easily be integrated into a domestic rural garden as a substitute for the usual lawn. With its succession of flowers and colours depending on the season, it will provide a haven for butterflies and act as a conservation area for rare flowers too.

How to create your own wild grassland

If you have a large garden, or indeed a field attached to your property, you can easily turn it into a beautiful wild flower meadow. Preparation and maintenance require a little bit of effort but this is nothing compared with the demands of lawn care, and you will be able to enjoy flowers up to the day of 'Saint Jean' (21st June - French gardeners often use Saints' days as references).

Start mowing the meadow in the summer, so that the plants do not spread or wilt. This will also stimulate fresh new growth in the autumn. However, do not cut the wild flowers you would like to keep for next season but let them go to seed. They will either self-seed a little later in the summer or be eaten and deposited by birds. Old favourites include: shepherd's purse, the big field daisy, yarrow, with its pale pink umbrellas, the lesser and greater celandines, buttercup, meadow anemones, and chickweed.

If you are starting with a shapeless piece of fallow land, you will need to tidy it up thoroughly first: pull out nettles, brambles, thorns and other bushes, remove any big stones, level and work the ground with a rotavator. You can also sow ray-grass, a tough grass originally designed for grazing, which will form a basic canvas, of which wild flowers will soon start to take possession. Ground preparation is best done in the autumn, then cover the ground with sheets of black plastic until the spring when you sow the seeds. Remember never to fertilise a wild meadow as this would merely encourage grasses, which would then choke out the wild flowers.

You can, of course, cheat to get even more colour into your

A meadow will bring
a more natural feel to
the garden than a lawn,
and for much less effort.

grassland during the spring. In the autumn, after clearing the ground of overgrown or dead plants and flowers, plant crocus, narcissus or snow drops, and early-flowering perennials such as cowslip, primroses, cardamines, wild geraniums etc. For summer meadow flowers, you can buy seed mixes of annuals and perennials, but make sure that the seed mix you choose is suitable for your soil conditions, otherwise the flowers are unlikely to re-seed properly. Choose the more hardy or wild species, which flower at different times of the year, are easy to plant and will look after themselves. You may otherwise deploy a lot of effort for a very short-lived result.

Looking after your meadow

One way of avoiding the potentially arduous chore of cutting the grass is to invite a local farmer to graze his cows, horses or sheep in your field. This may be only temporary, perhaps just a few weeks, but it is nevertheless recommended to charge rent, even if it is quite small, to prevent jealousy in other quarters of the farming community. The downsides are that you will not be able to use your land during this period, that the field may need to be fenced, either with barbed or electric wire, and there are, of course, the leftover cow pats. This option will be worthwhile if you only use the house in the summer, once the animals are gone.

Alternatively, if you intend to mow the long grass, or if you have agreed with a local farmer that he will cut it for you then keep it for hay, wait until the end of June when grasses have reached maturity and are about to enter a period of dormancy. The grass that will grow afterwards will be shorter and you should, ideally, cut it again in the autumn – once should be enough unless you want to be able to use the area for various activities in the meantime (or just lying on it!), in which case you will need to cut it every three or four weeks. The grass will start turning yellow from June onwards, brightening up the fields with its shades of straw.

THE POND

Pond life's hidden talents

Just like the meadow, the pond used to be a familiar part of farm and village life. It was usually dug in a carefully chosen location, designed to capture rainwater and groundwater draining from surrounding

**LANGUAGE LAB:
MEADOW AND FIELD FLOWERS**

Bell-flower : la campanule
Celandine (greater / lesser) : la chélidoine / la ficaire
Cuckooflower : la cardamine
Cowslip : la primevère, or le coucou
Crocus : le crocus
Daffodil : la jonquille
Daisy : la paquerette
Field : le pré
Grass : une herbe
Meadow : la prairie
Meadow crocus : la colchique
Ox-eye daisy : la marguerite
Narcissus : le narcisse
Pasture : le paturage
Poppy : le coquelicot (field poppy), le pavot
Shepherd's purse : la bourse-à-pasteur
Violet : la violette
Wild flowers : les fleurs des champs

For more on meadow flowers, see the Plant Finder p.165 and the Glossary p.210.

Whether it is the verdant scenery of the natural riverside (above) or the finer lines of a man-made fishpond (opposite), ponds will play host to many species of wildlife that will help maintain the ecological balance of the garden.

fields. In regions such as the Pays d'Auge where clay is used for building, ponds would form where the clay had been dug out, usually not far from nearby buildings. It was used as a watering hole for livestock, and as a useful water source in case of fire. If it was big enough, it would also be used to stock fish, grow various plants (like rush), and maintain small animals such as ducks and frogs. Chickens and other domestic fowl (referred to in France as the *basse-cour*) would also be kept nearby.

Although far from being pure, the water from the pond is perfectly suitable for cattle, as bacteria naturally present in the water clean the pond of organic waste (as long as the amount is not too great), while aquatic plants filter out particles suspended in the water.

Ponds have been neglected for a long time, or filled in, as they were seen as obstacles to modern farming and got in the way of tractors. Many dried up, and some were used as landfill sites or just wasteland. However, many French boroughs (*communes*) are rediscovering the benefits of ponds as reservoirs, which are useful at times of drought or fire, and also act as ecological conservation areas. Some voluntary organisations and public bodies are now providing technical or financial support for the upkeep or creation of ponds (see Address Book p.218).

Swarming with life, ponds are a vital source of food for wildlife. Like lakes, peat bogs, and flood plains, they combine the air, water and soil that are ideal for a vast number of plants and animals, many of which are rare species whose habitats are increasingly threatened by systematic drainage and levelling, new road building, riverside clean-ups and the drying of lakes. Some 30% of endangered species in France live in these wetlands, so having a pond in your garden will contribute to the eco-system and to the preservation of endangered species. In return, the pond will help keep the eco-system of your garden well balanced.

Finally, you will also be creating a beautiful setting: water lilies, irises, and rushes rustling in the wind, migrating birds that stop there to drink, the constant animation of frogs, newts, and all sorts of unusual insects. You could even introduce ducks or geese.

HOW TO MAKE A POND

Making a pond is a significant enterprise which will require careful planning and organisation.

Reeds, rushes, water lilies and other pond plants provide an ideal habitat for insects and wildlife (above). Reflections and shadows over the surface of the water create a slightly mysterious atmosphere (opposite).

Choosing the site

The best place to choose is a natural depression which already collects rainwater and surface water. Alternatively, you could direct rainwater into the pond, using an underground drain dug into the surrounding ground. The bottom of a valley is an obvious choice as the pond will blend in with an existing network of wet areas. Avoid locating the pond just below farmed areas as pesticides and fertilisers could pollute the water, although you might build a buffer zone - which could be either a hedge, a raised bank, or a gutter - which would act as a sieve and filter out pollutants.

If your pond is located near a road or houses, you will need to ensure that there is still a secluded area where wildlife can be left undisturbed and is able to prosper.

If the whole surface of the pond is to be exposed to direct sunlight, you may have problems with algae, and the pond could dry up. Ideally, only two thirds of the surface should be in the sun, which is vital to the preservation of life in the pond. But while you do need a bit of shade, make sure that the pond is not too close to trees, as autumn leaves falling into it will make the water dirty and could asphyxiate the pond.

The pond can be a wonderful feature of your garden, so you might want to site it so that it can be seen from the house. But you must take precautions if you have children: build a fence to make sure that they are not able to get near the pond when they are unsupervised. Remember also that the croaking of frogs in the spring can be extremely loud and that ponds can be a mosquito breeding ground in the summer. Finally, make sure you install an

overflow, whether a pipe or other system, that can take away excess water to prevent flooding.

How big should it be?

If you want to create a rich eco-system, then a pond of around 5 m in diameter and about 80 cm deep (12.5 cubic metres) is a good size. However, a pond of just 3 cubic metres is already big enough to attract a good number of wildlife species, but if you opt for this size, one side will need to be deeper to make sure that the pond

Savoir-faire:

Water will add atmosphere to your the perfect pond, which will be both a

does not completely freeze over in the winter. If you are planning on a pond any bigger than 20 cubic metres (5 m x 2 m x 2 m), prepare yourself for serious excavation work. You will also need to think of how you will dispose of the rubble, and making the pond watertight will be more tricky, particularly if it is not in clay ground.

Making it watertight

Avoid masonry material which will almost inevitably crack as a result of frost, and leak – particularly if you are building a larger pond. Pre-fabricated rigid ponds are an acceptable option but they tend to be quite small and are expensive to buy. A real natural pond is constructed with a layer of well-compacted clay at the bottom of the pit, covered in turn with a thin layer of sand or silt to protect it from drying out. Another solution is to use self-expanding clay known as *betonite*, if the underlying earth is not chalky. It can be worked into the underlying earth to a depth of 15-30 cm, unless you buy it as ready-made geosynthetic clay liner (such as Claymax or Bentomat – see Address Book p.218). Although this latter technique is used industrially to line landfill sites, there are mixed reports on ponds made with this material.

The most common (and cheapest) solution is to use a PVC liner – or better still, a low density polythene, which is more environmentally friendly, or a vulcanised butyl material (coloured dark green or black, which is less visible). Choose one which is thick enough (between 0.5 and 1 mm) that it will not get punctured and at the same time not so heavy that it will be difficult to handle. Note that, the more complicated the shape of the pond, the more difficult it will be to put the liner in place.

Filling the pond

After all this work, the moment of truth. Simply fill the pond, but not quite completely, with water from a tap – or better still, rainwater collected in a water butt if you have one. Then, wait for the

● **Digging the pond**
You will need to think about the distance between the deepest part of the pond and the edges. The circulation of water and oxygenation will depend on this, and if you get it right you will end up spending less time looking after the pond. To start with, cut off the surface layer of grass, but keep the slabs of turf as you may use them later for edging. Then, dig the pond, either by hand or with a mechanical digger.

Remember that if you are hiring a digger, or indeed have bought a liner that will be delivered in a van or lorry, you will need to make sure you have good access for vehicles to the pond site. As you dig, create the various levels or plateaux which will correspond to a particular zone of pond life (from shallow to deep). Mark the shape of the respective areas to be dug with a piece of hosepipe or string to ensure that the correct area is dug out.

creating a pond

garden but creating a pond should not be undertaken lightly. Here are a few tips to help you create joy for the eye and a haven for wildlife creatures.

● **Getting it level**

A way of checking whether the edges of your pond are level is to rig up the system shown in the diagram on the right. Simply cut up a couple of plastic bottles, and stick a hosepipe into the neck of each – either cutting through the lid for a narrow pipe, or putting the hosepipe directly through the neck of the bottle and sealing it with heavy duty hard-setting mastic from a DIY store.

Then, fill the whole system with water, and work your way round the edge of the pond to check the levels. Note, however, that although this method is simple in theory, it can be difficult to do accurately in practice.

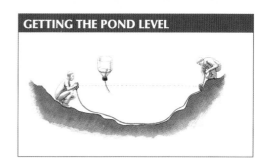

GETTING THE POND LEVEL

● **Levels and zones**

The first level in the pond will be just about 20 cm below the ground surface. This will constitute the edge of the pond, where marsh plants will be sited and animals will come to drink or bathe, as well as the place where the liner is held firmly in place, covered in earth or sand. It should be just slightly sloping towards the pond. Perfectionists can then create another level, this time about 40 cm beneath the surface. This will allow you to get better access to the pond to clean it or to tend to plants. Beyond this, simply dig down a steady slope to a depth of 0.80 to 1 m - the minimum depth to

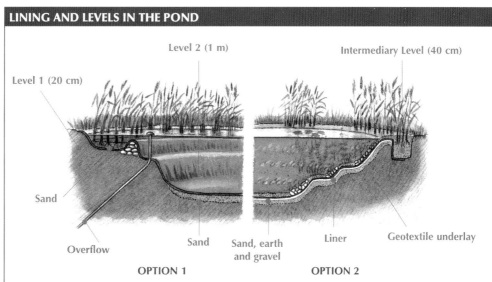

LINING AND LEVELS IN THE POND

Level 1 (20 cm)

Level 2 (1 m)

Intermediary Level (40 cm)

Sand

Overflow

Sand

Sand, earth and gravel

Liner

Geotextile underlay

OPTION 1

OPTION 2

prevent the pond from freezing through in the winter and from drying out in the summer. Once you have dug out the earth, remove any stones or roots, and firm it down carefully, especially around the sides. You can also put some sand down on the base to protect the liner from any remaining sharp stones in the ground, and put down a geotextile underlay to prevent root damage, or dam-age caused by burrow-ing animals. Old car-pets would be equally good. Put down the liner, starting at the centre of the pond. Think of enlisting the help of several people to unfold it, as liners can be very heavy. Remove your shoes if you need to walk on the liner. Cover the liner with 5-15 cm of earth, made up, ideally, of two parts gravel to one part sand and one part silt or mud.

The lush surroundings of this pond (right) are an idyllic setting for a bench with a view, tucked away on the edge of woodland. Hostas and bog irises are at home near the water (left).

rest to fill up with rainwater. The best times for making a pond are spring and autumn, which are the rainy seasons.

Once the pond has filled up, cut the liner, leaving about a metre beyond the edge of the pond. The outer rim of the liner is then buried in a trench cut all round the pond, just below the level of the edges. This can then covered over with rocks, gravel or plants.

You can top up the pond occasionally, but if you add water too frequently, you will upset the delicate eco-system which is starting to take hold. The temperature will change, and chlorine in tap water will kill off some of the micro-organisms you are trying to encourage. If the water is not being cleaned enough by the vegetation, you can help the situation along by buying pond bacteria to allow the pond to 'digest' some of the organic matter that it needs to process.

POND LIFE

A newly created pond will rapidly fill up with numerous aquatic plants which will grow from seeds - either blown in by the wind or stuck to the feathers of a passing bird taking a dip in your new pond. Nevertheless, the ground around the edges will settle more effectively if it is planted with a few specimens from the start. This will also encourage plant diversity and make the pond attractive from the outset.

What to plant in the deep section

You could plant water milfoil simply by leaving a clump under a stone and letting it grow in the water. It needs neither roots nor earth to survive.

Water lilies can be bought in a basket, already in their own earth. They flower in July and should be planted in the deep part of the pond. Put the roots in their ball of earth into a cardboard box and use a sturdy fishing rod to push it to the required spot if you do not want to, or cannot, wade into the water.

You can also put in some wild plants collected from other ponds, such as duckweed, hornwort, and Canadian pondweed, though the latter can spread very quickly and is difficult to remove once it gets a grip. Broad-leaved pondweed flowers from May to September - small frogs and many kinds of dragon flies love it – but it too can get a bit out of control. Water crowfoot and other members of the buttercup family come in numerous varieties, some of which are protected species. They help oxygenate the water, and provide food for insects and frogs. Members of the ceratophyllum family, such as the soft and rigid hornworts, are another good source of oxygen and a good habitat for insects. You do not need to plant them – just cut a few stalks from a nearby pond in the autumn, and throw them into your pond.

Around the edges

Flowering rushes, soft or compact rushes, reed, water forget-me-not, or common clubrush are ideal for the marshy edges of the pond. Planted in a clay soil, they will help stabilise the edges. Bullrushes provide a perfect natural habitat for songbirds and their seeds are also appreciated by many migrating birds. They are also used as a biological decontaminating agent in certain

---

**LANGUAGE LAB :
POND PLANTS**

Alder : un aulne
Ash : le frêne
Branched bur-reed : le rubanier dressé
Broad-leaved pondweed : le potamot
Buttercup : le bouton d'or
Canadian pondweed : une élodée du Canada
Creeping jenny : la lysimaque nummulaire
Duckweed : les lentilles d'eau
Gipsywort : la lycope d'Europe
Guelder rose : le viorne obier
Hornwort : le cératophylle
Iris (yellow) : un iris d'eau, or faux-acore
Loosestrife (purple / yellow) : la salicaire commune / grande lysimaque
Marsh marigold : le populage
Poplar : le peuplier
Reed : le roseau
Rush : le jonc
Sedge : les laîches, carex
Spearwort (lesser) : la petite douve, la renoncule aquatique
Water figwort : la scrufulaire aquatique
Water forget-me-not : le myosotis d'eau
Water milfoil : le myriophylle
Water mint : la menthe aquatique
Waterlily : le nénuphar
Willow : le saule

Rushes (joncs)
Bullrush : la massette
Flowering rush : le jonc fleuri, butome
Soft rush : le jonc épars
Compact rush : le jonc congloméré
Common clubrush : le jonc des tonneliers, scirpe

For more on pond plants, see the Plant Finder p.194 and the Glossary p.210.

Savoir-faire: pond care

It is a fact of nature: in the wild ponds are a transitory environment; without human intervention all ponds, even those with the right ecological balance, ultimately fill up and turn into a solid environment. Here are a few diagnostics and remedies to make sure that your pond lives on.

A pond will not look after itself indefinitely. At one point, you will have to step in – literally.

In effect, a pond is always in the process of filling up as dead vegetation and mineral sediments get deposited on the pond bed, and plant life starts to take over. So you need to keep an eye on it, and get tough with any plants that look like they are trying to muscle in and squeeze the others out. In the old days, ponds were regularly dredged, and the mud and slime used to fertilise the fields or vegetable patch. You can still do this today, but make sure you leave a good layer down at the bottom to help keep the pond base watertight. Don't dredge it out too often though - once every five years should be enough.

● **Silted up**
Remove half the gunge, taking plants out by hand first (or with a fork) making sure that you don't make a hole in the liner. This should be done in November, to minimise the effects on the wildlife in the pond.

● **Drying up**
There are several possible explanations. One is simply natural evaporation during hot weather. Another is a change affecting some of the water that used to drain off the fields and into your pond: a farmer may have installed a drain which has diverted groundwater. Alternatively, a heavy frost could have caused cracking in the pond bed. Or the dead roots of a nearby tree could be causing problems, behaving like canals that channel water away from the pond. If the problem is not with the supply of water to the pond, then you will have to bite the bullet, empty every-thing from the pond and examine its surface closely. Dig down to the layer of clay which is holding the water in place and clean it carefully. Any holes will have to be plugged carefully (with more clay) before you test the pond again to see if it is watertight and then replace everything.

● **Too much algae**
This usually comes down to too much nitrogen and phosphorus in the water, and warm weather. The best way to deal with this is to pull out the algae, and dig the pond a little deeper (simply removing silt from the bottom is the best bet) as this will leave more room for cooler water to circulate. Also, include plenty of plants which will help to stave off the growth of algae. If the problem is duck-weed, this is less seri-ous: simply skim the surface to remove it, and think about putting in some fish (such as carp).

● **Cloudy / green water**
This is caused by a microscopic algae in a pond which has a lot of mineral salts and, probably, too many fish. The fish eat the zooplankton, which feeds on algae and keeps it from spread-ing, so where the fish population is getting too large this balance is upset. The solution is to thin out the fish population (or place them temporarily in another pond), and put in some plants which purify the water. You can also apply crushed chalk which will push organic matter down to the bottom of the pond where it will set-tle. This should reduce the sludge to 10% of its original volume.

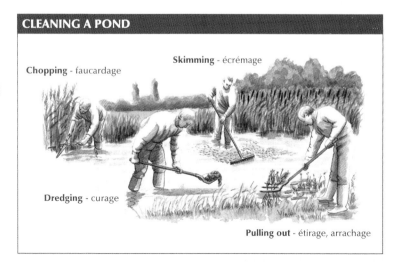

CLEANING A POND

Chopping - faucardage

Skimming - écrémage

Dredging - curage

Pulling out - étirage, arrachage

water treatment facilities, but it is another of those plants that will spread if not controlled.

Sedges help firm up the edges of a pond and they are used by spiders as suspension points and by the pupae of dragonflies for hatching out. Aquatic mint produces a lot of nectar which attracts insects; it produces light-purple flowers in August-September and its leaves, which are slightly toxic, are collected by female newts who fold them over their eggs.

Also worth considering are the bittersweet nightshade, the yellow loosestrife, creeping jenny, gipsywort, water figwort, the purple loosestrife, or the lesser spearwort. The yellow iris is a good choice for stabilising the borders and is another favourite of dragonflies. It flowers in May and June, even in the shade. Branched bur-reed is useful as it absorbs nitrates and purifies the water. It has striking round, club-shaped spiky flowers which turn brown in the autumn.

A little further away from the water's edge, you could plant alders, with their beautiful oval leaves, provided the surrounding are sufficiently marshy (the surrounds of a pond built with a liner may not be marshy enough). Guelder rose, with its pretty grapes of orangey-red berries, ash and poplar also grow well in these conditions. Willow, whose silvery foliage rustles in the wind, will be the delight of basket-weaving buffs, who will cut down the most supple boughs after pollarding the tree in the winter. Some tree suppliers will offer a number of different varieties of willows (see Address Book p.218).

All these plants are wild varieties, though some are available from commercial suppliers. You could take a few plants from a natural pond somewhere nearby, though make sure you do not take any protected species or take them from private property without the permission of the owner.

Go with a plant guide, and do not take more than one plant in ten. You should do your planting between March and June, bedding the plants in with a lump of clay. With plants that risk becoming very invasive, plant them in a tough box made of concrete, iron, or plastic which will help limit their spread through the pond.

The pond is alive with the flutter of butterflies and dragonflies (above) and the croaking of frogs (left)

Pond fauna

Given the chance, wildlife will quickly settle in your pond. First to arrive are the frogs and toads. Tadpoles and frogs are extremely useful to have around as they eat plenty of insects, but remember that it is illegal to scoop up tadpoles or frogspawn from other ponds as frogs are an endangered species. You will have to wait for them to find a way to your pond on their own.

Dragonflies have an extraordinary life, most of which is spent as larvae in the water, then as a pupa attached to a blade of grass in early summer. The insect itself will only live one season.

Other inhabitants of your pond may include newts and various water insects such as water scorpions, aquatic beetles, water boatmen, the common pond skater, salamander larvae and caddis flies.

You could also introduce fish into the pond, such as carp and stickleback, though their eggs may arrive independently, hitching a lift on the feathers of a passing heron. They will help control moquitoes, as they eat the larvae that swims on the surface of the pond. However, if the pond is too small, they could upset the balance of the eco-system, as they can be greedy and eat many of your plants and insects.

You should refrain from introducing exotic species, such as koi carp, goldfish, and terrapins, as these are predatory species that compete for food and territory with native species, sometimes causing their extinction. Terrapins for instance, have spread in European waters and invaded the natural habitat of the European Pond Turtle, a small water turtle now fighting for survival.

Birds will be regular visitors to your pond too. They will come to bathe and eat insects, including mosquitoes. When the water level drops, the dry pond sides often attract small wading birds on the hunt for worms. Ducks and geese are another possibility but they will eat your plants and you will have to live with cloudy water.

For more information about ponds, contact voluntary organisations such as 'Connaître et Protéger la Nature', a protection society with local clubs which organise outings and workshops on all things relating to nature and wildlife (see Address Book p.218).

Chapter 3

Hedges, fences & walls

❝ Each patch of earth could be considered as a patch of Earth; each garden just a fragment of an infinitely greater garden, extending to the very limits of the planet.❞

GILLES CLEMENT, THOMAS ET LE VOYAGEUR, ESQUISSE DU JARDIN PLANETAIRE

PARIS, ALBIN MICHEL, 1997

Fences have evolved since the Middle Ages, when the term was used to refer to the perimeter of a monastery only open to the monks and forbidden to members of the public (a situation reflected in words such as c*lôture* and *cloître*). Nowaday's fences represent a person's right to close off their property to others. As they started fulfilling their function as a boundary between the private space and the public space, fences also shaped the appearance of the countryside. However, fences, hedges and walls do not need to stand as impenetrable barriers so, before you start building your own, take a look around and find out about local methods and materials.

HEDGES

A rich heritage

There are a great many ways of parcelling up patches of land for cultivation, pasture, or grazing, which have evolved over the years. Originally designed to be temporary and movable, fencing was made of old branches threaded together (known as *haies sèches* or *haies mortes*) and, later on, from interwoven twigs (known as *plessis*).

From the Middle Ages onwards, when property limits were made permanent, the barriers became fixed and much more robust, hence the appearance of natural hedges formed from trees, shrubs or bushes.

The style of hedging can vary considerably from one region to another. In some areas, trees are left to grow freely; in others, they are regularly lopped both at the base and at the top to reduce the

Part and parcel: hedges, fences and walls divide up the land but also bring structure to the landscape and are an integral part of it. This dry stone wall in Brittany (opposite) blends so well with its surroundings that it could almost be a work of nature.

volume of foliage; or lateral branches are periodically sawn off, leaving just a long twisted trunk with a plume of leaves at the top. The trunk is later used for carpentry and the offcut branches for general woodwork or for burning.

Sometimes, hedges are simply made of a single row of bushes, and sometimes they are more complex and multi-layered. For the most common type of hedge, of intermediate height, smaller trees and berry-producing shrubs are usually used. These can include: hazel, willow, wild cherry, apple, hawthorn, blackthorn (sloe), and holly, either on their own or together with coppiced chestnut or hazel trees, and other medium-height trees pollarded a few metres above ground level. Below this, brambles and gorse are found alongside herbaceous varieties, providing nesting areas for small mammals.

Traditional hedges are trimmed every five to ten years, and it is a major task which can take weeks. The frequency and extent of the work is usually laid down in the lease of any tenant farm, as well as what should be done with the cuttings and who is entitled to them.

A *haie plessée*, or *plesse*, is a living fence, where young branches are platted through posts planted in the ground. Generally, thorny bushes are used, such as hawthorn. Training the branches needs to be done once a year in the winter (the *morte saison*, as it is also referred to in France).

THE LAW
Planning laws and hedges
Building a hedge is subject to prior notification to the local authority (*déclaration de travaux préalable*). The Town & Country Planning Code (*Code de l'Urbanisme*, article L.441.1 - 3) provides that, for general planning and environmental purposes, there may be local requirements concerning materials, height and appearance. These requirements, if any, will be found in the local planning guidelines (*Plan Local d'Urbanisme*, formerly known as *Plan d'Occupation des Sols*) which are available at your town hall (*mairie*).

There are records that this method was already used in Gaul before the Roman conquest, but it was little used in the Middle Ages, and today it is a dying art seen only in certain regions of France (Maine, Perche, Morvan, Sancerrois, Bourbonnais). However, some very old hedges, sometimes dating back hundreds of years, which are today maintained in the modern manner with clippers, started out as *plessé* and their core of woven branches is still visible.

A familiar sight in the north-western regions of France, Normandy in particular, is the *haie bocagère*, from the word *bocage*,

An unusual sight these days, the *haie plessée* is a wonderful example of man working with nature (above). A man-height hornbeam hedge (right) is easy to trim, acts as a good windbreak, and keeps its dried leaves through the winter.

In cold and rainy mountain climates, hedges help keep the soil on either side of the roads stable (left). *Haies de bocage* (opposite) were disappearing a decade ago but are now being replanted and maintained.

which refers to the division of farmland into small plots surrounded by dense hedges and used mainly as pasture for livestock. It is a high hedge, which usually mixes tall trees with shrubs and smaller trees, and is often grown on raised earth embankments (*talus*).

In some of France's oldest provinces, such as the Berry, hedges date from the Middle Ages, though generally most were planted during the 16th and 17th centuries. The current structure was established in the 18th century.

A more recent introduction is the mixed hedge (*haie mixte*), which is a combination of traditional species and ornamental ones.

The many benefits of hedges

In the past, the plants that went into a hedge were chosen for their usefulness. A hedge could supply wood for the fire, timber for building, berries and fruits, and be a refuge for animals, birds and insects, which in turn played their part in the agricultural eco-system.

Today, people are re-discovering the many benefits of hedges not just for the countryside itself but also for the farming economy.

Hedges also play a vital part in maintaining the balance of your garden. The parts of the plants that are above ground act as wind-breaks, they help shelter the ground and keep it comparatively warm, while the roots act as a drainage system, encouraging surface water into the ground and preventing it from drying out. Because they are often made of species that would not otherwise be grown commercially, hedges also contribute to biodiversity. And the wildlife that finds a refuge in hedges helps control the parasites and pests that might otherwise run riot in your garden.

But there are other more immediate and practical reasons for having hedges. Hedges look good throughout the year: they change colour with the seasons, grow new leaves, flowers and berries; they are good for wildlife; they live a very long time; and they are extremely resilient and inexpensive to look after. However, there are a few rules to follow.

Hedges & fences: before you start...

Here are a few practical and style considerations to take into account when planning a new hedge or fence:

- Take a look at traditional styles in your area and adopt the same proportions and materials
- Aim for consistency of style and materials, both with the house and garden, and with the environment (avoid 'mix and match')
- Make sure the design incorporates spaces for the electric meter box or the dustbins
- Use plants, either climbing over fences, or as hedges, particularly if the house is in the countryside.

Making a good hedge

A good hedge is one which combines different species, and the golden rule is to go for local varieties. These plants will be better suited to the local climate and soil conditions, will survive better, live longer, and cost less. Whether you choose deciduous or evergreen plants is a question of personal preference, but you might want to avoid conifers, which are not as easy to manage in the long term and offer less variety of colour.

To find out about local plants, look around and see what grows well in your area. Old, abandoned gardens, in particular, are a very reliable source of information on traditional rustic plants. Look out for species that appear to do well when trimmed, and for evergreen ones which bush up densely and will make the base of the hedge thicker (for instance, holly or box). Only when you have got enough specimens of those local species should you start thinking of using non-native ones which you might find interesting for their foliage, flowers or colour.

Avoid the all-too-common and monotonous hedges of thujas (the cultural equivalent of lleylandii in Britain) or cherry-laurel, which create a great, dense wall, as if of green concrete, and can leave you with unpleasant eddies of wind in the garden. They disfigure the landscape and provide very little support for wildlife; they can also grow very tall and get out of control unless trimmed regularly from the start, and tend to get a bit thin at the base. Further, they are prone to various diseases. Likewise, laurustinus (a member of the viburnum family), another often-used evergreen with thick glossy leaves and clumps of white flowers, tends to be attacked by insects, does not do well in heavy soil and does not withstand long cold spells and frost. For more on planting and trimming hedges, see pp.112-119.

A stunning hedge of tall beeches planted either side of a *talus* in Normandy (top). Various types of *talus* (right)

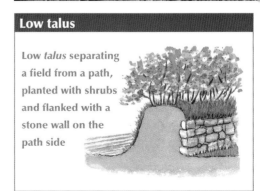

Low talus

Low *talus* separating a field from a path, planted with shrubs and flanked with a stone wall on the path side

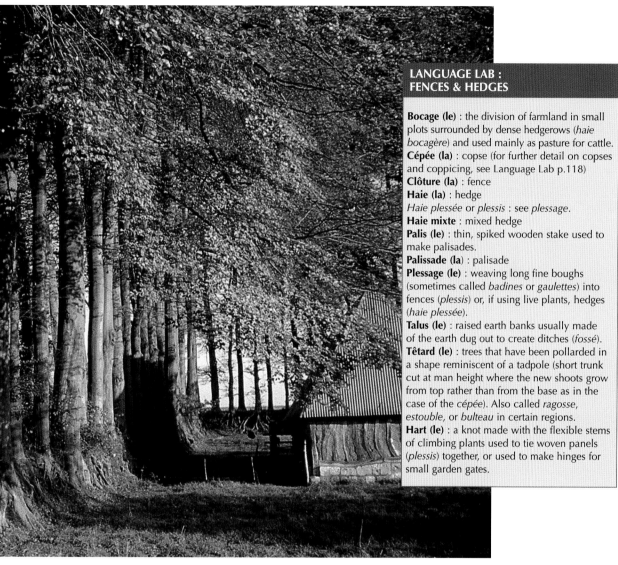

LANGUAGE LAB : FENCES & HEDGES

Bocage (le) : the division of farmland in small plots surrounded by dense hedgerows (*haie bocagère*) and used mainly as pasture for cattle.

Cépée (la) : copse (for further detail on copses and coppicing, see Language Lab p.118)

Clôture (la) : fence

Haie (la) : hedge

Haie plessée or *plessis* : see *plessage*.

Haie mixte : mixed hedge

Palis (le) : thin, spiked wooden stake used to make palisades.

Palissade (la) : palisade

Plessage (le) : weaving long fine boughs (sometimes called *badines* or *gaulettes*) into fences (*plessis*) or, if using live plants, hedges (*haie plessée*).

Talus (le) : raised earth banks usually made of the earth dug out to create ditches (*fossé*).

Têtard (le) : trees that have been pollarded in a shape reminiscent of a tadpole (short trunk cut at man height where the new shoots grow from top rather than from the base as in the case of the *cépée*). Also called *ragosse*, *estouble*, or *bulteau* in certain regions.

Hart (le) : a knot made with the flexible stems of climbing plants used to tie woven panels (*plessis*) together, or used to make hinges for small garden gates.

Tall and rounded talus

Tall and rounded *talus* planted with coppiced oaks and with a ditch either side for better drainage

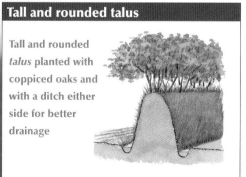

Wider talus

Wider *talus* with flat top, planted with full height trees for greater protection against the wind

Savoir-faire: building a *talus*

Building a raised bank or *talus* is a precise skill. It is labour-intensive and the bank will need to be sufficiently strong to prevent crumbling away with the first rainfall.

THE THREE STEPS TO BUILDING A *TALUS*

● **First, get some helpers** because it is a big job. Doing things properly, it will take a couple of hours per linear metre of earth bank, assuming you are building something around 1.5 m high and 1.8 m wide at the base. A mechanical digger will help (the cost of hire is approximately 250-300 for a day, or 50-60 per hour with labour included), but it will still be a labour-intensive job.

● **Do it in the winter**
The best time is between the beginning of November and the end of April, but not when it is freezing because the raw material – the earth – needs to be damp enough for it to stick together. The basic form has sloping sides, with a regular degree of slope all the way along. The top part of the bank must be convex so that water drains off easily. Because the water runs off, the earth at the centre of a talus tends to be extremely dry. Consequently, trees growing on the talus grow slowly, which means they tend to produce a much harder wood.

● **Building up**
Cut out wedges of turf that are at least six to eight months old, to a thickness of about 10 - 15 cm (A). Place the first pieces of turf on the ground, making two parallel lines which delimit the outer edges of the base of the talus. Fill the space between the two borders with earth, or with stones to start with. It is important that you press the turf firmly in place, possibly using a club, and compact the earth in the middle, using your feet. Then, add another layer of turf on top of the first one, slightly further in and overlapping the joins – you will need to think about the best angle slope (B). Then, again, fill the space in between, compress the earth and the turf, and repeat the process (C). When you reach the desired height, create the dome-shaped profile of the top of the bank so that the water will run off properly, and press it firmly.

● **Stabilisation**
It will take about two to three years before the *talus* is completely stable. You can help this process by planting bushes or trees along the top, whose roots will keep the earth in place, or sow flowers or grass to ensure that the soil is not bare and to prevent the *talus* from collapsing.

DITCHES AND EARTH BANKS

Ditches and earth banks (*talus*) often go together – not least because the latter are usually created with the earth dug to make the former. *Talus* help keep the soil in place, while ditches help channel rainwater away from the paths. They appeared in France in the 11th century, when land ownership began to be established and served as a barrier to keep in livestock. Many paths that ran in-between properties became 'sunken' between two *talus* as a result.

There are plenty of variants: faced with a dry stone wall; planted with trees; or with a drain on each side (see drawings pp.88-89).

Timber fencing, like these palisades in the Queyras, are a common feature of mountain gardens.

And there are regional variations. In Brittany, the *turon* is a talus more than a metre high, sometimes planted with trees or bushes, but without a drainage ditch, and the term *talus* refers to a low dry stone wall; and a *fossé* (which is a ditch anywhere else in France) is an earth bank: wide, high, crowned with trees, sometimes with a stone wall along the flanks, and with one or two drainage ditches. In Normandy, by contrast, *talus* are planted with beeches, tightly spaced and growing straight – forming majestic lines across the landscape (see pp.88-89).

TIMBER FENCING

Woven fences, palisades, gates and doors

The development of wooden fences has accompanied the evolution of the rural economy since the Stone Age. Although timber fencing preceded stone walls, the practice declined at the beginning of the 20th century but is now regaining a certain appeal, in particular the woven *plessis* type.

Most of the wooden fencing available in shops and garden centres these days is based on more urban, modern, or exotic styles, and is a far cry from the traditional French country fence work. However, Victorian palisades, which were so fashionable in the

A simple garden gate is perfect for a humble rural garden (right). Woven fences: criss-cross fencing with live willow boughs (above), and examples of *haie plessée*: a rougher weave where it is used to fence a field (opposite top) and a finer weave for a low border in the vegetable garden (opposite bottom).

19th and early 20th century, gained such popularity in France too that some of their features inspired many rural fence-makers, in particular the *palis* – the thin, spiked wooden stake used to make palisades which started to appear as fences around vegetable plots.

The oldest type of fencing is known in French as *haie sèche* or *haie morte* (dry, or dead hedge), so-called because it was made of dead branches roughly intertwined, usually hawthorn, blackthorn (sloe), wild pear or plum, dog rose, and bramble. These were originally designed to surround land that had been cleared in the forest and to protect it and its occupants from wild animals. As cultivation developed, the quality of these hedges improved and they became permanent, leading to the *plessis*.

The *plessis* is a more elaborate type of fence which is built using slender boughs woven through wooden stakes planted at a regular distance from each other, usually made of rot-resistant timber such as chestnut or oak. *Plessis* was widespread during the Middle Ages, and was still used in France

until the end of the 19th century. It was generally shoulder high, so that horses and dogs could jump it during a hunt.

Re-created in some restoration projects of prestigious medieval gardens in France, the *plessis* has started re-appearing in ordinary household gardens. It is undoubtedly a very pretty type of fence, which is easy to make (see p.94), and it deserves to resume its place in French gardens.

Another type of fence is the simple 'stockade' fencing (*palissade*), which works well with the character of a rural house. As with many outdoor wooden structures, chestnut is particularly suitable. There are two main types of *palissade*: either vertical slats nailed on to crosspieces (either flat boards or billets), or horizontal slats fixed onto stakes or boards with pointed or rounded tops. They can be held together with wire, for a more open design, or the planks can

Savoir-faire:

Timber fencing, like this simple gate (below), weathers well and will withstand the passage of time.

Making a wicker fence is very simple an boughs and branches, and a bit of patie

Weaving the boughs

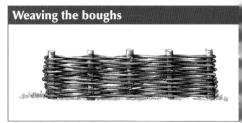

be fitted tightly together as protection against the wind or for increased privacy.

The criss-cross weave of boughs of hazel or willow to form a trellis is an unusual, though increasingly popular, option for a green and living fence. Preferably planted in damp ground, the trellis structure will start to bud and come to life rapidly, and will require regular clipping and maintenance as willow can grow very fast.

Making a wooden fence

Seek inspiration from local traditional types of fence, which are likely to have been made with wood that has been sourced locally and is both suited to the purpose and solid. Exotic hard wood may be equally rot-resistant, as well as resisting fungus, woodworm and other timber-burrowing insects, but will be more expensive. A more compelling reason not to resort to exotic species is that there is an environmental price elsewhere in the world in terms of deforestation, soil erosion, desertification and climate change. Not to mention the fact that the local population rarely benefits from this trade. Only hardwood that comes with a Forest Stewardship Council label

Threading the boughs around the end post

● **The posts**
Start by making the wooden fence posts, selecting timber poles of 4-8 cm in diameter, depending on the look you would like to create, or cutting bigger ones lengthwise down to the required size. For a fence of 1.2 m high, you will need stakes of around 2 m in length. Strip off the bark, sharpen the thickest end into a point, and chamfer the other end (to prevent the wood from splitting when you hammer them into the ground). Hammer the posts 60

- 80 cm into the ground, spacing them 30 - 80 cm apart, depending on the thickness of the stakes. A finer weave will be used around gardens and near the house, and a rougher weave in fields and pastures.

● **Weaving**
(remplissage)
Once the posts are in the ground, start weaving the fine boughs through, to 'fill up' the fence. You need to use fine, flexible boughs of between 1 and 3.5 cm in diameter (called *badines* or *gaulettes*), and from 2 - 4 m long. These slender branches are the younger shoots (one to three years old) of coppiced trees (*cépées*), usually found in woods and hedges, earth banks (*talus*) and river banks.

n be a good way of spending an afternoon for adults and children alike. All you need is a good stock of

the base, or pollarded at man-height (*en têtard* – in the shape of a tadpole) so that new shoots grow from the top of the tree. Other species that do well when coppiced or pollarded, and that produce strong, straight new shoots, can also be used. These include hornbeam, hop, and bramble.

● **Joining the panels**
Traditionally the woven panels (*claies*) would be joined using shoots of the more flexible varieties, such as willow or wayfaring tree, or the woven stems of climbing plants or bushes such as wild clematis, honeysuckle, hop or bramble. These would also be used as hinges for smaller wooden gates. These woven hinges are known as *harts*.

● **Securing the fence**
To avoid the fence being blown over in a strong wind, prop it up with wooden supports approximately two-thirds up, either tied to the posts or slotted into the weave of the panels.

● **The right materials**
Choose tender, flexible but nonetheless strong shoots, which will be easier to work with and more supple. They should be long, straight, and with no or few branches. Leave the bark on, but remove twigs, and if the branch splits into a Y-shape, cut off the thinner of the two boughs. It is possible to do all this preparatory work in advance and leave the wood in water to ensure that it remains sufficiently pliable. Then, thread the branches through the row of fence posts, twisting the bough at the end of the row as you run it around the end post and weaving it back in the reverse direction. Push the strips down close to each other for a tight weave and avoid overlapping the joins between the boughs.

● **Which wood is best?**
For the finer boughs (15-20 mm in diameter), the best varieties that are least likely to break include chestnut, wicker, wild clematis, elm, and goat willow. Within this selection, some are better than others: wicker and clematis are very flexible but have a short life span and will start decaying after four to eight years. Goat willow, white willow, hazel and alder will live just as long but are not as flexible. Chestnut is good because it is both flexible and long-lasting (12 to 20 years). Cut branches that are two years old for chestnut; two to three years old for elm and hazel; and for all other trees, cut one year's growth. For the latter, the trees will need to be *recépés* (coppiced again the following year) to stimulate new growth from

The cantilevered gate

Almost inevitably, if you build a rustic fence, you may need a rustic gate. The cleverest and simplest idea is the cantilevered gate, known in the Auvergne as *banlévo*, which can still be found on some rural paths deep in the French countryside. It works on the principle of a counterweight used, among other things, to draw water from wells.

How to make it : A solid timber post is embedded in the ground, and its top is carved out to leave a stout cylindrical peg emerging vertically from the top section of the timber. Onto this is inserted a long trunk of timber, roughly squared off, with a hole drilled in the underside about a quarter of the way down its length, to take the peg. The short end of the trunk is then hollowed out on top. Into this hollow section is inserted a heavy stone, held in place with large screws, or tied on with rope. This ingenious system will allow you to open and shut the gate effortlessly.

should be considered, as this has been cultivated from sustainable forests which respect the local balance of social, economic and ecological factors.

So, select local French wood instead. Chestnut, which is particularly suitable for lightweight picket fences, oak, the common locust (also known as 'false acacia') and the acacia are rot-resistant, sturdy woods that grow in Europe in managed forests. So are larch, red cedar, and Douglas fir. Other good resistant woods are hawthorn, dogwood, blackthorn (sloe), elm, holly, wild apple and pear trees. Rather less resistant to outdoor use are ash, maple, and alder. Cutting wood for fencing is best done in the winter, when the leaves have fallen and the branches are relatively sap-free.

Pine is a cheaper alternative but it must be pressure treated with a preservative, which for exterior use needs to be Class 3b. If the wood is to be in contact with the ground, a Class 4 treatment is required. Some of the substances used for the treatment of wood are toxic pollutants (some of which are banned) and they give the wood a rather unattractive greenish colour, although this will disappear after a while.

Wooden fence posts should be insulated from the earth to prevent them being affected by damp – for example, by resting them on a masonry base, or coating them with a bitumen-based product. Alternatively, burn the lower part of the posts that will be in contact with the soil to just above ground level. Remember to lay some gravel around the masonry base to help with drainage and to sharpen the top of the posts, giving them either a bevelled or rounded tip so that rainwater can run off.

WALLS

The walls that enclose land and property in rural France are generally built of the same stone as the buildings they enclose: stone, rubblestone, brick, a timber frame with an infill, or daub. These walls contribute to the character of many villages in France.

Timber fences can take all sorts of shapes. This one, with a simple gate, uses just enough material to act as a boundary without blocking the view.

Stone walls bring
unique charm and
warmth to gardens.

Stone walls

Dressed stone walls, with their even blocks
and smooth finish, have always been labour-
intensive and expensive to create, and were
originally only seen around chateaux, forti-
fied houses, and other buildings owned by
the nobility or the church. In the late 19th
century, however, they became more common, appearing around larger middle-class
houses and in villages. By protecting gardens from the wind and the cold, they create a microclimate beneficial to plants.

The town of Montreuil, where peach trees used to be grown on
trellises along rendered stone walls, offers a vivid illustration of the
use of walls for horticultural purposes (see Address Book p.218).
The walls acted as storage heaters, absorbing the warmth of the
sun during the day and releasing it well into the evening, while the
plaster render reflected sunlight toward the plants.

Boundary walls are usually covered with copings of some sort, generically known as a *faîtage*, to protect the wall from water ingress which might ultimately cause it to collapse. In its most basic form, the *faîtage* is just a big, flat stone extending either side of the edge of the wall, but more elaborate versions include pitched slate or tile roofs and rounded masonry coping made with small stones. Similarly, the jointing between the stones in the wall is important to ensure that water does not seep into the wall.

The best way to restore a garden wall is to use the same materials that were used to build the original wall. It is advisable to avoid repairing the foundations and the base of old stone walls with concrete, as the different density of materials may cause uneven settlement. Likewise, avoid grey cement for joints or skimming, as it is particularly unsightly. And never render a wall all the way down to the ground with a cement-based mortar, as it may stop the base of the wall from breathing and prevent the evaporation of rising damp.

In many regions, like the Bourgogne, the south-west, the Auvergne and Vivarais, fields are often divided with dry stone walls, sometimes with a hedge running alongside or on top. They are mostly the result of decades of field clearance. At crossroads they will usually be adorned with iron, wood or stone crosses to ward off the evil spirits. All too often these beautiful old walls are falling apart, buried under vegetation, and neglected.

However, dry stone walls are an important part of the French countryside, so if you are lucky enough to have one derelict on your property, you should try to restore it. You will find all the materials you need nearby (the stones will be lying around the wall) and, as the foundation and base are usually still in place, half of the work will have already been done. Building a dry stone wall is relatively simple – after all, there is no mortar involved – but for more complex projects you will need to acquire basic stone-fitting skills (see Address Book p.218). The top of the wall is generally made of larger, flatter stones, the weight of which keeps the smaller stones in the wall in place.

Colossal effort was required to build terraces in difficult hilly terrain in order to be able to grow a few square metres of fruit and vegetables.

Savoir-faire: building a retaining wall

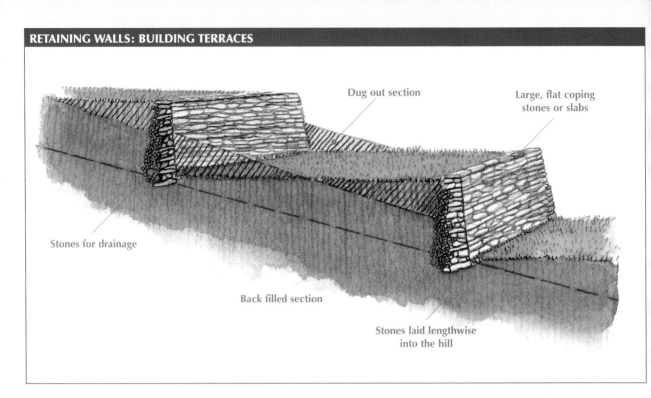

Dug out section

Large, flat coping stones or slabs

Stones for drainage

Back filled section

Stones laid lengthwise into the hill

Retaining walls are seen in many mountain regions in the south of France where they were used to prevent landslide and for agricultural purposes.

It takes a lot of effort and a particular talent to build or repair a retaining wall, but doing it yourself is often the only solution these days, and possibly the most economical one as there are very few people left with the required skills. The first step is to look at sections of the wall that are still in good condition, or, if you are starting from scratch, to inspect retaining walls in your area and talk to locals who still have the skills. Heritage organisations, such as a local *écomusée*, if you have

one, or the local representation of *Maison Paysannes de France,* will usually be able to help. Also, many preservation societies and most of the authorities responsible for national parks often run training courses (see Address Book p.218).

● **A traditional retaining wall** is built on a foundation of large stones or rocks – although a low wall might sit on a bed of gravel if it is not too high. The upper part of the wall should be made of stones packed

together tightly, with a back-filling of gravel or small stones between the wall and the earth it retains, for drainage. Retaining walls are best built as dry stone walls, allowing water to flow out easily and avoiding the risk of the wall being forced apart by swollen, damp ground behind it.

● **The main body of the wall** and the back-filling should be built up at the same time, and with a slight camber into the hillside. Stones should be laid lengthwise into the hill ('*en boutisse*'), helping

to anchor the wall to the ground behind it. Sometimes they are roughly hacked flat at the front, and the off-cuts are then knocked into the wall as padding to keep the stones firmly together.

● **The top of the wall** is then covered in large, flat stones, or with stones packed side to side vertically, sometimes with the top end rounded up. Staircases between terraces are either built into the thickness of the wall or made of projecting stone steps (*marches 'volantes'*).

TYPES OF EARTH WALLS

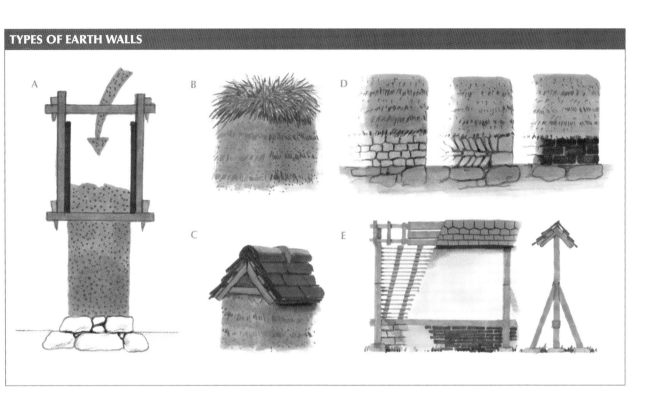

Cob walls (above from left): building a cob wall using a timber frame and gradually filling it with earth (A); cob wall topped with a straw matting (B) or a tile roof (C); three types of foundations using stone and brick (D); and an earth wall built on a timber frame and covered with lime-based render (E).

Retaining walls

In the mountainous regions of southern France, stone walls are also used as retaining structures, forming terraces that have been used for cultivation and to prevent landslips. Stone walls allow rain water to drain off, while at the same time keeping moisture in the soil. They absorb the heat of the sun during the day and radiate it back at night, creating a localised microclimate ideal for plants. The resulting terraces divide a hilly garden into discrete areas.

Cob walls

Original cob walls, made of daub (*bauge* or *pisé*), were mostly found in regions where stone is in short supply, like Normandy, the north-west of Vendée, or the Bresse. Usually they are topped with a small tile, timber or thatched roof, which is essential to protect the wall from the rain. The foundation and lower part of the wall are made of brick, stone, or flint. Earth walls are remarkably resistant as long as the foundations and the top are looked after. The flanks of the wall can be covered with a lime-based render, for added protection.

Chapter 4

Tricks of the trade

Sème à la St-Didier, tu auras des haricots plein ton panier (For a plentiful bean crop, sow on Saint Didier's day)'

FROM A COLLECTION OF TRADITIONAL SAYINGS COMPILED BY MICHAEL VIVIER,

LES JARDINS RURAUX EN BASSE NORMANDIE, CRECET, 1998

This chapter aims to share with the reader a set of elementary principles and techniques based on common sense and the *savoir-faire* of rural communities, which are essential in creating and maintaining a rural garden. The guiding principle here is that nature will only be tamed if it is obeyed.

DEALING WITH DERELICT GROUND

Whether it is an old house being restored, or a new house that has just been built, the garden is generally found in the same condition: devastated by the building work and in need of attention.

Clearing overgrown land

If the ground is overrun with brambles, you will probably want to get rid of most of them but ask yourself whether it might not be useful to keep some at the edge of the garden to form a natural barrier, or for their blackberries in the autumn. Brambles are also a great habitat for birds and insects. If you do decide to keep a few, make sure you cut them back every year, otherwise they will soon spread back again.

To clear overgrown land there is no quick and easy solution. Cut everything down, dig out or pull out the roots of brambles, nettles, couch grass and other unwanted plants. Then remove rocks and stones, branches and other debris.

Glass bells (opposite) are ideal for growing young plants outdoors early, keeping them protected from the wind, the cold, and from pests and animals.

Whether the garden is overgrown or its soil compacted, bringing it back to life will involve clearing, digging and nurturing before plants and vegetables can grow again.

Improving the soil

The next stage is to improve the quality of the soil. Weeds tend to thrive on compact ground, so once the plants you have dug out have dried up, dig up the soil to loosen it and make it easier to work. The plants you have removed will decompose and provide humus; some of them, nettles for instance, are a good soil enhancer.

Once this is done, make sure you do not leave the ground bare for too long. Plant mint, for instance, which will establish easily where nettles used to grow, or wild flowers or grasses (see The Meadow, p.64). For even more effective soil improvement, sow green manure (*engrais vert*), that is, plants like lucerne (alfalfa) whose roots aerate the soil and whose leaves, rich in nutrients, will feed their goodness into the soil when they have been cut and left to decompose on the ground before being dug into the soil. Rye works well with lighter or sandy soil. This is best done at the end of the summer, when the soil is still warm but beginning to get a little damp; the buried leaves will decompose over the winter.

Alternatively, dig well-rotted manure or compost into the ground. If the soil is quite chalky, resist the temptation to remove all the stones, as they stop the ground getting too heavy and help it warm up in the spring.

Weeding

To prevent grass growing in-between paving stones and through gravel, cover the ground underneath with a geotextile liner; or top dress the soil at the foot of trees or around the vegetable plot with mulch. This should minimise having to resort to chemical weed killers, which are toxic and pollute the soil – they should be used with caution, and away from wells and streams. Glysophate-based weed killers seem to leave fewer toxic residues. However, they are only effective during the growing season (so you must take care not to spray the surrounding plants) and they are ineffective on certain species of weeds, such as nettles, ivy,

Regenerating a courtyard will be a painstaking task requiring proper planning and good organisation.

thistle and horsetail. It is also worth remembering that the consequences of using some of the more recent and complex molecules are not yet known and that they can easily find their way into the food chain.

Tougher weeds can be eradicated using simpler molecules like ammonium sulphamate which will not affect grasses and will turn into nitrogen. The most effective solution to keep stone surfaces clean for up to 12 months is sodium chlorate, which will biodegrade into sodium. However, it is not as good for the soil and is a water pollutant.

Tree stumps

To remove old tree stumps, which can harbour contaminating fungi or throw up new shoots, drill holes of at least 3 cm depth into the stump and fill these cavities with saltpetre (potassium nitrate) or sodium chlorate, then leave for approximately six months. Be careful when handling these products as they are technically classed as explosives, so wear gloves and make sure there is no naked flame. When the six months or so have elapsed, burn the remains of the stump (this could take from a few hours to a few days depending on the size). An alternative method is to drill holes in the stump, pour ammonium sulphamate into them and seal them. The stump will then decompose of its own accord.

A slower, but far less toxic, method is to place garlic cloves in the holes, and seal them with clay. This will speed up the decomposition of the stump, and within a couple of years it will have disappeared.

However, you may not need to resort to any of these methods. Most stumps will decompose naturally, or can be dug out – albeit with a mechanical digger for the bigger ones. Bear in mind that a dead tree will be home to many insects and birds so you should consider keeping it if there is no compelling reason to remove it.

If the trees in your garden are damaged, judicious pruning will usually bring them back to life (see p.116), whilst if they are affected by parasites, a coat of limewash on the trunk should get rid of them.

LANGUAGE LAB :
REGENERATING DERELICT GROUND

Brambles : les ronces (f)
Compacted soil : une terre compactée
Digging : bêcher (digging the garden); creuser (digging a hole)
Improving the soil : améliorer le sol
Improver (soil) : un amendement (will refer to any component which will improve the soil, e.g. manure to fertilise, sand to improve drainage, etc.)
Fertiliser : un engrais
Green manure : un engrais vert
Overgrown : envahi
Pebbles : petits cailloux, gravillons
Rocks and stones : pierres (f) et cailloux (m)
Root : une racine
Scrub : les broussailles (f)
Stump : la souche
Weeds : les mauvaises herbes (f)
Weeding : désherber, enlever les mauvaises herbes
Weedkiller (chemical) : le désherbant (chimique)

For more on weeds and dealing with derelict ground, see the Glossary p.210.

PROTECTING THE GARDEN DURING MAJOR WORKS

Rubble : Renovation work and regenerating a garden usually result in piles of rubble. Try to keep them off the areas intended to become part of the garden, as they will compress the earth and leave it rock hard. The best option is it to throw the rubble directly into a skip; alternatively, stock it out of sight of the house until a skip can be arranged.

Repairing compacted soil : Land that has suffered from building work will first need to be regenerated. Aerate the soil with a bit of light digging, and then fertilise by laying over a carpet of ferns, hay or compost (but without burying them) topped with a covering of straw.

Trees : If a tree or shrub is in the way, transplant it, preferably to a spot which will be its new permanent home, rather than a temporary place which will involve moving it again. Before moving the plant, prune it, taking advice from experts at your local garden centre or nursery if necessary.

PLANTING TREES AND SHRUBS

Knowing how to plant a tree is an invaluable skill – whether it is to repair a hedge or build a new one, brighten up a courtyard, create a bit of shade, grow fruit, or just admire a beautiful silhouette.

MINIMUM DISTANCE FROM BOUNDARIES

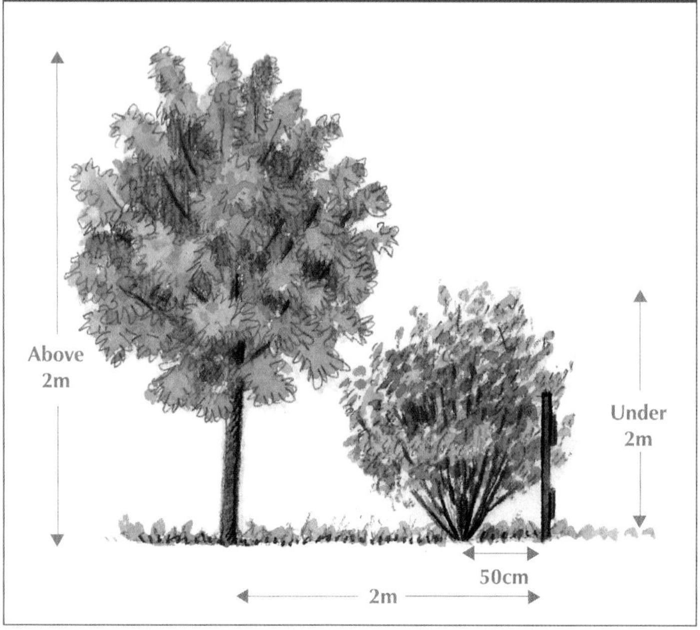

Above 2m

Under 2m

50cm

2m

First, make sure that your garden is of a suitable size: bigger trees will generally need a radius of 15-20 m of free space around them. Then, consider the nature of the soil: what is its depth, is it acidic or alkaline, light or heavy, damp or generally dry, and is there enough of it to allow the roots to spread? Watch out for trees which spread through suckers, like acacias or aspens, as they can be hard to keep under control.

Trees are essential components of the landscape (opposite). In smaller gardens, they must be planted 50 cm from the boundary if growing to less than 2 m. If more, they must be planted at least 2 m away.

You will also need to have an idea about how fast a tree will grow, how long it is expected to live, and how tall it will be when it is fully mature. As a rule of thumb, there should be 5 - 10 m between trees in the open, and between 1 and 2 m for trees planted in hedges (30 to 60 cm for shrubs). However, these general indications do not need to be applied literally: trees planted closer to the house will contribute to the charm of the property and they rarely cause much damage provided they are no closer than 5 m. Do be careful with conifers, though, as they are fast-growing, block light and can become dominant and dense.

Lime trees are impressive either planted singly in the centre of a courtyard, or in rows. Thirsty poplars are also good planted in rows alongside rivers or in marshy grounds. Keep them well away from buildings because their shallow roots mean they can be uprooted in strong winds and cause damage.

If you are going to plant a hedge between you and your neigh-

THE LAW
The French Civil Code (Articles 670 - 673): trees and neighbours

Trees growing to no more that 2 m may be planted up to 50 cm from the boundary of your land, and taller trees (over 2 m) must be planted at least 2 m away. You can plant trees within this 2 m limit, provided you keep their height trimmed to less than 2 m – as with fruit trees planted along a boundary wall, for example. Claims of unlawful planting may be brought up to 30 years after the date that a tree was planted, but there is no time limit if the tree causes or threatens to cause damage.

If branches overhang your neighbour's garden, he can ask you to cut them, but he is not allowed to do this himself without your permission. Any work must be carried out at your own expense.

If, on the other hand, the branches of a fruit tree overhang your garden, you are not entitled to the fruit of the tree unless they have fallen to the ground in your garden unaided. Again, it is the responsibility of your neighbour to cut the branches (if you want them cut).

If the roots of a tree push into a neighbour's garden, the neighbour can cut them himself, up to the boundary between the two properties. The owner of any tree, even lawfully planted, is responsible for any damage caused to the neighbour's property by the roots. Trees planted down the boundary between two properties are shared by the two households. If they die, are cut or pulled out, the wood and any fruit are shared equally. Looking after these trees is the responsibility of both neighbours, and must be paid for jointly. There may be local regulations requiring property owners to clear their land regularly of brambles and thistles, thus restricting fires – particularly in dry regions. Find out from the *mairie* (town hall) or check with your regional authority (*Direction Départementale de l'Equipement*).

Sowing seeds

Sowing seeds may seem like a technical skill that should be left to professional gardeners, but sowing your own seeds means that you will have a much greater choice of plants than if you buy potted seedlings, and you will be able to grow plants in greater quantities. It is also much cheaper. Here are a few essential principles:

1 : If instead of buying seeds you choose to harvest them from existing plants, select healthy, strong plants (not from hybrid varieties) when the fruits are ripe and just beginning to dry. Keep the seeds in paper bags in a cool, dry place away from light.

2 : Some seeds need to be kick-started into germination: a period of cold, a little nick cut into a hard seed, or by soaking in water for a few hours. Usually, though, all it takes is prepared soil which is warm and damp, and a bit of sunshine.

3 : Most plants can be sown directly into the ground. Prepare the ground first, breaking it up with a rake and removing any weeds. Small seeds (mixed with fine sand if they are very small) should be sown by scattering a handful across the ground. Larger seeds are sown in 'pockets', putting a few in a hole together and then keeping only the best seedling of the bunch. You can also sow in a line, as you would in a vegetable garden, thinning out as required.

4 : Some plants (tomatoes, peppers, aubergines, etc.) need heat to germinate and reach maturity in the season and should be sown indoors, or in a greenhouse or cold frame during the winter. The seeds are sown in clean, light soil in shallow containers and kept just moist. They should then be gradually introduced to the colder, exterior temperatures, before being planted out.

bour, do not forget the strict rules in the French Civil Code (see The Law p.111). As a general rule, use tall trees if you want your hedge to act as a wind-break, either leaving them to grow freely or trimming them so they thicken up in the centre. For a more compact hedge, plant two rows side by side, mixing taller and shorter species, deciduous and evergreens. If you want greenery throughout the year, consider holly, box, privet, yew, or rhododendron if the soil is acidic; holm oak or bay in the southern regions; or hornbeam which will keep its red leaves during the winter.

For a decorative hedge, train climbing roses over it – they can reach a good 6 - 8 m. Hold them in place with some twine or trellis at the lower part of the hedge.

How to plant trees

It is always best to plant a tree when it is dormant, between November and March, although pot-grown trees can in theory be planted at any time of the year, but they are more expensive, which could increase your budget significantly if you are planning to plant a lot of trees. If you do decide to plant in the summer, keep a close watch on the trees and water them well.

Bare-rooted trees are best planted in November-December, leaving the plant time to grow hair-roots and to settle in properly before the cold sets in.

If you have a lot of trees to plant, it will be worth getting in touch with a local farmer or landowner with a copse or forest, who may allow you to take away some saplings. If so, choose healthy-looking plants that are growing nice and straight.

Younger plants (0.6 to 1.3 m) are likely to transplant more easily, grow better, and they are cheaper. For fruit trees, choose a one-year-old tree (known as a *scion*) that has already been grafted, and preferably 2 m tall if it is to be planted out in the open.

How to plant a hedge

Dig a trench the whole length of the planned hedge, to a metre deep, and put the soil to one side. Make sure that the top soil is kept separate from the sub-soil. Loosen up the sub-soil with a fork. If the soil looks a little poor, add some compost or well decomposed manure (*amendement organique*), or a few handfuls of bone meal mixed in with the top soil, and then spread onto the bottom of the trench.

Without disturbing the root ball too much, cut off thin, broken

PREPARING A BARE-ROOTED TREE FOR PLANTING

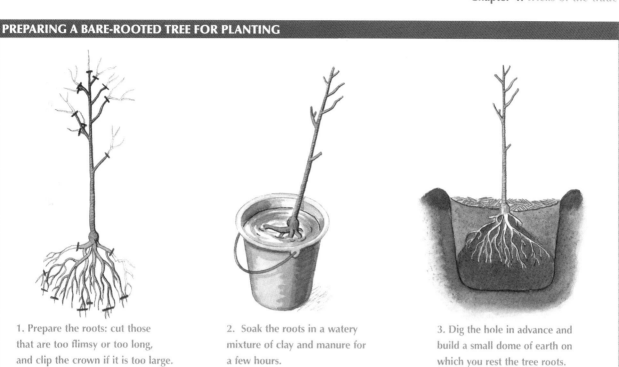

1. Prepare the roots: cut those that are too flimsy or too long, and clip the crown if it is too large.

2. Soak the roots in a watery mixture of clay and manure for a few hours.

3. Dig the hole in advance and build a small dome of earth on which you rest the tree roots.

PLANTING A HEDGE

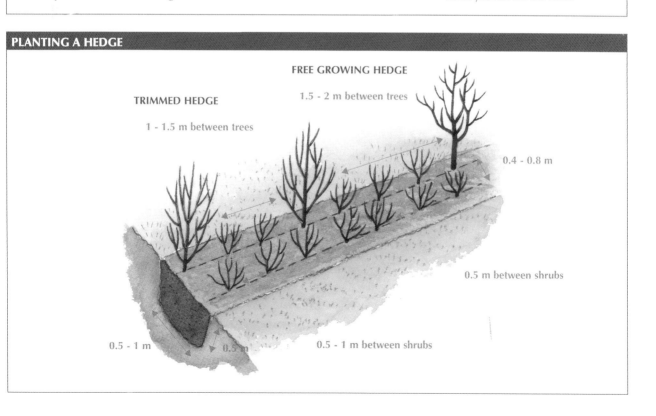

FREE GROWING HEDGE

1.5 - 2 m between trees

TRIMMED HEDGE

1 - 1.5 m between trees

0.4 - 0.8 m

0.5 m between shrubs

0.5 - 1 m   0.5   0.5 - 1 m between shrubs

A cold frame
is particularly
useful fo sowing
early vegetables
(above right).
Glass bells create
a warm and
damp atmos-
phere ideal
for seedlings
and young plants
(above left).

or damaged roots (*habillage*), and trim the crown of the tree, if necessary, to prevent evaporation through any remaining leaves. Then, in a bucket, mix up clay soil with fresh cow pat and water, and soak the root ball in this mixture, to both feed and protect the roots (*pralinage*). Alternatively, simply soak the root ball in water.

Start the planting, in either one or two lines, spacing young saplings 1 - 2 m apart, and shrubs and bushes at intervals of around 50 cm, depending on the type of hedge you want to create (closer for a trimmed hedge, further apart for a free-growing hedge). At the bottom of the trench, make a dome-shape with some good earth and spread the roots of the tree onto it. Make sure the roots do not come into direct contact with the layer of fertiliser at the bottom of the trench.

Then, fill up the trench with the remaining earth, and leave a bowl-shaped depression around the base of the tree, to help channel water to the roots. Water in well, but do not stamp on the earth to firm it up. You can also add a layer of straw to help prevent water from evaporating.

Follow the same procedure for a tree planted singly. Dig a hole around 50 cm deep and put some compost at the bottom. It is better to dig holes in advance so that the soil has time to settle before you plant the tree. And do support the tree with a stake if it is planted in a part of the garden exposed to wind.

Looking after your trees

The first three years are vital in making sure your trees get off to a good start. A tree that manages to develop good roots quickly will thrive as it becomes more resistant to bad weather and parasites, and will live longer. The trick is to encourage root growth from the earliest stage by watering well in the first few years, especially in spring and summer.

A young tree establishing itself needs a lot of water, which helps the sap to circulate and then evaporates through the leaves. By way of comparison, a man weighing 70 kg (11 stones) needs 2.5 litres of water per day; a tree of the same weight will require at least 70 litres of water per day.

It is also essential in these early stages not to do anything that might affect the supply of water the tree receives, such as diverting a stream or back-filling a pond. However, too much water can also hinder root growth and cause root damage through waterlogging.

Remember to protect the tree with a fence if there are horses or

---

**LANGUAGE LAB :
PLANTING TREES & SHRUBS**

Bare-rooted tree : un arbre à racines nues
Dormant : au repos
Graft : la greffe
Roots and hair-roots : racines et radicelles (f)
Sapling : un jeune plant
Shrub : un arbuste
Tree : un arbre
Wind-break : le brise-vent, le coupe-vent

Before planting
(see diagram p.113)
Habillage : preparing the tree for planting by removing damaged or broken roots, and those that are too fine.
Pralinage : a traditional method which consists of soaking the bare roots in a watery mixture (*barbotine*) of clay and manure to protect and stimulate the roots.

PRUNING LEVELS

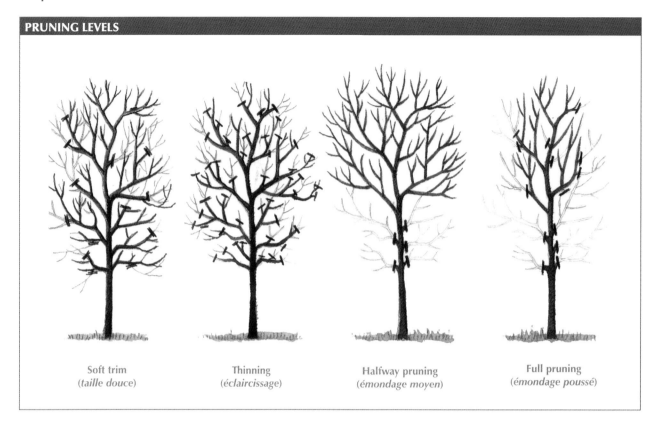

| Soft trim
(*taille douce*) | Thinning
(*éclaircissage*) | Halfway pruning
(*émondage moyen*) | Full pruning
(*émondage poussé*) |

goats, or even deer, in the vicinity, so that they cannot chew the bark of the trunk.

Pruning tips

Pruning is often necessary in smaller gardens, but you will need to find the right balance between cutting too hard too often, and radical emergency pruning.

● The golden rule: **interfere as little as possible** and ideally only when the tree is still young, to train it into shape. Avoid radical pruning, such as harsh horizontal cuts which can be traumatic for the tree - the resulting new growth will be very dense, preventing air and sunshine from penetrating the crown; the bark will start peeling off around the deformed, stunted branches; and the wood will ultimately succumb to rot and diseases.

● **Forked branches** : Sometimes trees are pruned to take off one arm of a Y-shaped trunk, so that there is a single, central bough rising from the trunk of the tree. Cut off new shoots coming out

Pruning is not technically necessary unless a specific effect is required or to achieve a particular purpose such as lightening the load of branches, letting air into the tree crown (above) or stimulating new growth from the stump (*recépage - opposite, bottom*). In all cases, make a clean cut (opposite, top) of the trunk, and any branches on the lower part of the trunk, to raise the crown of the tree as it grows. Smaller branches can also be removed to stimulate the growth of the main branches.

● **Infected branches**: do not be too determined about removing all rotting branches, as the tree will use its own bio-chemical defence mechanisms to create protective barriers containing fungicides and antibiotics. Furthermore, dead branches are a good home for small insects and spiders in the winter, which you will want to welcome back into your garden in the summer.

● **The cut** : make a good clean cut with sharp secateurs. Pull the branch down as you cut it, making sure the cut starts at the upper part of the branch.

Pruning a tree or a shrub

Spring-flowering species, such as fruit trees, should be pruned after the flowers have appeared, as new leaves form on the previous year's growth. Conversely, if the flowers appear after the leaves have come out, then pruning should take place in the winter. In either case, pruning will stimulate new growth.

If a tree is a bit listless, producing few flowers or fruit, then a more thorough clean-up might be in order. Cut older branches at the base and any flimsy, unproductive branches. Also take off any damaged or dead branches, and branches which are rubbing against each other. This will help the sap circulate and allow more sunlight and air into the crown of the tree. Finally, simplify the branch structure, cutting off some of the smaller branches sprouting from the ends of longer ones, and reducing the number of large branches running from the main trunk.

Pruning a hedge

In smaller gardens, or if a hedge borders the road, pruning is necessary to stop the hedge spreading. It also helps thicken it at the base. Do not be too harsh: tackle the growth from inside the hedge, and avoid square edges unless it is a formal hedge.

A young hedge can be cut back hard in the first three years or so if it includes trees or bushes that resprout from the base (*recépage*). You should end up with a good, thick hedge from the base up. If a hole appears in your hedge, just stick one of the cut branches into the ground, or train lower branches horizontally to fill the gap.

PRUNING TECHNIQUE

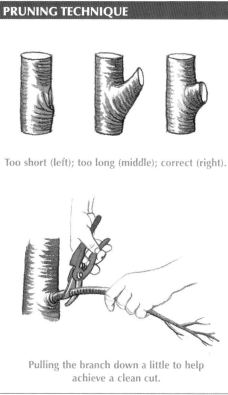

Too short (left); too long (middle); correct (right).

Pulling the branch down a little to help achieve a clean cut.

COPPICING (*RECÉPAGE*)

Cut a non-grafted one-year-old tree horizontally just above the stump (see Language Lab p.118).

Recépage (coppicing) is a technique used to stimulate a tree to grow new shoots from the base. Not all trees respond well to this treatment. Hazel, hornbeam, willow, oak, and thorny trees work well for hedging and produce strong new shoots which thicken the base of the hedge. A coppiced tree is known as a 'coppice' (*arbre recépé*) and a woodland or row of coppices is a 'copse' (*cépée*).

How it is done : Choose a one-year-old, non-grafted tree and cut the trunk just above the base (grafted trees will develop new shoots below the graft, reverting to their wild variety). The resulting stump is sometimes known as a 'stool' (*souche mère*). The technique is also used to regenerate trees that have been damaged by fire, or fruit trees that have been left unpruned for too long. In this case, only one of the new shoots is kept as the new trunk after a few years.

Pruning a living woven hedge (*haie plessée*)

The *haie plessée* (woven hedge) is a rare sight these days in France. Tightly woven to keep livestock from roaming, these hedges require a fair amount of work, which many farmers can no longer justify when they can achieve the same objective using barbed-wire fences.

All species can be trained into a *plesse* but those with supple branches work better. Hazel, hornbeam, hawthorn, blackthorn (sloe) and oak are good candidates.

The *plessage* (hedge laying) should be done in the winter. Choose a young hedge (seven to 12 years old) and distinguish between the strong, straight trees (sometimes called *guettes*), which will be used as uprights, and the long, more flexible branches, which will be woven around the uprights. Remove other shrubs and older specimens (*dérinçage*). Cut the uprights 1 m above the ground, add fence posts if necessary, to ensure that there is a vertical support every 30 cm or so. Then cut a gash in the longer, flexible trunks and branches at a lower point, so the wood almost splits but does not break. Bend these horizontally and weave them through the uprights.

This procedure will give you the main structure of your living hedge. The next step is to fill the gaps, weaving in loose branches here and there. In the first few years the operation should be repeated every year in the spring; thereafter, you will simply need to trim the hedge.

Creating a *haie plessée*: volunteers at the traditional craft museum in the Perche demonstrate the *plessage* technique. The main trunks are notched at the base so they can easily be bent sideways and grow horizontally.

Watering with a watering can (left) is more labour-intensive than watering with a hose (above), but it allows you to control the amount of water more precisely. Mulching (opposite) helps the soil retain moisture, reducing the frequency of watering.

WATERING AND IRRIGATION

Water is a valuable and expensive commodity and, as gardens can consume a lot of it, it is essential to use it wisely.

When and how

● **Preparing the ground.** Before planting, dig deep to break up compacted earth. A loose and crumbly soil will absorb water more easily. It is a good idea to gently hoe the surface of the soil regularly, especially when it tends to form a dry and hard crust during the dry season. This will help keep the weeds out. Hoeing after heavy rainfalls also prevents the soil becoming too smooth and letting the water run off and away.

● **Mulching.** Mulching (covering the soil surface with straw - thus the French word for mulching: *paillage* - or other dry material) will prevent evaporation. Flax straw works well, keeping in the moisture and enriching the soil. Ordinary straw from cereal crops is a natural option, and very 'rural', but can be blown away by the wind and does not always allow water penetration in lighter rainfalls. Alternatively, dried ferns and grass clippings provide a good mulch (but they must be allowed to dry first or they will rot), as do shredded branches and leaves which biodegrade and enrich the soil. Mulch also protects plants from the cold in the winter and keeps weeds out. Peat bogs are disappearing so you should avoid using peat; use coconut shells, coir or hemp instead.

Among modern materials, one of the most effective ground protections is a plastic film, or woven polyethylene sheeting, but this might also be a serious aesthetic faux-pas.

● **How much to water.** Plants that are well adapted to the soil and climate will not need much water at all, even in the summer. However, recently planted trees, the vegetable plot, and more delicate flowers may require watering. If so, it is better to water generously twice a week, rather than water a little every evening. Less fre-

quent but thorough watering will encourage plants to put roots into the soil in search of water.

● **Check the soil type.** Sandy soil will not retain water, so there is nothing to gain from prolonged watering; instead, water less but more frequently (twice a week should be adequate). For a clay soil, which retains water, watering once a week should be sufficient.

● **What time of day?** Water in the morning until May (to protect against the risk of overnight frost). In the summer, water early in the morning or in the evening, so that the water does not evaporate. This will also avoid sending the plants contradictory information: during the heat of the day some plants contract their leaves to reduce evaporation, so if you water them at this time the leaves are likely to open and lose moisture. In direct sunlight drops of water can also act like a magnifying glass, burning the surface of the leaves.

● **The right amount.** Seedlings, bulbs, fruit and vegetables, and newly planted trees need plenty of water. However, too much water can weaken a plant and, in the case of fruit trees, can produce large but rather bland fruit.

● **Using fertiliser.** Put in a good layer of fertiliser before planting, such as blood, bone meal, or nettle compost mixed with soil. The plant will feed on these nutrients as it grows and push down deep roots, making it more hardy and able to withstand the heat of the summer. You could also water plants with liquid plant feed, made with nettle or comfrey (see p.131).

● **Where to water.** Watering at the base of the plant is most effective, especially if you create a hollow around the stem or trunk to stop water running off. The most economical solution is a drip system (*goutte à goutte*) running around the garden, which allows water to seep out exactly where required, or use a microporous hose buried just beneath the soil surface. This can save up to 50% of the water you would otherwise use, and it can save time too. The disadvantage of these systems is that the roots are not encouraged to penetrate the earth and may remain superficial and close to the water source. For this reason you should also give the plants a good, thorough watering occasionally if it has not rained for a while.

Regular hoeing of the ground will help water penetrate into the soil more easily (above). It is commonly assumed that plants will need a lot of, and regular, watering but this is not always necessary, even in the heat of the summer, if the plants are suited to the soil and climate (opposite).

LANGUAGE LAB :
WATERING

Hose-pipe : le tuyau d'arrosage
Sprinkler : l'arrosage par aspersion
Water (to) : arroser
Water tap : l'arrivée d'eau,
le robinet
Watering : arrosage, arroser
Watering can : un arrosoir
Watering rose : une pomme
d'arrosoir
Drip system : un 'goutte à goutte'

Did you know...
Arroser ('watering') is also used
metaphorically to mean something quite different: '*un repas
bien arrosé*' refers to the large
quantity of alcohol consumed
over a meal.

● **Hosepipe versus watering can.** A hosepipe makes watering so much easier but you need to watch out that it does not get caught on – and cause damage to – other plants as you move through the garden. With a hosepipe, it is easy to over-water too. Using a watering can involves more effort but allows better dispersion and is more economical.

● **Lawns.** Sprinklers are an option but an expensive one, as lawns need a lot of water and almost inevitably turn yellow in the summer in most parts of France in any event. It may be more sensible to let the grass suffer (grass is tough and it will green up again with the first rainfall), or grow a more informal meadow instead (see The Meadow, p.64).

● **Vegetable plot.** Sprinklers should be banned from the vegetable garden, as damp foliage retains moisture which can lead to plant diseases. A simple option is to create small irrigation channels alongside each row of vegetables, and run water from a hose into these periodically.

What water to use

Most gardeners agree: rainwater is best (see Recycling rainwater, p.154). Water drawn from a well is too cold and contains too many minerals, and tap water is a little too chlorinated and expensive as all water is metered in France.

However, if you do have a well it is a pity not to use it. The simplest way is to connect a pump to your hosepipe; most garden centres will have several types on offer. If the water is more than about 7 m deep, you will need a submersible pump to bring it up effectively. If the well has been left abandoned for a while the water level may be very low, but it will rise as you start pumping and using the well again.

IMPROVING THE SOIL

Various improvers (*amendements*) can be added to fertilise the soil or modify its balance.

Organic improvers (*amendements humiques*) add organic matter to the soil, such as manure, compost, leaf mould, and various other organic mulches, which turn into humus. Mineral based improvers (*amendements calciques*), such as crushed limestone, quick lime, and slaked lime, are used to correct the pH balance of the soil. Although

Wells left unused for some time can become blocked with earth, branches and other debris; contact a local *puisatier* to clear it and get it working again (right). Some gardeners recommend not hoeing organic fertilisers too deep into the soil and letting the earth absorb them gradually (opposite).

The compost heap can be a fenced area in a corner of the garden (top) or an old bin with perforations to ensure circulation of air (bottom).

using soil improvers requires some expertise, clay and cold soils can be made more workable and warmer, and overly acidic soils can be toned down effectively. An easier alternative is to add sharp sand and compost to a heavy soil to improve drainage.

Organic fertilisers are generally added in the autumn, or at the end of the winter, to soil that has been loosened with a fork. This is particularly important for the vegetable plot, but may also benefit more difficult areas of the garden. Organic fertilisers can be dug into the soil if already well-decomposed, or left on the surface as top-dressing where they can be slowly digested into the soil through the combined action of the sun, rain, and earthworms. In the meantime, they keep the soil moist and prevent weeds.

Compost

Traditionally, the compost heap consisted simply of garden and kitchen waste, mixed with manure, in a corner of the vegetable garden where it would slowly turn into humus. Egg shells were also kept and used as a soil improver as an alternative to lime. The technique is still the same today and achieves two purposes in one go: it helps reduce waste and it produces humus and trace elements that improve soil density in the garden.

Making compost is simple: choose a corner of the garden, in the shade and out of sight, where you can heap together grass cuttings, dead leaves, straw, small branches and twigs, and biodegradable kitchen waste (including coffee and tea, even teabags or filter papers). Avoid any diseased plants or rotten branches, citrus peel, leftover meat and fish (they smell and attract cats, dogs, and rats), wood treated with chemicals, dairy products and bones.

The compost heap can be simply a pile on the ground or contained between two wooden panels but there are more sophisticated options: building a structure with wooden boards or old pallets, or recycling an old container (remove the base so the compost is in contact with the ground; this will encourage fermentation and will allow useful activating creatures like earthworms and insects into the heap). Or buy a ready-made compost bin.

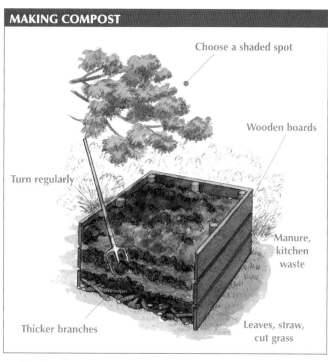

MAKING COMPOST

Choose a shaded spot

Wooden boards

Turn regularly

Manure, kitchen waste

Thicker branches

Leaves, straw, cut grass

At the bottom of the compost heap, place a layer of twigs or straw which allows air to circulate and absorbs excess water. Throw on a few handfuls of earth or manure, or water with a nettle concoction to start the composting process, before adding biodegradable waste to the heap.

The best compost, which decomposes quickly, combines thin layers of carbon-rich material (straw, dead leaves, dried grass clippings) with damp, nitrogen-rich materials. Turn the pile over from time to time to help the air circulate, prevent compaction, and to encourage bacteria to do their work. The compost must also be kept moist but you can cover it with a lid or plastic film in the winter to keep it warm.

The mixture slowly decomposes and it takes six months to a year for the compost to be ready. It should be crumbly with a dark colour, and smell of humus. Use the compost which is at the bottom of the pile and is most decomposed first.

Green manures - the all-in-one solution

Green manures (*engrais verts*) are crops sown in the winter or in-between growing seasons to avoid leaving the ground bare. They prevent leaching (erosion by rainwater) and inhibit the growth of weeds, while producing green organic matter that quickly breaks down into humus. They also stimulate the soil's biological activity, keep the soil soft and workable, and act as temporary storage for nutrients (nitrogen, potassium, magnesium and trace elements) which are then released back into the soil the following spring. Some plants in the leguminous family (peas, beans, lupins, etc.) are able to collect nitrogen from the air in their roots and fertilise the soil. When they reach maturity they are simply shredded with a mower and left on the ground for a few days to decompose, before being dug into the soil. Yet another advantage of these plants is that they more or less look after themselves.

Comfrey is rich in potassium, and can be used to make a liquid manure or for compost. **White mustard** grows quickly and produces quantities of compost, and if it is sown in October it will decompose during the winter. Likewise **sainfoin** or **vetch**, which are suited to dry or chalky soil and often associated with rye. Vetch is good on heavy, alkaline soils, where it can improve the structure, and it can improve poorer soil by fixing nitrogen from the air into the ground.

Buckwheat also grows fast, and softens up the earth with its long roots. The lovely **phacelia** (also known as scorpion weed), with its blue flowers, discourages couch grass and nematodes, and attracts bees. **Lucerne** (alfalfa) and **purple clover** are rich in nitrogen, while the **yellow lupin** is very good for sandy soil. As many of these plants also produce colourful flowers, you can create an attractive mix of yellows, purples and whites by sowing a combination of these across a field.

Natural fertilisers

Fertilisers should provide three vital ingredients for your plants: nitrogen, which stimulates leaf growth; phosphorus, which helps to build up strong roots and produce flowers, fruit or vegetables; and potassium to give the plant strength to fight frosts, droughts and diseases. Plants also need calcium for wood growth, magnesium and iron, which help plants produce chlorophyll, and trace elements.

There are many natural fertilisers, which should make it unnecessary to use chemical fertilisers. Those tend to be more expensive, not as effective, and can be harmful to the environment. Synthesised nitrogen, for example, if used in excessive quantities can leach into ground water and leave toxic residues; as does phosphorus, which has found its way into rivers where it encourages the growth of algae, thereby choking aquatic life.

The soil can obtain all the various nutrients it needs from ordinary potting compost, garden compost or manure, and plants then assimilate these gradually. Remember to aerate the soil to encourage the work of microorganisms and earthworms, and to rotate the crops in your vegetable plot, as not all have the same requirements (see pp.56-59).

Natural, organic fertilisers include manure, sea weed, guano, urea, dried blood, and bonemeal. They are slower than chemical fertilisers, as they need to be absorbed by the soil before they can be assimilated by plants, and greater quantities are usually required. It is best to allow organic fertilisers to decompose fully by natural fermentation. They can then be dug into the soil, either mixed with compost or left

Cut grass is an ideal compost material (left). Just add the cuttings to the heap and turn over occasionally.

LANGUAGE LAB :
ORGANIC FERTILISERS

Ash : la cendre
Bone meal : la poudre d'os, la farine d'os
Compost : le composte
Fertiliser : un engrais
Green manure : un engrais vert
Guano : le guano
Hornmeal : la corne torréfiée
Liquid plant manure / feed : le purin de plante
Mulch : le paillage
Manure : le fumier
Poultry manure : le fumier de poule
Seaweed : une algue ("or brun" - brown gold -
is a mixture of manure and seaweed)

Did you know...
'Organic' can be translated literally as
'organique' but this will usually refer to
processed material (e.g. manure). A more
idiomatic translation is 'biologique'. For
instance, the French equivalent of the phrase
'organic farming' found on food products is
'issu(e) de l'agriculture biologique'. This will
often be abbreviated to just 'bio', as in 'légumes
bio', for 'organically grown vegetables'.

A typical sight of French rural life: the farmyard with its manure heap (right). Manure, the organic fertiliser *par excellence*, is often available directly from farmers.

in layers on the soil surface (top dressing). Be sure to get manure from organically-reared livestock, as it could otherwise contain residues of weedkiller or antibiotics used to treat animals. You should also avoid peat taken from peat bogs, which are a rare, fragile and threatened environment.

Liquid plant feeds (see box opposite) are useful for their high content of trace elements and they are just as easy to prepare as they are to use. Finally, green manures (see p.128) are equally useful and provide ground cover for bare earth, especially in crop rotation.

Horse manure The king of manures. Rich in nutrients, it warms up quickly and therefore takes effect rapidly. Recommended for lightening up heavy, clay soil, for roses and fruit trees.

Cattle manure Colder than horse manure and not as rich, it can be used in large quantities without risk. It suits all vegetables and soils, thinner soil in particular, which are able to retain moisture more effectively. Mix it with straw before composting, as it is otherwise quite dense on its own.

Guano and poultry manure Possibly the most active fertiliser, suitable for all crops. It is rich in nitrogen and lime, and contains phosphate and potassium. However, it should be used in small quantities, and preferably mixed with sawdust to prevent it burning the plants. Put it down towards the end of winter and early spring.

Ash This works quickly, and is rich in phosphorus, potassium and trace elements.

Animal horn, ground or roasted Rich in nitrogen, hornmeal can be either ground or roasted and is released slowly over a long period. Ground horn has the longest lasting effect and is recommended for trees and shrubs as well as alpines. Roast horn is also used for vegetables, flowers and lawns.

Fish bone meal Rich in phosphorus, fish bone is particularly good at encouraging the development of the plant's root system through slow release. It is used for flowers, including annuals, and is also effective for bulbs and roses.

Savoir-faire: plant concoctions

Many plants, including garlic, onion, tomato and rhubarb leaves, can be used in concoctions that are sprayed onto plants to protect them from pests and fungus, or watered on the soil as fertiliser. But the organic gardener's favourites are nettle, comfrey and horsetail.

The stinging nettle (above) is one of a number of weeds which can be turned to good use as a liquid plant feed and is a favourite of organic gardeners.

Nettle concoction

Stinging nettle macerated in water to extract its key substances has many useful qualities: it stimulates plant growth; protects from diseases; and speeds up the transformation of organic matter into humus. Liquid nettle feed is rich in minerals, trace elements and vitamins. Spray it over newly planted crops to help them take root, and over plants in bud to encourage fruit growth and prevent aphids.

Making it : Soak 1 kg of nettles (leaves, stems and roots) in 10 litres of rainwater. The concoction can be quite smelly but adding a few angelica leaves will take care of this.
Using it : *Against aphids*: leave to stand for 12 - 24 hours, remove the nettles and spray the plants with the liquid without diluting it. *As liquid feed*: leave to ferment outside for about two weeks (at a temperature of 20° C). Small air bubbles should appear in the liquid; when these have disappeared the liquid is ready for use. Filter it, and then dilute 1 or 2 litres in 10 litres of rainwater (10 - 20 %). Spray or water the diluted mix onto the ground and onto plants (but not onto fruit) once a fortnight. The liquid will keep in jerry cans. Nettles can also be used as top dressing, either as they are or roughly chopped, to discourage weeds and keep the soil moist while improving it at the same time.

Comfrey concoction

Comfrey is rich in potassium and trace elements, though not quite as rich in nitrogen as nettle. It is both a soil improver and a fertiliser. Use it later in the season, when nettles start flowering and are no longer suitable for concoctions.

Making it : Soak 1 kg of leaves in 9 litres of water, for three to five weeks.
Using it : *As liquid feed*: strain out the leaves and water directly on the garden, watering around the base of plants. The leaves can be thrown on the compost heap, or around potato plants and small fruit bushes.

Horsetail concoction

Horsetail is another weed that can be turned into a multi-purpose fertiliser. A bushy sword-shaped plant, it looks as if it has no leaves or fruits and can be found growing on the side of many countryside roads. Liquid horsetail manure is very rich in silica and is used to prevent fungus, mildew, and other spotting or marking diseases in fruit. It is also known as the 'scouring herb' because of its abrasive qualities, and was often kept near the kitchen sink for this purpose.

Making it : Boil 1 kg of horsetail in 10 litres of water for about half an hour and let it cool.
Using it : Spray plants that are at risk from mould or mildew. Alternatively, mix it up with clay soil or cow dung, and apply it to the trunks of fruit trees in the autumn.

A balanced
eco-system
will naturally
minimise the
devastation
caused by insects
(right and oppo-
site). Fruit trees
can be protected
by applying a
lime-wash
around the
trunks (above).

TREATING SICK PLANTS

Useful garden creatures

In the days before synthetic pesticides and insecticides, people used all sorts of tricks passed on from generation to generation to keep bugs at bay. To get rid of slugs or caterpillars, for example, people used to put a ring of ashes or sawdust around the plants, or they simply went out early in the morning to collect them and feed them to the chickens – same with the potato beetle. Other less effective techniques steeped in superstition included leaving a handful of caterpillars to dry out near the stove, or even hanging the body of a dead mole, field mouse or bird, on a tree, as a warning to others.

In Limousin, cabbages would be covered with freshly cut broom leaves to deter caterpillars of the cabbage white butterfly, which would be repelled by the strong smell of the broom. Another technique consisted in planting sticks between each cabbage and placing halved egg shells on the top of each one; cabbage whites would be attracted to the upturned egg shell and lay their eggs inside.

Natural solutions to garden protection are being re-discovered following the growing interest in environmentally friendly practices. Protection begins with prevention, which includes crop rotation, companion planting (see p.56), and planting mixed hedges and nectar-rich flowers which attract useful insects – all of which will maintain the natural balance of the garden. Remember also to encourage animals such as tits, hedgehogs, and shrews, which help keep the pest population down, by providing nests and shelters.

An invasion of greenfly or slugs, or the appearance of mildew, are generally the consequence of an imbalance in the local ecosystem: too much water, too much nitrogen in the soil, or too much acidity. The solution is gradual but natural: cut down on the watering, do not put any manure down in the spring, and correct the acidity of the soil by adding calcium in the form of seaweed such as lithotamme.

LANGUAGE LAB :
BOUILLIE BORDELAISE
(BORDEAUX MIXTURE)

Bouillie bordelaise is said to have been invented by vine growers in the Bordeaux region -thus the name - who used the mixture to treat vineyards against mildew.

A traditional all-round fungicide used widely in agriculture and gardening, *bouillie bordelaise* is a mixture of copper sulphate and lime, to which sulphur is sometimes added. Copper is toxic and, in recent years, excessive use of *bouillie bordelaise* has been criticised by the French agricultural authorities. Fruit and vegetables should be thoroughly washed before being eaten.

Using it: the mixture comes in powder form and should be diluted with water. The resulting blue liquid is sprayed onto plants affected by mildew or other fungal diseases. Spray preventively in the autumn after the leaves have fallen, and at the first signs of attack in the spring. Do not exceed the recommended amounts as this could cause leaf burn, and avoid using on hot summer days.

Savoir-faire: traditional remedies

In most rural gardens, protecting plants was more a matter of keeping pests and diseases under control rather than complete eradication. Working with nature was the best way of ensuring that the garden could look after itself.

SLUG TRAP

MOLE DETERRENT

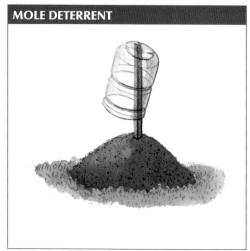

1 : Mildew, leaf blight, blistered leaves, canker. The traditional preventive remedy used by French gardeners against fungal diseases is known as *bouillie bordelaise* (sold in Britain as 'Bordeaux Mixture'), which is a powder on a copper sulphate base. It stays on the plants, resists rainwater, and works for a long time. However, use sparingly as copper is toxic and do not let it go into the soil. (see Language Lab p.132).

2 : Powdery mildew on trees. Cut off all the branches affected and burn them. If this does not stop the problem, spray with a regular fungicide. Wash any fruit or vegetables before eating.

3 : Birds eating your fruit and vegetables. Scarecrows, wind-chimes, or bits of metal, mirror or glass suspended on a piece of string work with various degrees of success. The main problem is that birds get used to them. Netting is the most effective measure but it is not particularly aesthetic in a rural garden.

4 : Moles. Knock a wooden stake through the molehill into the soil as far down as possible and put a flower pot or half a plastic water bottle over it. This will move around in the wind and create small vibrations that the moles will be able to sense under the soil, causing them to move away. Mole pellets are very poisonous, and poisoned worms are not very effective.

5 : Slugs. Slugs cause the most trouble when it is wet. Slugs have trouble getting over powdery or shifting surfaces, so a ring of sawdust, ashes, pine needles or shells around your plants will keep most of them out, but you will have to repeat the operation after heavy rain fall. In hotter weather, gently raking the surface of the soil will stop them burying themselves into the ground. Trapping them with potatoes, marrow, or grapefruit peel can work too. Beer traps are also effective: bury a small glass of beer just above ground level and half cover it with a piece of wood; the slugs will topple in and drown. The best solution, though, is a hedgehog. However, if there are hedgehogs in your garden do not use slug pellets as they are toxic for hedgehogs too.

6 : Aphids, green or black flies and other insects. There are good ecological solutions, such as ladybirds, lace-wings, and syrphe larvae which are keen predators of aphids. You should be able to find them in local garden centres easily – but remember if you do opt for ecological solutions, do not use insecticides which would kill off useful insects. Tits love aphids too, so feeding them in the winter should ensure that they will come back to your garden the rest of the year and keep pests under control. Another traditional remedy is *savon noir*, a mixture of linseed oil and ash, which is diluted in warm water (1 to 3 %). Spray the plants liberally as soon as the problem appears, in the evening. It is effective against aphids, scale insects, whitefly and thrips. Boiled tobacco leaves (*not* cigarettes, which contain toxic residues) can be used for the same purpose. Finally, an effective and traditional method is to apply a thin coat of lime onto the trunks or woody stems of plants. This will keep parasites at bay, prevents moss and lichens, but still allows the plant to breathe. There is also an organic insecticide called *roténone* which is made from tropical plants, and which is effective against aphids, flee beetles and potato beetles. However, it will also kill helpful insects so use it with moderation.

7 : Ants. Place walnut leaves or salt across their way. On fruit trees, you can wrap a grease band (picture opposite) around the trunk.

8 : Apple blossom blight. This is caused by a fungus which affects blossoms and fruits. Plant turnips at the foot of the tree, every year and for a few years. This is a slow process, and in the meantime you will need to take off any affected fruit and destroy it. The problem will slowly disappear.

Chapter 5

Landscaping

❝ Tell me (since you are so sensitive to the power of architecture), have you not noticed, walking through this town, that of all the buildings which populate it, some say nothing, others seem to speak; and others, finally, which are the rarest of all, appear to sing? It is nothing to do with their purpose, or even their general appearance, which seems to animate them to such a degree (or reduce them to silence). They owe it to the talent of the developers, or perhaps to the Muses smiling down on them. ❞

PAUL VALERY, EUPALINOS, PARIS, GALLIMARD

As muses are not expected to smile down on buildings these days, developers and architects provide the main source of inspiration for both building the house and landscaping the garden. This is particularly the case where major building works are anticipated for lighting, drainage and water disposal – not to mention swimming pools. Such landscaping work should be planned and preferably carried out before any planting is done in the garden as it is likely to cause major upheaval.

AROUND THE HOUSE

Paths, pavements and tracks

Being able to get around the garden without getting your feet wet or muddy implies that the paths and alleyways of your garden let rain water drain away rapidly into the soil and remain dry. This is the main argument against using cement, tarmac or interlocking concrete slabs, as instead of letting water permeate and drain into the soil, these materials divert it away from the path into other areas of the garden. This can cause serious problems if the path runs alongside a wall: water will gradually seep into the wall and damage the foundations and the building. In addition, these materials can be particularly unsightly and unsuitable for rural houses.

Where a path runs along a wall, especially if the roof above has no gutter, using stone, brick or slabs laid on a bed of sand is often

Drainage and water disposal systems may require extensive ground work which is best done before tackling the garden.

Opposite: many earth paths or tracks are the result of repeated passage (main); simple cobble or stone paths where the grass is allowed to grow work best in a rural environment (far right).

The garden gate

The entrance to the garden creates the first impression and should be in sympathy with the spirit of the garden.

● **A small garden gate** in a low wall in the countryside should be kept simple, possibly made with unsawn timber. A solid timber door works well in a village setting.

● **A main entrance gate** in a wall is often made of long vertical slats or boards, usually painted rather than varnished.

● **Railings and metal gates** are suitable in vil-lages or for 19th century buildings, possibly with wrought iron features, as a sign of refinement, but they should nonetheless be kept simple and unpretentious to fit in with a rural setting.

● **The gateway itself** is often constructed of stone and, depending on the scale of the property, can be adorned with a roof or canopy, carved stones and other decorative features.

● **Spur-posts** are useful if the gateway is also a vehicle entrance.

the best solution, with a drainage channel sloping toward a water collection point. And you could still plant flowers along the wall.

In the north of France, for instance, people used to use reject bricks that got 'burnt' (*briques brûlées*) because they were too near the centre of the kiln during firing and were deemed unsuitable for buildings. Slightly uneven in shape but extremely hard, they were used for the surfacing of paths between a farm building and the main road as they would not break under the weight of cartwheels, and allowed people and vehicles to cut across the heavy clay mud found in much of the region in the winter.

A paved walkway around the house can be widened to create a terrace but, again, it should be very slightly sloping to make sure that rainwater drains away from the house. Water can then be ducted to a pond or another collection point in small, open drainage channels lined with flat stones, for instance.

Paving patterns and techniques are often specific to each region. In the south, surfaces made with stones and pebbles taken from the river bed are called *calades*. In the Dordogne, *pisé* refers to floors made with polished pebbles, while in Charente, the local term is *pichat* for paving made with smaller cut stones often framed with borders made with larger flat stones. These river stones were a cheap alternative to flagstones, sourced from quarries, which came at a price. People could simply pick them up from the local stream. Laid in decorative geometric patterns, these small river stones can be slippery when wet, and laying a whole floor or path is an arduous and time-consuming task.

A simple earth track is also fitting for a rural garden, particularly in the middle of the countryside or in the mountains. If it is to be used by vehicles it ought to have a gravel or stone surface which will provide a better grip and avoid muddy grooves, and drainage ditches on either side. Think of checking with the *mairie* (your local town hall) whether the road to your property is a public road (*route communale*), in which case it will be their responsibility to maintain it.

Footpaths of compacted earth or sand are perfect for a modest rural garden, particularly in the vegetable patch. Wider paths should be designed with a slight camber and a drainage ditch so they do not turn into a muddy trench.

Grassy paths are also quite attractive, although they need more upkeep. For ease of maintenance, create a border of bricks on either side of the path, sunken into the ground to just below path level which will allow you to mow right to the edges, and will stop earth or rainwater encroaching on the path.

Low ground-covering plants are useful in-between paving stones. Try *sagina procumbens* (procumbent pearlwort), with its tiny white flowers, which has a part-grass part-moss appearance, or wild rock plants. In the south, plants that work well include sedum, another small scale but quick-growing ground cover plants, and grasses.

For little-used paths, creeping thyme (*thymus serpyllum*) is effective, as are Corsican sandwort (*arenaria balearica*, a lawn-like perennial which also grows in holes in a wall), and members of the potentilla family such as tormentil (*potentilla erecta*) or Spring cinquefoil (*potentilla tabernaemontani*), both with small golden yellow flowers.

Along the edges of the path or on more rocky ground, try flowers from the erigeron family (producing masses of small daisy-shaped white or pink flowers), bellflower (*campanula*), Mouse-ear (*cerastium*), or aubrietia (*aubrieta*) - all of which grow easily on thin soil and are very pretty.

Paving: how to make it or repair it

Natural stone does not have to be that much more expensive than reconstituted stone, and it weathers well. Try to source stone from a nearby quarry, which is more likely to match that of the house.

River stones (*calades*) are used in the southwest to make stunning paving (above). Flagstones in the lawn make a perfect rural path along the house (opposite, main). Low-growing ground-cover plants brighten up the side of the path (opposite, right)

141 •

Stone for outside paving needs to be very hard, and 7 - 10 cm thick. Where bricks are used, it is worth noting that the darker coloured ones are generally more durable.

If your paving has become wobbly, it will need to be re-laid. Take up all the stones, and remove any vegetation that is growing underneath. If you need to dig down to get a better surface, put gravel or crushed stones as a base (a layer called *hérisson* – 'hedgehog'), and then add sand, before flattening this all down vigorously, to get a smooth, level surface. The same technique should be used for laying new paving from scratch. Remove the topsoil or grass, compact the earth, and then add a layer of sand. Ensure that you have the correct slope or camber for water run-off.

There are several possible methods for laying paving. One is to lay the slabs or bricks straight onto the sand, as close together as possible. Then, run sand into the gaps between the bricks and brush it in carefully, going over the surface several times. The final stage is to pour in a slurry (*barbotine*) of hydraulic lime which fixes the sand in place. Wash the paving to remove any milky residue from the lime.

Alternatively, paving can be held together with a lime mortar (1 unit of lime to 3 or 4 of sand), which is first poured onto the site to a depth of about 8 - 10 cm. Paving stones are then laid in place on the wet mortar, leaving a reasonable gap between each, which, in turn, is filled with mortar. This may leave the terrace a little bare and sometimes it is preferable to leave the gaps between some of the paving stones unmortared, filling them instead with earth to encourage grass and small plants to grow between the slabs. Otherwise, a paving stone may be omitted here and there in order to grow a small plant or bush in the space.

Laying timber decking

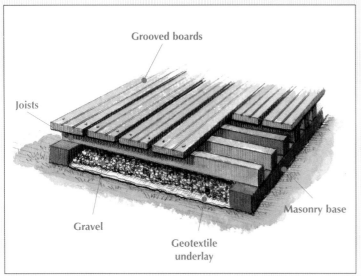

Grooved boards

Joists

Gravel

Geotextile underlay

Masonry base

1 : Use rot-resistant timber such as Atlas cedar, or acacia, both of which are grown in Europe. Alternatively, use other types of wood and treat with yacht varnish – preferably one that does not contain any chemical additives.

2 : Wood should not be in contact with the ground. Nor should the joists supporting boards. These should be set on a masonry frame about 10 cm from the ground. Lay a plastic or geotextile film over the bare earth beneath the decking and cover it with gravel. This void beneath the decking needs to be well ventilated to allow the wood to dry out after a rainy period.

3 : Thickness. The boards need to be at least 280 mm thick by 100 mm wide. Any thinner and they might warp.

4 : Fixing the boards. Decking planks are permanently under stress, swelling up in wet weather, and bending and flexing as you walk on them. Use nails designed for the task such as annular ring shanked nails (*clous annelés crantés*), in galvanised steel or protected from corrosion with wooden stubs or polyurethane putty. Leave at least 20 mm between the nail and the edge of the plank.

5 : Groove. Wet wood is very slippery so make sure that the boards are grooved on the surface.

PAVING MATERIAL

BRICK

COBBLES

With time, cobbled paths will get a little uneven and grass will grow in-between the stones, creating a bucolic atmosphere in the garden.

A cobbled street in Corsica, with a gutter in the middle to drain away rainwater.

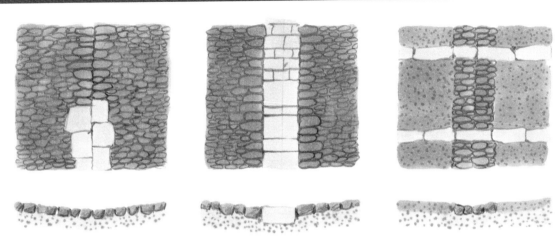

Examples of paving with central gutters using different types and colours of stone (above).

Street paving stones set on sand, with gutters on either side. The sand bed beneath is for easy drainage.

Open joint paving (*dallage à joints vifs*) (above left); the side of the path can be made into a distinct paved area (above right).

Two examples of drainage: a simple slope which carries the water away from the paved area (left), or collects the water in a channel in the path (right).

Hiding the trappings of modern life

Many rural properties have somewhere to park cars under cover and out of sight: in an old barn, behind a hedge or wall, under an awning, etc. If you have to build a new garage, use similar materials to those of the main building and adopt a similar style and shape, or build it in a place where it will be hidden from view behind a hedge or a wall.

Satellite dishes do not have to be white. They can be painted green, grey or brown. A tree in front of the dish will not be in the way as long as it is perpendicular to the aerial in the centre of the dish. Instead of being fixed to a wall, an aerial may be fixed to a post and hidden behind a bush out of sight.

A good place to install a barbecue is in an open building – barn, dovecot or other outbuilding – where it can be used in bad weather, but remains out of view most of the time.

Exterior lighting

Subtle lighting is often much more pleasant than bathing your garden in the glare of halogen spotlights and creates a much more intimate, enjoyable atmosphere – and at 250-500 watts halogen lights are expensive to run too. Think about putting lights into trees, hanging lanterns on walls, or burying spotlights in the undergrowth

Lighting shoud be discrete and matched to the house (above). Old barns are good for parking cars out of sight without having to build a garage specially.

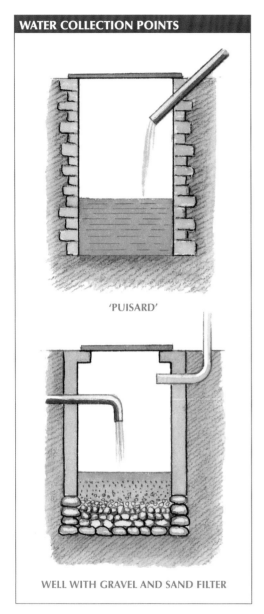

WATER COLLECTION POINTS

'PUISARD'

WELL WITH GRAVEL AND SAND FILTER

to light up the branches of trees. From a practical point of view, remember to light dark steps or narrow paths.

Any external cabling should be laid in plastic ducts, and all fittings should conform to the CE mark (*Conformité Européenne* – or 'EC') or NF mark (*Norme Française* – the equivalent of 'British Standard') for exterior electrics. Remember to make lighting installations robust enough to withstand bad weather.

DEALING WITH WATER

Waste water from the house

Dealing with waste water means dealing with two types of waste – that of your WC, and the waste water from baths, sinks, washing machines, etc. If you are planning a garden, it is essential to make sure the domestic drainage system is up to scratch before you start on the garden.

Many properties in the French countryside are not connected to any mains drainage, which means that a septic tank (*fosse septique*) or filter bed system is required to deal with household waste water. A modern septic tank is highly efficient and, combined with a grease trap for kitchen waste, should not give you much trouble.

However, many old rural houses have primitive forerunners to the modern septic tank. One of these is the so-called *fosse d'aisance,* designed to handle only waste from the WC. In the old days, other kinds of waste water were simply channelled out straight into the ground. This is no longer legal. A *fosse d'aisance* has two main disadvantages: it frequently blocks up, needs regular servicing, and will usually release an unpleasant smell from time to time.

Another antique water treatment system is the *puisard* (cesspool) – essentially a hole in the ground with watertight sides, where wastewater would sit until it seeped into the ground water. A variation on this method is a hole with gravel at the bottom, which acts as a rudimentary filter. Like the old *fosses d'aisance, puisards* are no longer allowed although existing ones are tolerated.

Modern septic tanks are a far cry from these old cesspits. They treat both WC waste and all other wastewater (*fosse 'toutes eaux'*), and they use biological action to treat the waste before it is drained out onto the land. If you are planning such a system from scratch, you should check at your *mairie* before you start. They may have imminent plans to connect mains drainage, for example, or they may

Different systems of soakaway depending on the lie of the land

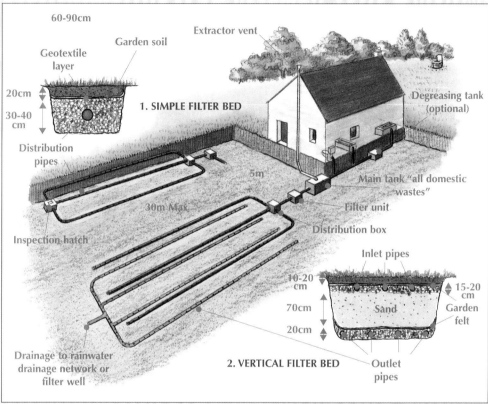

60-90cm

Geotextile layer

Garden soil

Extractor vent

20cm

30-40 cm

1. SIMPLE FILTER BED

Degreasing tank (optional)

Distribution pipes

5m

Main tank "all domestic wastes"

30m Max

Filter unit

Distribution box

Inspection hatch

Inlet pipes

10-20 cm

15-20 cm

70cm

Sand

Garden felt

20cm

Drainage to rainwater drainage network or filter well

2. VERTICAL FILTER BED

Outlet pipes

● **Permeable soil.**
If the soil allows water to drain away, then a soakaway for a septic tank is a relatively straightforward operation. The waste liquids from the tank flow into perforated pipes which then drain slowly into the soil. This needs a reasonable area for the network of drains (up to 30 m of pipes for a typical household) arranged in a grid system. In addition, the water table must be more than 1.5 m below the drains which in turn need to be about 80 cm below the ground surface, to avoid freezing up in the winter in cold regions. The pipes are laid on a layer of gravel to allow liquid to drain through, and covered with a sheet of geotextile, and then topsoil. This works on reasonably level ground, with a slope of less than about 4%. If there is a slope, even a gentle one, the pipes should be arranged perpendicular to the slope. The system should ideally have an air intake at each extremity, and should have a filter that allows the liquid to be channelled in equal volume through the network of pipes. Grassing over the surface is the best way to cover the septic tank , but take care never to let vehicles park on this area as this could damage the pipes.

● **Less permeable soil (such as clay).** In this case, sand is used to create a filter bed instead of soil. The principle is the same as the classic run-off described above, with the perforated drains releasing waste into a 70cm or so layer of sand, before the waste seeps into the surrounding soil.

● **Rocky ground, with a requirement to direct treated effluent to a** nearby water course. A filter bed of sand (as above) is used, but at the bottom of the filter bed is a second network of perforated pipes, which take away treated effluent away to a nearby watercourse. The area for each sand filter bed must be equal to 5 sqm per room in your house, with a minimum area of 20 sqm.

● **Rocky ground, on a sharp hill, with limited space.** In these difficult conditions, the filter bed is created as vertical layers of gravel and sand in an excavated pit, with the liquid in effect being filtered as it flows more or less horizontally.

● **Restricted or totally impermeable ground.** The solution here is to excavate a well, boring down to a level where the ground becomes permeable. The waste is filtered through layers of materials (sand, gravel and so on) as it seeps down and is finally absorbed by permeable ground at the bottom. The top must be just above ground, and covered with a lid to allow ventilation and servicing.

have certain standards that must be met when you build the system. The *mairie* must be contacted in any event as their authorisation (*permis de construire*) is required to install a septic tank. Expect to pay between €2,500 and €5,000 to have a new *fosse* installed.

A modern system operates in three stages: pre-treatment, purification, and drainage into the surrounding environment. The pre-treatment is carried out by the septic tank itself, with a grease trap between the tank and the kitchen if the tank is more than 15 m from the house. (The reason for this is simple: the further greasy water has to travel, the more likely it is that it will solidify in the pipe).

Bacteria in the septic tank will liquefy the waste, and anything solid that is not biodegradable in this way will be retained in the tank and cleaned out at a later stage. Septic tanks need regular attention, with new bacteria being added from time to time (particularly important in a second home where the house is not used constantly) and a complete pump out and service every two to five years.

A by-product of the cleaning process is the emission of hydrogen sulphide gas (that rotten-egg smell) which requires the installation of an air vent to allow the gas to escape via a pipe running to the ridge of your roof.

The ecological *lagunage* system for the treatment of waste water uses ponds which integrate easily into a natural landscape.

The next stage is for the treated waste to flow through a long series of pipes where it gradually drains out into the soil. The soil surrounding these run-off pipes develops into a cleaning filter where purifying bacteria develop and thrive.

If the soil is not sufficiently deep, or the ground is more or less impermeable, a filter bed is required. In this case, the treated waste is brought from the septic tank to the top of a filter bed and released for purification. By the time it filters to the bottom, it has been cleaned due to the bacteria action that develops during the process. This liquid then enters drainage pipes at the bottom of the sand bed, and runs off into the ground water (see box p.149).

Purification using plants

An alternative way of treating waste water is a system the French call *lagunage,* which, as the name suggests, makes use of small ponds or

LAGUNAGE: HOW IT WORKS

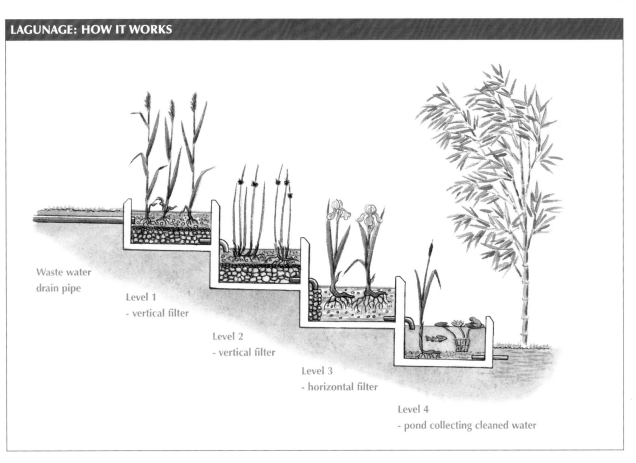

Waste water
drain pipe

Level 1
- vertical filter

Level 2
- vertical filter

Level 3
- horizontal filter

Level 4
- pond collecting cleaned water

lagoons. It is not used much by private households yet, but is being developed successfully in many small villages and hamlets. Instead of relying on sand filters, soil and microbes to filter the waste, the system uses plants.

There are many variations but the system works on the same basic structure involving marsh plants, rocks and gravity. Waste water is allowed to flow slowly through a succession of small ponds arranged in steps down a gentle slope. These ponds contain a bed of pebbles and a very absorbent volcanic rock, pozzolana, and are planted with aquatic plants such as reeds, rushes, great reedmace, and other macrophytes. Micro-organisms living around the roots of these plants are able to break down the residue in the waste water.

This system needs regular attention, such as opening sluices to shift water through the system once or twice a week, a complete clean-out once a year (after the second or third year of operation), and a comprehensive clean of the first filter every ten years. Nor is

The lagunage *system works by filtering waste water through ponds on various levels, each populated with bacteria that break down the waste.*

BUILDING DRAINS TO PROTECT WALLS

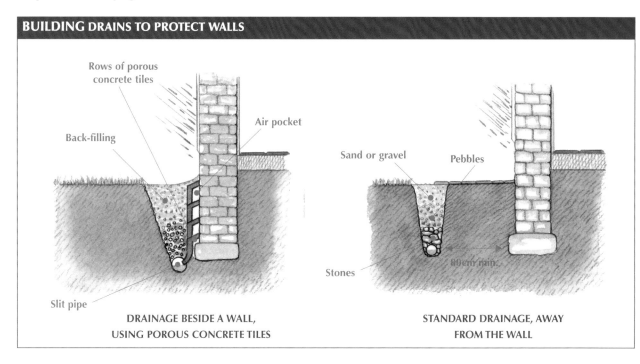

Rows of porous concrete tiles

Air pocket

Back-filling

Sand or gravel

Pebbles

Stones

80cm min.

Slit pipe

DRAINAGE BESIDE A WALL, USING POROUS CONCRETE TILES

STANDARD DRAINAGE, AWAY FROM THE WALL

LANGUAGE LAB : LANDSCAPING & DRAINAGE

Cobblestone : un pavé
Drainage : le drainage
Drainpipe : le drain
Gate : le portail (meaning both 'gate' and 'gateway')
Gutter : la gouttière (on the edge of a roof); le caniveau (on the side of the road)
Lighting : l'éclairage
Mains drainage : le tout-à-l'égout
Pipes : les tuyaux
Purification : l'épuration, la purification
Rainwater : l'eau de pluie
Septic tank : la fosse septique
Spur-post : le chasse-roue (low bollards either side of a gate preventing vehicles from running directly into the gate-posts)
Waste water : les eaux usées
Water treatment : le traitement de l'eau

the system suitable if it is not used regularly in the first few years, for instance, if the house is unused for more than two months in the summer, or if the house is at 1,200 m above sea level, as the ponds may freeze over in the winter.

The advantage of *lagunage* is that it takes away most of the risk of polluting groundwater. This risk remains even with a standard soakaway, as the water quality of the treated waste is rarely tested. It is also odour-free, and you end up with treated water that is ideal for watering the garden. The succession of ponds, planted with vegetation, built onto a slope, also have a pleasant landscaping effect.

On the downside, you need special permission from the *département,* and this will only be granted if it is not possible to install a standard soakaway.

Disposing of rainwater

Rainwater running off the roof of the house is not meant to go into the mains drainage system (assuming the property is connected) because it bulks up the volume of water that needs to be treated at the local water purification plant. But if you really have to get rid of it, it is not illegal to release it into streams.

Protecting the walls of the house

Houses react to damp. Old buildings are built with traditional materials that 'breath', such as stone, earth or lime. The walls made with these materials absorb moisture and then allow it to evaporate. The stonework can withstand reasonable levels of humidity without suffering any damage.

For this reason, there should not be any cement over the foundation as this might prevent damp from evaporating, and a drainage system should be put in place to keep water away from the walls. Making sure that the ground slopes away from the walls of the house is sufficient if the area is not too damp, but if water run-off is important a drain pipe or channel should be built (see diagram on opposite page). The latter is essential if there are no gutters to the roof, as was the case with many rural houses.

Tanking the walls provides increased protection. The standard technique involves lining the section of the wall that is below ground with a waterproof membrane. An alternative to the water-proof membrane is to stack rows of porous concrete tiles along the foundations. The tiles prevent contact between the foundations and the ground, duct the water to the drain, and allow air to circulate around the stone.

In areas that are particularly damp or susceptible to flooding, trees such as poplars help keep water levels under control and prevent the ground from becoming water-logged (above).

Draining a damp garden

If the ground around the house takes days to dry out after a period of rain, it might be worth installing some drainage. However, wet ground should not systematically be drained: wet areas are reservoirs through which water travels to reach the sub-soil, thus preventing droughts. Also, many plants also thrive in these conditions, which might be useful for green gardeners: horsetail, buttercup, autumn crocus, various bulbs, comfrey, hop, and marsh plants love damp soils. Similarly, certain trees enjoy damp ground and will absorb plenty of water. These include: poplar, willow, alder, silver birch and mountain ash.

However, draining the ground close to your house may be wise. First, you will need to check with the *mairie* where the drained water can be run-off to, and you will need to consult with neighbours. The water should be channelled into a holding area, such as a small pond or an underground chamber (*puisard*) before being directed to its outflow.

Draining the ground involves digging deep trenches and installing perforated drainage pipes on a bed of gravel. Typically, these drainage pipes are around 5-10 m apart, and converge on the drainage pond. If the ground is particularly uneven or sloping you will need to get specialist advice. Once the soil has been drained it will need to be well-fertilised before planting.

Recycling rainwater

Very few houses in rural areas have a pond that serves as a water source for irrigation purposes. More common is a water butt, or a water tank, sometimes buried in the ground, designed to store rainwater.

Tank systems are becoming increasingly sophisticated, so that they not only serve for watering the garden, but also for other purposes where tap water is often used: washing the car, flushing the WC, washing clothes, cleaning the house, or even the shower (if

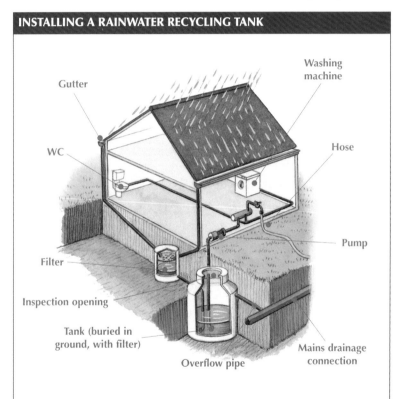

INSTALLING A RAINWATER RECYCLING TANK

Gutter

Washing machine

WC

Hose

Filter

Pump

Inspection opening

Tank (buried in ground, with filter)

Overflow pipe

Mains drainage connection

the water is sufficiently filtered) – altogether representing approximately 50% of the water consumption in an average household. Furthermore, rainwater is low in mineral content, which means that it is softer to use, does not create scale in the plumbing system, and less soap and detergent need to be used.

Investing in a rainwater filter, tank, pump and plumbing (around 4,500) will eventually pay for itself from the savings made on tap water consumption.

How it works:

● **The tank.** This needs to be either buried in the ground, or kept in the cellar, away from the light (to avoid the appearance of algae), and protected from important variations in temperature (to avoid the risk of frost).

● **How much water can you get?** First check the average rainfall figures for your region. Then work out the surface area of roof which will be feeding your tank. Just 1 mm of annual rainfall corresponds to a collection rate of 1 litre per square metre of roof surface.

● **How much water do you need?** An average household will typically use around 1,000 litres per person per year, so a tank of 4-5,000 litres will be sufficient.

● **Keep connections short.** The siting of the tank should be chosen to minimise the length of pipe-work both to the tank and from the tank to a pump and points where it will be used.

● **Mark the pipes.** It is a legal requirement that the pipes from the rainwater tank must be easily identifiable so they are not confused with the drinking water network supplied by your water company.

● **Filters.** Rainwater from the gutters will collect a certain amount of decomposing material (such as dead leaves) and should be filtered before entering the tank. In addition, the water should pass through a filter of 90 microns before leaving the tank for household use. This level of filtering is sufficient for most household applications other than drinking. If you want to use rainwater in the shower, you will need a much finer filter (1 micron). And if you want to drink your rainwater, you will need to buy a purifying system for indoor use, which eliminates all bacteria, viruses and nitrates.

● **What kind of tank?** A concrete tank is generally more reliable than a plastic or metal one. The overflow pipe from the tank should be connected to either a soakaway system or a nearby stream, but not to the mains drainage.

WATER TANK BUILT ON ROCK WITH PEBBLE FILTER

Intermediate filter tank

WATERBUTT BY THE SHED

You will not need a particularly sophisticated system if you only intend to collect rainwater to water the garden. You should be able to have a tank built to your specifications by a local builder or *maçon* for a modest outlay. It is still worth fixing a pre-filter to stop dead leaves and insects from entering the water, and filtering the water flow through gravel, sand or even charcoal.

Alternatively, you can buy a ready-made water butt in PVC with a capacity generally between 200 and 800 litres, sometimes supplied with a kit containing the various parts required to connect the butt to the gutter, hose-pipe and overflow. Choose one with a cover, which will prevent the formation of algae, and which is preferably lockable to protect children from the risk of accidents.

Or you could take the simplest route of all: install a water butt sitting under the guttering of the garden shed.

SOMEWHERE TO SWIM

A question of integration

Modern swimming pools do not necessarily fit in very well with a traditional rural garden. Also, their upkeep can be costly, especially if only used for a few months in the summer.

However, it is possible to integrate a swimming pool in a rural setting providing you choose materials that will blend into the surroundings: stone or reconstituted stone rather than concrete for the paved area; wooden decking or even terracotta if you live somewhere free of winter frost; and tiles rather than a liner for the pool itself. If you do go in for a liner, choose natural colours, like sand, which will give the water a pale green hue, or white, which will make the water look pale blue – but try to avoid bright turquoise which is far from natural and is rather harsh in a countryside retreat. Dark colours, such as brown, grey, or green, will give the water a sense of mysterious depth. The final effect, though, depends on the colour of the sky, and on the plants and trees nearby that are reflected on the surface of the water.

Certain pools built of concrete can be painted with mineral-based paint, or else rendered with a finish that resembles stone, which gives the pool a natural look. There are also a few examples of man-made rock pools in certain regions, created by digging out the rock and injecting the stone with a silicon resin to make it watertight. A pool will often look a little dreary in the winter, so it may be worth

Using natural material will help blend the pool into the rural setting of the country house.

Natural alternatives: simple lines and natural materials work best for a man-made pool (opposite), but natural alternatives, such as a pool dug into the rock (above) or a *lagunage* system using plants to filter the water (right), blend perfectly in a rural setting.

screening it from the house, if there is room, with a hedge, low wall, or a line of trees such as hornbeams, which keep their dead, dry leaves throughout the winter until these are pushed out by new ones in the spring. Beyond this aesthetic touch, you will also need to comply with legal requirements on pool safety, which provide that either a child-proof fence, pool alarm, or robust cover should be fitted over the pool.

When it comes to planting around the pool, avoid plants which will make the pool water dirty: trees in particular, which shed their leaves in autumn or plants which release a lot of pollen. Remember also that thorny plants might make it uncomfortable to walk around the pool with bare feet, and fragrant plants may attract wasps.

The most suitable plants are the shrubby varieties which do not lose their leaves: oleander; or the Mexican orange tree further south; and trees that form a good screen – though make sure they are far enough back so as not to block out the sun.

An alternative: the natural pool

This is a rare thing indeed, and is known in French as *la piscine écologique*. Inspired by the water purification technique of *lagunage* (see p.151), water flows first into a pool where aquatic plants are growing, such as irises or bulrushes, which have a biological cleaning action on the water. It is then filtered through sand before flowing on into the swimming pool itself, a little lower down, which is either built of concrete or, in some cases, constructed like a pond using a layer of impermeable clay. A pump is then used to circulate the water, so it is kept clean.

The sand filters the water very effectively but the water is not as sterile as that in a classic swimming pool using chemicals. However, it is well oxygenated, germ free, and is of a similar quality, in terms of suitability for swimming, to the water in a lake.

This pool will be the perfect waterhole for a natural rural garden, both aesthetically pleasing and ecologically advanced.

Plant Finder

CLIMBING PLANTS 162

COMMON FLOWERS 165

HERBS 176

This compendium provides a selection of plants that might commonly be found in rural gardens throughout France. The flowers, vegetables and trees listed here with their characteristics and history will help you recreate the true spirit of a traditional French garden.

VEGETABLES 178

FRUIT TREES & SHRUBS 190

POND PLANTS 194

TREES & SHRUBS 198

Climbing Plants

Vine was the plant traditionally grown along façades and it is still a favourite of French rural gardens today, often combined with a climbing rose. Here are a few other popular climbers.

Bignonia or Trumpet Vine
La bignone ou
jasmin de Virginie
(Campsis sp.)

The yellow, orange or red (*C. grandiflora*) trumpet-shaped flowers of the bignonia cheerfully spread colour over whole walls throughout the summer, especially in sunlit spots. Its hardy vines climb rapidly, though its base should be kept shaded and in cool soil. Beware of its tenacious tendrils.

Clematis
La clématite
(Clematis sp.)

The Japanese clematis (*C. montana*) adorns itself with a multitude of small, delicate, light-pink flowers and does best in shade and dry soil. The hardy *clematis tangutica*, with yellow bell-shaped flowers, prefers moist soil and flowers all summer long. Both types of clematis should be planted in a spot where the base is shaded and the branches reach the sunlight.

Honeysuckle
Le chèvrefeuille
(Lonicera)

Honeysuckle has been a common sight in gardens since the Middle Ages. It also makes good hedging and will cover several square metres. It grows easily in all soils, in or out of shade, and is propagated through soft or hard cuttings, or seeds. Its berries are poisonous, whilst its roots can be used to make blue dye. Because it needs plenty of space, it is advisable to mount a trellis against a façade, a few centimetres from the wall. Some white-flowered varieties are evergreen.

Ivy
Le lierre
(Hedera helix)

This evergreen is ideal for hiding an unattractive building, concealing a post or a dead tree trunk in hedging and covering north-facing walls. It prefers shaded locations and is tolerant of all soil types. Beware of its tendrils: once they adhere to a wall, it is almost impossible to strip the area clear of them and they will root into the wall. Ivy is not parasitic, although it has been known to suffocate a tree by covering it completely. It provides precious sustenance to certain rare insects and to blackbirds, although its berries are poisonous to humans. It can be used for green dye.

Nasturtium
La capucine
(Tropaeolum majus)

Climbing nasturtium (*la capucine grimpante*) is a variety of nasturtium. See 'Nasturtium' in the Common Flowers section, p.165.

Roses
Les rosiers
(Rosa)

For details of climbing and creeping roses (*rosiers lianes ou rosiers grimpants*), see under 'Rose' in the Common Flowers section, p.165, which provides a detailed list of popular rose varieties.

Vine
La vigne
(Vitis vinifera)

If the weather in your region can be inclement, plant your vine against a south-facing wall and choose a variety best suited to your area: late-fruiting in the south, early-fruiting (quick-ripening) north of the Loire to avoid frost. INRA (*Institut national de la recherche agronomique*) has developed *vitis* vari-eties resistant to disease, requiring no further treatments, such as the 'Perdin' variety, whose golden grapes are adapted to northern climates, whereas the 'Aladin' (black grapes without a lot of taste); and 'Amandin' (Muscat-flavoured white grapes) varieties are best suited to southern cli-

mates. In the north, also try the 'Muscat de Hambourg', a very old and hardy variety with delicious bunches full of large black grapes, or even 'Sulima', a crisp and fragrant white grape. The 'Teinturier' variety, loaded with tannins, offers blue-tinged, black grapes and displays leaves that take on a glowing-red shade from June. The 'Teinturier' is also used in herbal teas to promote good circulation in the legs. The 'muscat à petits grains', imported by the Romans, or the 'chasselas muscat' are also delicious and easy to cultivate. However, the 'Muscat d'Alexandrie' or 'Malaga', originally from Africa and introduced in the 17th, does best in the South of France as it requires a lot of sun. Obtaining healthy grapes

means you have to prune the vines every year to avoid unwieldy growth. But this is very simple as long as you bear in mind that new shoots come from the previous year's branches, and that each shoot will bear fruit every other year. Cut back the previous year's branches so that at least two buds remain as your future shoots. Prune at the beginning of March (or at the end of February in the South) when growth has already begun and the frosts are over, then again if necessary between May and June if there is an excessive number of long shoots. Prune carefully: cutting back too hard will produce a few long shoots with few grapes, not pruning enough will produce an overabundance of stunted grapes.

Virginia Creeper
La vigne vierge
(Parthenocissus)

Easy to recognise with its large, pointy, trilobed leaves, the virginia creeper (*Parthenocissus tricuspidata*) grows easily just about anywhere, even on a north-facing wall. It grows fast, with dense foliage and is ideal for covering a drab or unseemly wall quickly. Like the tendrilled variety, whose thinner, jagged leaves form five lobes (*Parthenocissus quinquefolia*), it displays vibrant red autumn colours. Be aware that the tendrils, though self-clinging, are best supported with wire netting or a trellis.

Wisteria
La glycine
(Wisteria sp.)

Although it dislikes chalky soil, wisteria is easy to grow in sunlit spots. Most wisteria flower in springtime before their foliage appears, then flower sporadically until autumn, lighting up walls or railings with their subtle, sweet-smelling bunches of mauve blooms. The Chinese wisteria (*W. sinensis*) is vigorous and grows fast, but buy it in bloom and preferably potted to be sure that it flowers. It needs support as it grows, but be careful of the tremendous strength of its branches: they are known to bend even the strongest of railings.

Common Flowers

There was little room for flowers in the original rural garden. Flowers mostly grew in the wild and in meadows, although some were allowed in the vegetable garden because they helped protect crops from pests. Flowers which grew from seed sowed by the wind would be left in corners of the garden for a bit of colour. Here are some of the more traditional specimens.

Anemone, Pasque Flower
L'anémone pulsatille, coquerelle
(Pulsatilla vulgaris)

A pretty, purple perennial, the meadow anemone flourishes on sunny hillsides and dry, mountain pastures. Its flowers, which bloom at the first sight of spring, are covered with a silky down. It is distilled into a medicinal aid for headaches.

Angelica
L'angélique
(Angelica)

This large umbellifer thrives in moist soil. Associated with the angel Gabriel, it was thought to protect against ghosts and the plague. Young, green angelica stems can be eaten candied and were once frequently used by confectioners. Angelica is a well-know tonic and good for the stomach, which is why it was also grown for its roots, used in numerous after-dinner drinks.

Borage
La bourrache
(Borago officinalis)

Cultivated since antiquity, borage grows on fallow land and in rubble. Its leaves and flowers were once put in wine, to relieve sadness and reduce fever. Its small, purple flowers, quilted with a fine white velvet, liven up salads; the leaves are eaten cooked. It is also good in herbal teas, and in oils for its richness in essential fatty acids. In the kitchen garden it keeps the cabbage butterfly away from other plants.

Camomile

La camomille

(Anthemis nobilis)

Very often used in herbal teas and in hot drinks to alleviate fever and stomach ache, as well as in compresses to aid in the treatment of conjunctivitis and skin problems, camomile was once a common sight as a border to vegetable gardens. The leaves can be dried in the sun, then kept in a cool dry place. Camomile does best in the sun and in rich, sandy soil.

Chicory (Wild Chicory)

La chicorée sauvage

(Cichorium intybus)

A hardy plant with blueish-mauve flowers, chicory is widespread in pastures and on roadsides. It is said to work as a stomach tonic, a depurative and a light laxative. One variety with large roots grown in the North of France is served as a coffee substitute (also see Vegetables, p.178).

Comfrey, Black Wort, Consound, Ass-ear

La consoude, herbe à la coupure, oreille d'âne

(Symphytum officinalis)

Comfrey is a large perennial with small bell-shaped flowers varying from white to mauve. It thrives in wet climates and enjoys the shade. Its woolly leaves are reputed to have healing, anti-inflammatory and suppurative properties, although they can be poisonous in large quantities. Rich in potassium, it is also used as fodder and as liquid plant feed.

Cornflower

Le bleuet

(Centaurea cyanus)

The bright blue cornflower once brightened up corn fields but is now found only rarely as a result of the large scale use of weedkillers. In the Middle Ages, magical powers were attributed to it. Since the 19th century it has been used in compresses for to soothe irritated eyes.

Cowslip
La primevère, ou coucou
(Primula veris)

In early spring, cowslips bring meadows and undergrowth to life with their small, fragrant, bell-shaped yellow flowers. In the mountains, pink-coloured or odourless species can also be found. The leaves and flowers are edible. The flowers are known for their emollient quality and are effective against headaches. Cow-slips macerated for a month in white wine add a fine, aromatic flavour to it.

Cranesbill, or Geranium
Le géranium
(Geranium sp.)

Of the numerous varieties of meadow geraniums, *Geranium Robertianum* is the most widespread, growing in thickets and hedges and forming 20 to 50 cm clumps of tiny pink flowers. In open spaces, this hardy plant can live for years in the same spot, requiring very little main-tenance. The equally hardy meadow cranesbill has large, purplish-blue flowers, while the wood cranesbill has smaller, mauve-coloured flowers.

Dahlia
Le dahlia
(Dahlia)

Dahlias often line the edges of vegetable plots. When dahlias first arrived from Mexico in 1802 they were planted in the *Jardin des Plantes* in Paris as an edible plant, but no one, not even animals, would eat them: the leaves and bulbs had too strong a smell and the roots were too fibrous. Dahlias recently returned to country gardens in hybrid form, where they are regaining popularity as a decorative plant.

Dandelion
Le pissenlit, dent-de-lion, laitue des chiens, salade de taupe
(Taraxacum officinale)

Dandelion is prolific in meadows. There are sev-eral species, all of which are content in any soil. It is one of the most widely picked wild plants, eaten in salads, of course, or cooked in soup. It is effec-tive in cleansing the liver: Boiling fresh roots or leaves to make a tonic was once recommended against loss of appetite and to ease digestion.

Forget-me-not
Le myosotis
(Myosotis)

The field forget-me-not (*M. arvensis*) is pale blue and grows on bare, sandy, dry ground. The richer blue garden forget-me-not (*M. silvatica*) prefers woods and meadows. The water forget-me-not (*M. scorpioides*) is a creeper. So, there should be a variety suitable for any garden, and indeed, the forget-me-not is a common sight in rural gardens, where it often grows along walls, flowering from May until mid-October. It re-seeds freely.

Heartsease
La pensée sauvage, violette des champs
(Viola tricolor)

The yellow-violet heartsease is typical of old-style gardens. Covering well-drained, cool, shaded soil, it flowers until November. It was once thought to be effective against skin ailments. The flowers are used in salads.

Hellebore
L'hellébore
(Helleborus sp.)

Bouquets of stinking hellebores (*helleborus foetida*) were once hung in stables to ward off snakes and illness - no doubt because hellebores are poisonous. When an animal had fallen ill for an unknown reason, as a last resort, an incision would be made into its limb and a section of hellebore stem would be inserted into it, tied to a woollen thread that would be left hanging out. The wound formed pus, which stimulated the animal's immune system. When touched, the stinking hellebore releases a strong smell. The black hellebore (*H. niger*) flowers in winter; thus its other name, the 'Christmas rose.'

Honesty, Moonwort, Moneywort
La monnaie du Pape, lunaire, herbe aux écus
(Lunaria annua)

Perhaps because of its strange translucent seed pods, honesty was long considered a magical plant, which protected from "everything that hovers over the surface of still waters, from everything with cleft hooves that gallops in damp moors, and from 'white ladies'; it opens locks and even hearts" (Michel Vivier, see Bibliography, p.219). Lovers on postcards were once pictured surrounded by honesty. It is planted in September in light, cool soil.

Hop
Le houblon
(Humulus lupulus)

Hop often climbs along river banks and through hedging. The variety bearing yellow flowers, Golden Hop, is especially attractive. Its young, hazelnut-tasting shoots can be eaten like aspara-gus, and its fruit gives beer its particular flavour. Hop is also good as herbal tea to help cure insomnia.

Houseleek
La joubarbe, artichaut sauvage
(Sempervivum tectorum)

The sap of this little, plump plant, which looks like a small artichoke, is said to treat burns and verrucas. Popular culture also claims that it can ward off lightning, which explains why it is often planted at the apex of thatched roofs. Houseleek thrives between paving stones and in low, dry stone walls or in a pot, where it requires little attention.

Iris
L'iris
(Iris)

This beautiful flower is often planted under the edges of roofs because its leaves guide waterdrops to the ground. The roots absorb the humidity and carry it up to the leaves, which are evergreen. Its rhizomes, once peeled and dried, can be used to perfume washing. It is thought to be a remedy against colds thanks to its expectorant properties. Understandably therefore, the iris is commonly found in many gardens. The yellow iris (*I. pseudacorus*), or yellow flag, grows on the banks of wild ponds.

Lavender
La lavande
(Lavandula anguistiflolia)

Lavender thrives in dry, rocky and chalky soil in sunny locations. Used in herbal teas and essential oils, essence of lavender has stimulative, tonic and antispasmodic properties. It appeared in the gardens of monasteries as early as the Middle Ages, but it was not until the 19th century that it became widespread in the French countryside. Small sachets of its flow-ers perfume linen and deter insects. The larger-stemmed *Lavandula latifolia* variety provides a less subtle fragrance.

Lily
Le lis
(Lilium)

A symbol of virtue and purity, the white Madonna lily is the quintessential flower of the Church. One variety however, the arum lily, has a more controversial origin, according to Greek mythology: it grew from a drop of milk fallen from the breast of the goddess Hera. Aphrodite, jealous of the lily's dazzling whiteness, took revenge by endowing it with an enormous pistil which recalls "*la verge d'un âne*". Kept in alcohol, the flower of the lily was once used as a disinfectant, and in oil, to treat bruises. In Flanders, the blossoming of Saint Joseph lily signalled that the coming harvest was but one month away.

Lily of the Valley
Le muguet
(*Convallaria majalis*)

Lily of the Valley is found in undergrowth beneath beech and oak trees. This luck-bearing, May flower, linked with the worship of the Virgin Mary, is not found in the Mediterranean region. The entire plant is used for cardiac infections, as an antispasmodic and a light purgative. But be careful because it is poisonous in large doses. Its crushed leaves cause sneezing.

Mallow
La grande mauve
(*Malva silvestris*)

This beautiful plant, which can grow a metre high, is found in uncultivated terrain, fields, hedges, rubble and even on village streets around houses. Its large, decorative flowers with five, heart-shaped petals are coloured a purplish-blue pink. The tea made from these flowers is used in popular medicine as an emollient and is supposed to be very effective against persistent constipation. It is also used to brighten up salads, as its young leaves and tender flowers can be eaten raw. There are other varieties, such as the smaller and paler (*Malva neglecta*), as well as the tree mallow (*Lavatera arborea*), with crimson veins.

Marigold
Le souci
(*Calendula officinalis*)

This very hardy flower seeds easily and stays in bloom for a long time during the summer months. Many varieties can be found in country gardens. The large double-flower heads of some varieties are used in herbal teas or in extracts for treating wounds, chilblain or burns, as they encourage healing and soothe skin ailments. Marigold petals were once distilled and used to colour unacceptably pale butter.

Marsh Mallow
La guimauve
(Althaea officinalis)

The marsh mallow, as the name suggests, grows mostly in marshes or on water banks. It requires light, deep, cool soil. Its delicate pinkish-white flowers, which look like those of the holly-hock, can be used in teas to soothe an irritated throat. Its roots used to be given to children to chew as a delicacy.

Meadowsweet
La reine-des-prés
(Filipendula ulmaria)

This large, hardy flower with its fragrant, diaphanous, cream-coloured flower heads is commonly found in swamps, hedges and damp wooded areas. It is a traditional remedy in herbal teas to cure headaches and particular-ly rheumatism and gout. Ancient medicine claimed that this plant, because it is mainly found in wet places, treated ailments caused by damp. It was once also given to cows when they were in calf.

Nasturtium
La capucine
(Tropaeolum majus)

Nasturtium is a native of Peru. Its leaves and flow-ers are used to bring out the flavour in salads or to decorate meat dishes. The flower buds can be macerated in vinegar as 'faux capers'.
Nasturtiums are easy to grow, especially the climbing varieties, which are very attractive trained on wire netting or fences, cascading from a pot or crawling over empty spaces. The dwarf variety is the most common in rural gardens.

Nettle
L'ortie
(Urtica)

Considered an irritant and judged unattractive, net-tles are widespread in meadows and along low walls in moist, rocky, alka-line soils rich in nitrogen. The white dead nettle, which does not sting and has larger, white, double-rimmed flowers, is in fact not a nettle but a member of the mint family *(Lamium album)*. At first somewhat repellent, the nettle actually hides a treasure of virtues. Nettle concoction is an effective insecticide against aphids and a good fertiliser for kitchen gardens (see Natural Fertilisers, p.128 *et seq.*). It also has medicinal properties: extraordinarily rich in vitamins and min-eral salts, it is considered an anti-diabetic, antidiar-rhoeic, cholagogue (aids in the secretion of bile), depurative (cleans the blood), diuretic, haemo-static (helps to stop bleed-ing), resolvent (dissolves congestion in organs) and, above all, a restorative. Nettles are also used as feed for livestock (in Denmark, it was traditional to add a handful of dried nettle seeds to horse feed) and even as food for humans - its young buds are eaten cooked, like spinach and in spring, it makes a very tasty soup. It is claimed that nettles help raise milk and cream produc-tion, and prolong the lay-ing period of hens - hence the proverb from Picardy: "Nettle in the henhouse is one more egg in the basket". Finally, the strong fibres of its stems were used to make fabric (grass cloth), ropes and even paper in the Middle Ages. This continued until the 20th century in eastern Europe and Scandinavia.

A yellow pigment can also be extracted from its roots, and a green pigment from its leaves.

Peony
Le pivoine
(Paeonia officinalis)

Folklore about the peony varies according to the regions and period in history. Since the 12th century, various properties have been attributed to the roots of the wild peony. More recent species, brought back from China since 1784 have been used to create wonderful hybrids, which were planted in rural gardens especially after the Second World War. At the end of the 19th century, it was believed that its leaves, tucked in stockings or in socks, acted as a contraceptive. And hanging a dried bou-quet in the house was all that was needed to ward off storms and evil spirits.

Periwinkle
La pervenche
(small: Vinca minor;
large: Vinca major)

This graceful, hardy plant with climbing stems grows in cool, wooded areas, hedges and on shaded rocks. It can also be found in Southern regions as it can tolerate some dryness. The leaves are used in herbal teas to help with digestion. It is a popular anti-lactation remedy, though its effec-tiveness is questionable.

Pinks and Carnations
L'oeillet
(Dianthus)

A plant with a long history, it is claimed that the carnation was brought back from the Crusades by Saint Louis. It has met with a lot of breeding success since then and there are now numerous varieties. Hardy varieties are sometimes planted in borders, while other, more frost-tender vari-eties are commonly used as ot plants.

Poppy, Field Poppy
Le coquelicot
(Papaver rhoeas)

Since the introduction of weedkillers, field poppies are a rare sight in the countryside, although they can still be spotted on stream banks and slopes. Generally they re-seed easily in the right conditions. In the spring, its leaves can be eaten with vegetables. The petals can be added to salads for decoration, or dried and used in herbal teas for sore throats or coughs (though its tea should not be given to children). The seeds of the field poppy can be used in cooking and baking as a substitute to the seeds of the blue poppy, which are more commonly used.

Rose
La rose
(Rosa)

The rose was honoured during the month of Mary and Corpus Christi, and its petals were scattered during religious celebrations, processions and the Eucharist. Old-fashioned roses with fragrant flowers are disease and pest resistant and require very little care. A frequent choice in rural gardens, according to old roses specialist Eléonore Cruse, was *Paul's Scarlet Climber*, possibly because of its intense red flowers and the fact that it grows very easily, flowers late into the season and is extemely resistant to diseases. The *cabbage rose* (*R. centifolia muscosa*), originally from the Caucasus, and the

four seasons rose, a pale pink, fragrant and repeat flowering rose, is often found near vegetable plots, as is the famous *Provins officinalis*, with semi-double red blooms, introduced to Provins after the Crusades. It grows to 1.5 m tall, flowers in June-July and is often found in hedges and thickets, especially in the centre of France and in Alsace. Its aromatic and astringent flowers are used in mouth gargles and to make rose jam and rose honey. The *Centifolia major*, the rose with an hundred petals, produces large, full, deep, sweet smelling blooms in June. The *Resht rose*, which has a bush habit, and small, deep-pink, red flowers growing in a dense bush, comes from Iran. It is very resistant to the cold, repeat flowers and has a wonderful scent. The *Rosa rugosa* hybrid roses are good for coastal and mountain climates, and parts of nothern France. All rose hybrids of the *R. wichuraiana* and *R. luciae* varieties, as well as the climber *R. helenae*, tolerate chalky soil.

Among bush roses, easy varieties include *R. alba*, *R. gallica*, *R. damascene* and *R. centifolia*. *Blush Noisette*, also called *Bride's Bouquet*, produces pinkish, white flowers with a spicy scent and will grow in partial shade. The rambling 'pompom' rose *Dorothy Perkins*, first bred in the United States in 1901 is quite widespread, blooming densely in June. It is sensitive to mildew, but generally recovers with strong growth the following year. It has small, bright pink flowers and fine, rambling and very thorny branches. The *Excelsa*, launched in 1909, also in the United States, is similar, but with red flowers. Neither are fragrant. *Madame Alfred Carrière*, first grown in 1879, has white, flesh-coloured blossoms that repeat flowers until the frosts. It is a very romantic variety with a soft and subtle fragrance. The *Albertine*, sturdy and thorny, produces large, light salmon-pink flowers that can perfume an entire garden. In the South of France, the long cultivated

R. sempervirens hybrids are semi-deciduous and appreciate warm weather, as do the roses from Bengal, known as 'perennial Chinese roses'. In the Bordelais region, the latter are traditionally planted near grapevines as a 'test' for diseases, as they catch diseases earlier than the vines. In Mediterranean regions, the most common variety is the *Albéric Barbier*, easily recognisable by its glossy, semi-evergreen foliage, its luxuriant vegetation and its double, white flowers with lemon-scented hearts. This variety tolerates shade and is seen in the narrow lanes of villages. Finally, a mention for the thornless, densely-flowering *Lady Banks' Yellow Rose* (*R. banksiae lutea*). Discovered in 1825 in China by the English, who then intro-

duced it to France, it contributed to the new charm of many gardens in Provence and the Riviera at the beginning of the century.

Planting and looking after your roses:

Buy a bare-rooted bush from a specialist grower at the end of the autumn or in winter and plant it immediately in well drained soil, with well rotted compost. Rose cuttings usually mature more gracefully with a fuller habit than grafted rose trees. In the spring, water with liquid plant feed (nettle or comfrey). Garlic planted nearby protects from fungal diseases, and lavender deters aphids and ants. For black spot: burn affected leaves; spray preventively with a copper-based product or a horsetail decoction in winter (see pp.131 *et seq*.).

St John's Wort
Le millepertuis, herbe aux piqûres, herbe de la Saint-Jean, chasse-diable (Hypericum perforatum)

This hardy perennial with golden yellow flowers, common throughout Europe, grows in colonies on hillsides where it needs no special care. The leaves contain tiny pockets of translucent oil, hence its French name meaning 'plant with a thousand holes'. The flowers can be picked and made into dried bouquets. St John's Wort is also a popular remedy used to treat burns and cuts when dissolved in hot oil or macerated.

Meadow Salsify, Showy Goat's Beard
Le salsifi des prés, barbe de bouc (Tragopogon pratensis)

A familiar sight at the edges of footpaths, this yellow flower is from the same family as the dandelion. Its downy pistils are carried on the wind. The flower buds can be eaten before they open, like other salsify varieties.

Soapwort, Bouncing-Bet
La saponaire, savonnière,
herbe à foulon,
herbe à savon
(Saponaria officinalis)

The soapwort has lovely, pale, pink petals. Its rhizomes allow it to grow and spread easily, whatever the soil or altitude. It also has a number of qualities, in particular its use as soap: since antiquity, it has been used to remove grease stains from wool and to clean fabrics. The rhizomes have tonic, cleansing and dermatological properties.

Tansy
La tanaisie
(Tanacetum vulgare)

The fragrant tansy has small, button-shaped, yellow flowers and grows on the side of sunny paths in rich, cool, slightly dry soil. A tonic which also helps to expel parasitic intestinal worms (anthelmintic), it was once used as a medicinal wine, as a spice in *crêpes* (French pancakes) or omelettes. It was effective against fleas and mites and was added to the bedding straw of farm animals and placed in wardrobes where linen was kept. Tansy also repels certain insects harmful to vegetables, such as the cabbage white butterfly or the potato beetle, and was often planted in the vegetable plot.

Teasel
La cardère,
chardon à foulon
(Dipsacus fullonum)

Teasel looks like a thick thistle in its cultivated form. Its dried heads were once used to 'tease' (disentangle) wool – thus the name *cardère* in French. Teasel grows in rough or poor soil. The bases of its rigid leaves retain water, attracting thirsty small birds that also pick at the many seeds when the plant matures in its second year (teasels are biennials).

Violet
La violette
(Viola)

The hardy violet grows in any soil but multiplies best in rich shady soil beneath trees, where it blooms from March to May. It is easy to transplant if watered well at the start. Many varieties exist, some more fragrant than others (*V. odorata*, with deep-purple flowers, is highly scented) and in many colours (*V. alba* is white, *V. canina* is sky-blue). The flowers, which have sudorific and expectorant properties, were used to flavour wine in the Middle Ages. The leaves are emollient and diuretic, its roots purgative and emetic. The violet is also used in perfumery and confectionery.

Herbs

Wormwood

L'armoise

(Artemisia vulgaris)

Considered the plant of
Artemis, the goddess of
hunting and nature, this
large aromatic plant was
used to induce abortions
and against pain and
discomfort. It forms
large greyish-green
tufts with clusters of
small yellow flowers
which invade uncultivated
land and screes.

Yarrow, or Milfoil

**L'achillée millefeuille, mille
feuilles,**

herbe aux coupures

(Achillea millefolium)

The name milfoil derives
from the plant's narrow
leaves divided into multiple
points. Its small flowers
form lovely white or pink
corollas. They thrive in
acid soil and on sloping
ground, in grassy areas or
moors and in hedging.
Yarrow was credited with
magical qualities: protecting
from malign influences and
bringing good fortune to
the newly-wed. Its leaves
mixed in poultice were
reputed healing agents and
in herbal teas were considered a tonic. Its sap was
added to beer, aperitifs and
butter as flavouring, but it
was said to provoke bleeding (school children would
use it to fake illnesses).

Most herbs will grow
happily in all regions
of France, although
some prefer the drier
soils and warmer
climate of the south.
Here are a few of
the most common
herbs found in
French gardens.

Basil

Le basilic

(Ocinum basilicum)

Introduced to western
Europe in the 16th centu-
ry, basil thrives in warmer
climates of France where
it can rapidly turn into a
bush 90 cm high with
large green leaves. Sow in
a cold frame or green-
house in March and bed
out in May-June.
Alternatively, sow directly
in the ground from May.
Basil prefers fertile well
drained but cool soil. An
annual, it flowers at the
end of the summer and
dies back completely
during winter.

Chives
La ciboulette
(Allium schoenoprasum)

Chives will grow happily in most soils but prefer rich, moist and well-drained ground. Either sow seeds directly in the soil from March or obtain a small clump from a fellow gardener when he divides an existing clump. Division should be done every few years so the plant continues to grow healthily. Chives deter many garden pests and are perfect companions for many vegetables and flowers.

Marjoram
La marjolaine
(Majorana hortensis)
Oregano
L'origan
(Origanum vulgare)

Marjoram and oregano are very similar, as both form tufts from which fragrant, tiny purple flowers emerge. Cultivated marjoram is used in herbal teas but it was once a beverage drunk only among women. It is alleged to be effective against insomnia, nervousness, colds, bruises, and is said to aid digestion. The leaves were also smoked as tobacco substitute. In southern regions, the leaves of the *origanum majorana* and of the *origanum vulgare* varieties develop an intense flavour, well known as a seasoning herb.

Parsley
Le persil
(Petroselinum)

Curly and decorative, or flat and fragrant, parsley species are a constant of the French herb garden. Parsley is used extensively in everyday French cuisine but must be used fresh, as it rapidly loses its flavour, and raw, as cooking kills its vitamin content. Parsley is biennial and will grow almost anywhere but prefers light fertile soil. Sow directly in the soil between February and September.

Rosemary
Le romarin
(Rosmarinus officinalis)

Rosemary is evocative of the south of France but it is a frost hardy plant that can grow in cold climates too. It prefers dry, well-drained, chalky soil and full sun. Its spikes of purple-blue flowers, produced from April to early summer, are a favourite with bees. Rosemary is an evergreen shrub that can grow to 1,5 m. It does not require pruning but you can trim to keep the shape in late spring. An essential cooking herb of many *provencal* dishes, it is used to flavour lamb, pork, and vegetables.

Sage

La sauge
(Salvia)

Sage, from the latin meaning 'cure' is credited with many medicinal properties. Sage is quite hardy but grows best in warmer, well drained soil. A bushy plant, it can live for many years. It produces purple or mauve flowers in the spring and keeps its leaves in the winter. Regenerate the bush now and again by pruning back or cutting out some of the main branches.

Thyme and Creeping Thyme

Le thym *(Thymus vulgaris)* et le serpolet *(Thymus serpyllum)*

Thyme and its ancestor the wild, creeping thyme both like dry, rocky or sandy soil. Creeping thyme can be left to grow between paving stones for a natural decorative effect. Both can be used in cooka

Vegetables

The vegetable plot was the food factory of the rural household. We have listed here a few of the more traditional vegetables that used to be grown widely in rural gardens. Some varieties became rarer but many are now easily available again from specialist seed growers.

Amaranth

L'amarante à feuilles
(Amaranthus gangeticus)

The amaranth is immediately noticeable for its enormous clusters of bightly coloured seed pods. It was imported from South America, where it was highly regarded for its high content in vitamins and minerals. These days, it is mostly known as an ornamental plant, or as a weed, but its leaves can be eaten like spinach, either raw or cooked. The seeds are edible too.

Artichoke,
Globe Artichoke
L'artichaut
(*Cynara scolymus*)

The genetic ancestor of
the globe artichoke was a
variety of cardoon (*cynara
cardunculus*) grown in the
Mediterranean region and
developed in Spain in the
12th century before
spreading to Italy and
France. The head and
stalks of the wild varieties
have been consumed
since prehistory. Keep
artichoke plants well protected under straw in winter and they will grow
again the following spring.

Aubergine, Eggplant
L'aubergine
(*Solanum melongena*)

The aubergine belongs to
the same family as tomatoes
and potatoes but, unlike
them, it arrived not from
America but from Asia via
Italy during the Renaissance.
The Kokopelli association
(see Address Book p.216)
has several rare varieties.
The aubergine is widely
cultivated in France but it
is sensitive to frost and
fungal diseases and needs
warmth. It has shallow
roots, so make sure the
ground around it is clear
of weeds, as they would
compete for water.

Bean
Le haricot
(*Phaseolus sp.*)

Beans are natives of
South America, where
they have been cultivated
for thousands of years.
Green, dwarf, or flat,
there are 4,000 different
varieties. The common
'green' bean as we know
it, with an edible pod and
minuscule beans, is a
19th century creation.
Prior to that, the bean
pods were shelled and
only the seeds were eaten.
Most bean varieties grow
easily in all conditions and
are good croppers.

Beet
La betterave
(*Beta vulgaris
esculenta Gürke*)

The beet belongs to the
same family as chard.
There are three species,
of which only the garden
beet varieties can be used
for human consumption.
The tubers of the garden
beet take various forms
and colours, from dark
purple to golden yellow,
and have a sugary taste.
Beet grows in all soil types
rich in organic matter.

Broad Bean
La fève
(Vicia faba)

Cabbage
Les choux
(Brassica oleracea)

Carrot
La carotte
(Daucus carota)

This is one of Europe's oldest beans. It went into decline in Europe after the 16th century, when people started to prefer the finer white bean, although it continued to be eaten in purees in India and the Middle East. Broad beans grow in moist soils with good drainage, and will even improve poorer ones through its nitrogen-fixing roots. In the south, the seeds can be sown in the autumn and the pods picked in the spring. In the north, sow in spring for summer picking. The seeds, rich in proteins and fibres, are tasty raw or cooked; steamed or sautéed with onions and shallots.

A winter vegetable of various colours and shapes, the entire cabbage family can be put to good use: as a vegetable and in soups or as animal fodder. The leaves are also used as packing for fragile items such as butter, cheese and small fruits, and the dried stems as fuel. Cabbage resists the winter cold and keeps easily. It was once common to plant 400 to 500 on large farms. There are several related varieties: broccoli, originally from the Meditarrenean; the smooth-leaved white cabbage, which includes species such as *coeur de boeuf* or *quintal d'Alsace*, used to make *sauerkraut*; red cabbage, used in many dishes, is particularly rich in vitamin C; Brussels sprouts, grown since the 19th century and which are harvested in autumn and winter, Savoy cabbage, with curly leaves; cauliflower, another Mediterranean import which has become widespread in France; curly kale, an old cabbage variety, which used to be very common in vegetable gardens, and should be picked leaf by leaf rather than cutting a whole head; kohlrabi, eaten like turnip or in *gratin*; and fodder kale, grown as fodder for animals but whose young suckers can be eaten in salads or steamed.

Records show that the carrot was already used in antiquity, although it was sometimes confused with parsnip. It became widespread in Europe in the 16th century, when orange and purple varieties were popular. It is believed to originate in central Asia but the white variety is a European native, although it has become rare today.

Celery, Celeriac
Le céleri, le céleri-rave
(Apium graveolens)

Wild celery used to grow in marshes in coastal regions and was used in death rituals by the Egyptians. It was appreciated until the Middle Ages for its medicinal properties, in particular as a diuretic, and grown for its fragrant seeds, which were used as flavouring in wine and bread. Improved in the 19th century, there are now two main varieties, one grown for its stalks (known as celery) and one for its root (known as celeriac).

Chard, Swiss Chard, Spinach Beet
La bette ou blette, côte de blette, carde
(Beta vulgaris cicla)

This is a variety of beet cultivated for its leaves, rather than its tuber, which can grow to large proportions. Red, yellow, or white chard can be spectacular. A native to Europe, it appears to have been grown by the Celts. Charlemagne ordered that it should be cultivated throughout his empire and the plant became popular in the Middles Ages in all French regions, which explains the number of different names it has. A good winter green, chard is eaten cooked and is delicious with *béchamel* sauce.

Chervil (turnip-rooted)
Le cerfeuil tubéreux
(Chaerophyllum bulbosum)

The turnip-rooted chervil is a very old vegetable which arrived in France from Northern Europe in the 19th century, but is practically unknown today. Its white-flesh conical root has a taste reminiscent of dill and with hints of flowers. Extremely rare on market stalls, it is highly prized by gastronomes and can be eaten raw, mashed or sautéed with a drizzle of oil.

Chicory
La chicorée
(Cichorium intybus)

The beautiful blue flowers of the wild chicory are set atop rigid stems are often seen growing along roadsides. Successive breeding has produced the endive and varieties of delicious, red chicories from Italy.

Cress, Garden Cress
Le cresson alénois
(Lepidium sativum)

An indigenous, very hardy plant that adapts well to any environment, garden cress grows fast and can be planted from seed all year round. It has been harvested from the wild for a very a long time. Its leaves have a sharp taste, contain vitamin C, stimulate the appetite and have digestive properties.

Cucumber
Le concombre
(Cucumis sativus)

The cucumber reached Europe from India, where it has been grown for over 3,000 years. It was also sought after in Egypt and the Middle East for its high water content.
There are numerous varieties: thorny cucumbers from the West Indies; smooth-skin cucumbers from Asia; and orange cucumbers, some with small fruits, and some with round fruits, such as those grown in Russia and eastern Europe, which are resistant to cold and easier to grow.

Evening Primrose
L'oenothère ou onagre
(Oenothera biennis)

Also called 'earth ham' because its edible roots, which are delicious raw in salads, turn pink when cooked, and taste like salsify. The evening primrose arrived in Europe from North America in the 18th century, and first spread extensively in the wild. For the past fifteen years it has been cultivated in particular for the oil extracted from its seeds which is used to fight numerous ailments.

Gherkin
Le cornichon
(Cucumis sativus)

The gherkin is, in fact, merely another member of the cucumber family. A French native, the cream-coloured 'blanc petit de Paris' is a traditional, though now rare, species. Some cucumbers are as big as marrows. They grow in abundance and the only real requirement is that they need to be picked as soon as they are ripe or they will grow as large as cucumbers. They are then eaten in salads, like cucumber.

Good King Henry
Le chénopode bon-henri
(Chenopodium bonus-henricus)

Of Asian origin, this plant has spread far and wide since antiquity. It was a common sight in kitchen gardens until the late 19th century and was eaten like spinach. It is still often found in the wild near homes or in meadows. It is a perennial, so you can collect a few seeds from a specimen in the wild and sow them in the spring in your garden, preferably in moist and well-drained soil, and it will grow back every year. It is eaten like spinach but tastes slightly less acidic, and with hints of hazelnut.

Ice Plant
La ficoïde glaciale
(Mesembryanthemum crystallinum)

The silver leaves of the ice plant, covered with miniscule pockets filled with a salty liquid, make a wonderful impression as a border plant. It resists heat and dryness well and, as a native of the Mediterranean coast, enjoys rich, sandy soil. Its leaves can be eaten raw throughout the summer.

Jerusalem Artichoke
Le topinambour
(Helianthus tuberosus)

The Jerusalem artichoke is once again being seen on French market stalls after decades of neglect. Until recently, it was still suffering, like swedes, from its association with the Second World War, when it was one of the few vegetables available. It is a delicious tuber, with a delicate nutty flavour reminiscent of artichoke hearts. It can be eaten raw or cooked, boiled or steamed, with a knob of butter or a drizzle of oil. It is a hardy perennial that grows in almost any soil and will keep in open ground during winter.

Lamb's Lettuce, Corn Salad
Les mâches
(Valerianella locusta)

Lamb's lettuce was harvested in the wild until the 19th century and valued for its restorative qualities (it contains a high level of vitamin C and beta-carotene). Hardy varieties are frost-resistant and self-seeding; let a few of them go to seed in your garden for the following year and, in the meantime, they will provide greenery in the winter.

Leek
Le poireau
(Allium porrum)

Leek is a member of the liliaceae family, like garlic and onion, tulip and hyacinth. Leek has been grown since Roman times and used to be planted in vineyards as a perennial. It became popular in the Middle Ages as one of the vegetables 'for the pot' (*potée* and *pot-au-feu*) and can also be eaten cold with *vinaigrette*. Leek likes mineral- and nitrogen-rich soils and, with a bit of protection, will grow throughout the winter.

Lettuce
La laitue
(Lactuca sativa)

Lettuce grows in the wild in Europe but without forming a head. It has been improved over the centuries and the varieties found in gardens are annuals that are grown from spring to winter. There are several varieties, which include the classic *batavia* or *romaine* (cos) lettuces. Their milky sap explains the latin name 'milk grass'.

Malabar Spinach
La baselle
(Basella rubra)

Originally from tropical regions of Asia and Africa, Malabar spinach is an easy plant to grow, very decorative, and tastes good. It is worth discovering. The edible leaves are similar to spinach leaves but it is a climber growing to 2 m. Sow in March under cover, plant seedlings out in May and train up poles as you would beans. Given enough water and heat, Malabar spinach is productive all summer.

Marrow, Courgette, Pumpkin, Patipan
Les courge, courgette
(Cucurbita pepo), citrouille, pâtisson, et potiron
(Cucurbita maxima)

Cucurbita (plants in the marrow family) are natives of Latin America. The vast number of varieties available means that there will always be one to suit any type of garden and any type of cooking: edible and decorative, salty or sweet, cooked or raw, orange, white, green, black, blue or striped, smooth or bumpy; the choice is endless!

Melon
Le melon
(Cucumis melo)

The melon comes from eastern Africa, and reached our shores via India. It belongs to the marrow family but is quite difficult to grow because it requires a lot of sun and heat, plenty of water, and a rich but well-drained soil. There are numerous varieties, from the 'peach-melon', the size of a peach which is used to make jams, to the bigger, sweet cantaloupe melons. They grow well on top of compost heaps where bacterial action keeps the humus warm.

Nasturtium (tuberous)
La capucine tubéreuse
(Tropaeolum tuberosum)

The tuberous nasturtium is related to the climbing nasturtium and produces edible tubers in the shape of small, purple-white contorted pears. It should be sown in May in well drained soil, in the sun. The tubers, which can be collected from the end of September, are eaten cooked, with other vegetables and white meat for instance.

New Zealand Spinach
La tétragone cornue ou épinard de Nouvelle-Zélande
(Tetragonia tetragonioides)

This is one of the few vegetables grown in western Europe originating in Australasia. With its deep-green, triangular leaves, New Zealand spinach looks like spinach and nearly replaced it in the 19th century when it became very popular with the middle classes, but it was never really successfully commercialised.

Nutsedge, Yellow Nutsedge
Le souchet comestible
(Cyperus esculentus)

The yellow nutsedge is a member of the papyrus family which grows around the Mediterranean, in Africa and in the Middle and Far East. It has small tubers and prefers moist, sandy soil. It should be planted in June after the tubers have been left in water overnight to trigger new buds. It can be eaten dry, like currants, and has a nutty flavour, or can be cooked in syrup or in cakes.

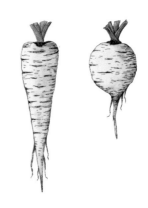

Oca
L'oca du Pérou
(Oxalis crenata Jacq.)

Oca arrived in Europe at the same time as the potato but failed to become as popular. It has small pink or purple wrinkled tubers which should be planted under cover in March in light, rich and moist soil. It requires a warm climate and is not hardy in France. There are pink, yellow and white varieties with dense, low-growing foliage. Leave the tubers to dry out in the sun for a few days so they lose some of their acidity.

Orach
L'arroche, Bonne-Dame
(Atriplex)

The garden orach *(Atriplex hortensis)*, with its triangular leaves, looks very much like spinach. It was a frequent sight in the gardens of the Middle Ages and of the Renaissance and is well-known for its laxative properties. There are three species, which all grow easily and quickly to a height of up to two metres. It is self-seeding.

Parsnip
Le panais
(Pastinaca sativa)

Another root vegetable known in Europe since prehistoric times, parsnip was recommended for its fortifying properties. It is quite hardy and if left to grow it makes an attractive plant rising to 2 m tall. The root is eaten like a potato, and the yellow leaves can also be eaten, either in salads when young, or in soups when older and tougher. It used to be grown widely but is now not as popular in France as it is in Britain. It is still found in the wild under the subspecies *'urens'*, a reference to the skin rash it can provoke.

Pea
Le pois
(Pisum Sativum)

Peas have been grown around the Mediterranean for a long time. The smaller variety, the garden pea, is the most common, but there are several others: shelling peas, mange-touts, pole, dwarf peas. Field peas were once grown in most farms up to 1,000 metres altitude in the Auvergne. They were dried and kept to make soup in the winter.

Pepper and Chilli Pepper
Le poivron et le piment
(Capsicum annuum)

Peppers were brought back from Mexico in the 16th century to be used as a substitute to pepper which was then an expensive, sought-after spice. Peppers spread rapidly around the Mediterranean, and in Africa and Asia. One of the best known chilli peppers grown in France comes from the Basque country, and is the *'piment d'Espelette'*, which is now a protected denomination of origin. Bell, or sweet, peppers are a variety of *capsicum annuum* developed for its fleshy fruit and with little or no capsaicin (the compound responsible for the hotness of chilli peppers).

Physalis, Cape Gooseberry
Le physalis ou coqueret du Pérou
(Physalis sp.)

The Cape gooseberry (*P. peruviana*) has a delicate mango and clementine flavour. This bushy plant grows in a similar fashion to the tomato and will re-seed freely if protected from frost. The small, tomato-shaped berries are wrapped in fine, lace-like skins. They can be eaten as they are or dipped in sugar or chocolate. Other species of physalis commonly known as *amour en cage* or *lanterne japonaise* (alkekengi, or chinese lantern) are not edible.

Potato
La pomme de terre
(Solanum tuberosum)

Native of the Andes, the potato has only been grown in France since the 17th century and has now become the most cultivated vegetable in the world. It is very productive, grows easily and more rapidly than cereal crops, keeps well and is easy to cook. Although only a few common varieties are found in the shops, there are in fact hundreds of varieties. Experiment with different varieties so you can discover which work best in your garden, and which one you would like to see on your plate. There are even black and purple varieties, which are now more easily available. Its leaves are mildly toxic.

Purslane
Le pourpier
(Portulaca oleracea)

A creeping plant with crisp leaves, purslane grows wild in gardens where it self-sows and flourishes with little or no upkeep. It is well known for its richness in fatty acids and omega 3 and makes refreshing salads. It has reappeared recently after a long absence.

187 •

Radish
Les radis
(Raphanus sativus)

A standard feature of rural gardens, radishes grow quickly and can be planted in spring or autumn. The Chinese traditionally use them against intestinal troubles. Black radishes are particularly well know for regulating the gall bladder. They are often confused with horseradish - a plant grown for over 3,000 years and used to prevent scurvy, horseradish looks like a fat, white radish with a very hot flavour, used as mustard and to treat boils, coughs and bronchitis. It is still found widely in eastern Europe.

Rhubarb
La rhubarbe
(Rheum)

A must in any rural garden, and very easy to look after, rhubarb is extremely hardy and grows without any maintenance. Its roots have purgative properties but the green part of its leaves, held by thick, edible stalks, can be toxic. Plant it well away from other plants as its broad, spreading leaves take up a lot of space. Replant by detaching a part of the base with roots and leaves attached.

Rocket
La roquette
(Eruca sativa)

Rocket has an incomparable taste and was even cultivated in Charlemagne's garden. The crushed seeds make a flour similar to mustard. It also has a reputation as an aphrodisiac and is said to prevent scurvy. In winter it should be planted in deep furrows to protect it from the cold. The leaves are eaten in salads, or used as a stuffing. It can be cultivated nearly all year round in cool climates and should be watered frequently to ensure that the leaves do not become too bitter.

Salsify and Scorzonera
Les salsifis
(Tragopogon porrifolius) **et les scorsonères**
(Scorzonera hispanica)

Native to Spain, salsifies and scorzoneras have been cultivated for a very long time. The former have white roots and the latter black roots with a more pronounced taste (unless you peel the skin). Introduced, in the 17th century they were reputed to cheer people up and chase away sadness. A vegetable for special occasion, it is served as an accompaniment to chicken in cream sauce in Normandy. In the Perche region young salsify leaves were eaten in salads, and the flower buds like asparagus. Both form new buds after each picking.

Skirret
Le chervis
(Sium sisarum)

Skirret is a hardy plant in the umbelliferous family, related to the carrot, chervil and celeriac. A perennial with clumps of grey-ish roots, it was once greatly appreciated by the kings of the 16th century for its delicate flavour similar to salsify, but sadly has completely disappeared from market stalls today.

Sorrel
L'oseille
(Rumex)

Sorrel is a hardy perennial which prefers rich, cool soil and tolerates shade. It used to be very common in old gardens and the leaves would be picked through the winter. Propagate by division in spring or autumn. It is one of the earliest greens available.

Spinach
L'épinard
(Spinacia oleracea)

Spinach came from Persia and spread with the Arab conquests to India and China. It arrived in France from Spain and became widespread in the 16th century. It was one of those 'plants for the pot' ('*plantes à pot*'), like Good King Henry, orach and New Zealand spinach, which would be cooked to a mush. Unlike them, spinach requires rich soil and plenty of water.

**Sunflower Root,
Pale-leaved Sunflower**
Hélianthi
(Helianthus strumosus)

This member of the *helianthus* family originating in North America is similar to Jerusalem artichoke, both in taste and in appearance, although a little smaller and with a smoother skin. It has only been grown in France for a hundred years. It is a hardy annual. The rhizomes should be planted in March, 50 cm apart in rich cool soil but in the sun. They can be lifted for consumption from the end of October and through the winter providing the soil is covered in a straw mulch for protection. The plant can grow to 2 m.

Tomato
La tomate
(Solanum lycopersicum)

There are hundreds of varieties of tomatoes, all of different colour, size and shape, from the small cherry tomatoes to the chunky 'beef-heart'. They are rich in vitamin A, C and beta-caroten, particularly the tasty, lesser known orange tomatoes. Some develop very little and reach a manageable maximum height, while others have no finite growth and must be staked, cut back and pinched. Tomatoes like rich soil,   so when re-planting the seedlings, mulch with a compost or nettle leaves.

Turnip and Swede
Navets (Brassica rapa)
et rutabaga
(Brassica napo-brassica)

Turnips and swedes are native European vegetables from the cabbage family, grown for their roots rather than their leaves, and have been a staple of rural households or centuries. There are many varieties, usually specific to a region, such as the 'noir de Pailhardan' with has a very distinctive taste. The yellow 'boule d'or', or 'navet jaune' which is extremely rich in minerals and is known as 'swede' in English. In France, swede was traditionally used in *pot-au-feu*, but it is not as readily available as in Britain these days. Turnips prefer cool, wet climates.

Fruit Trees & Shrubs

Whether trained against a south-facing wall or planted in an open orchard, fruit trees and shrubs were an integral part of the rural garden.

Apple
Le pommier
(Malus)

Apple trees were cultivated and grafted as far back as 2,000 ago. They were grown in Greece in 600 BC but it was only in the 18th century that serious breeding started. Apples are grown throughout France, and all regions have their own local varieties; there are now over 6,000 apple varieties for eating. Apples are used in all sorts of dishes: raw, dried, in *compote*, in cakes and tarts, to make vinegar, with meat, in French black pudding, etc. And they keep well: stored in a cool attic, or sliced thinly and then dried in the oven.

Apricot
L'abricotier
(Prunus armeniaca)

Originally from the temperate regions of China, the apricot was first introduced to Europe by the Romans, who imported it from Armenia (thus its Latin name). It arrived in France in the 10th century when the Moors invaded southern France, but it was only in the 15th century that it reached the Loire valley. There are many varieties, some sturdier than others. Most are disease resistant but some do not cope well with the cold, and spring frost, in particular, can have disastrous effects on the early flowering varieties. Make sure you choose a variety that is right for your region.

Cherry
Le cerisier
(Cerasus = Prunus)

Sweet cherry originates in the region between the Black Sea and the Caspian Sea. Birds and the Roman armies transported it to Europe and Asia. The cherry tree is very robust and adapts to almost any conditions. It is one of the first fruit trees of the summer and there are now many grafted varieties.

See also Trees and Shrubs, p.201.

Blackcurrant
Le cassissier
(Ribes nigrum)

Blackcurrant is particularly rich in vitamin C. Like most fruit shrubs, it grows well in cooler regions and it is not particularly demanding. Some varieties are self-fertile. Older branches should be cut off in September to stimulate fruit growth. Some of these branches can then be planted approximately 30 cm into the ground to propagate a new bush using hard cuttings. Alternatively, blackcurrant can be propagated by layering (*marcottage*).

Fig
Le figuier
(Ficus carica)

The fig tree is believed to have originated in Turkey or Syria and there are reference to figs in all civilisations around the Mediterranean sea. In France, it mostly grows randomly in the garden rather than in orchards. The fig tree is not particularly demanding and will grow in most types of soil, although it prefers rich, sandy or chalky soils. It is well adapted to dry weather and thrives in the sun. It can be found in northern France but is unlikely to produce fruit.

Medlar
Le néflier
(Mespilus germanica)

A native of Armenia and the Caucasus, the medlar was later introduced to the forests of Gaul and Germany (thus its Latin name) and grows in the whole of the northern hemisphere. The fruit is eaten late in the autumn, not before the day of Sainte Marguerite (16 November), according to a saying in the Limousin. It is slightly tart and sweet at the same time, just a little bit astringent, and very rich in minerals. It used to be grafted on hawthorns.

Mulberry
Le mûrier
(Morus)

The mulberry is found almost exclusively in the south. A tree with an elegant bearing and bulky trunk, it is often pruned in the shape of a parasol. The white mulberry was once cultivated in the silkworm nurseries of the Cévennes and Haute-Provence, as silkworms eat its leaves. The large, black, juicy fruit of the black mulberry often get squashed on the ground in summertime, causing formidable stains. Their taste is similar to that of blackberries, although less acidic. Mulberry syrup is a treat.

Peach
Le pêcher
(Prunus persica)

A native of China, the peach tree quickly reached Persia and the Caspian Sea before being introduced to Gaul by the Romans. By the 6th century it was grown in most French regions and the varieties producing larger fruit arrived from Italy in the 16th century. Early varieties are picked in May in the south of France, and late varieties in August-September. Peach trees can be grown in orchards or singly, trained as a straight stem, or in fan or candelabra shape. Treat with Bordeaux mixture (*bouillie bordelaise*) at the first signs of peach leaf curl, to which it is very sensitive.

Pear
Le poirier
(Pyrus communis)

The common pear tree has been grown for over 4,000 years. It originates in the Middle East and is doubtless the result of cross-breeding. Pear trees can live a few hundred years and used to be grown with cherry and apple trees along fields and near houses. In the Middle Ages, the varieties grown in France were so bitter that they required cooking. In the Auvergne, pears were left to dry overnight in the oven where bread had been baked and were treated as a delicacy. Most varieties today are 19th century. There are very few winter varieties left, the 'Passe Crassane' being the most well known.

Plum
Le prunier
(Prunus)

The origins of the plum tree are unclear. It is possibly a descendant of the blackthorn, commonly found in hedges, but it is also likely that varieties from Greece and Asia Minor had a role in the development of modern varieties. It can grow in almost any soil and its only real enemy is the wind. There are many varieties: mirabelle plums and quetsche plums in the north-east, greengage in the sout-west, and several local varieties in most regions. Depending on the variety, some plums will keep well as dried fruit (prunes) or better as jams. The traditional advice to prune plum trees severely is now being questioned.

Quince
Le cognassier
(Cydonia oblonga)

Quince is one of the oldest trees grown in European gardens. Pliny and Plutarch claimed its fruit warded off malign influences. During the Middle Ages, it held a central place in monastery gardens.The fruit is turned into jelly and paste, and quince water was said to be effective against diarrhoea in children. It is also delicious cooked and served with a meat dish. Quince wine is used in gargles for mouth and gum infections. Quince is very robust and its May flowering means that it is unlikely to be affected by spring frost but quinces fruit need a lot a sun to ripen in late autumn.

Raspberry
Le framboisier
(Rubus idaeus)

The raspberry is related to the bramble and produces fruit even in semi-shade. It likes well-drained, rich soil. Add manure to the hole before planting. Double-croppers, which fruit in springtime on the previous year's branches and in autumn from the current year's buds, should be cut back hard in January and thinned out in July to stimulate the second crop. Single harvest bushes which fruit only in spring, are best pruned after fruiting. The canes produce fruit in the second year and should be replaced every ten years or so.

Red Currant
Le groseillier
(Ribes rubrum)

Like the raspberry and the blackcurrant, the red currant bush does best in cool climates and does not mind shade. The fruit does not keep long after being picked. It is grown as a single bush or in rows. New growth should be pruned back by half or one third in winter and re-trimmed in summer, keeping a bush of approximately 15 cm tall. Red currants are rarely affected by diseases or aphids.

Walnut

Le noyer

(Juglans regia)

The walnut tree comes from central Asia and the Himalayas, from where it gradually moved west, through Uzbekistan, Iran and Turkey to western Europe. It has been present in France since the prehistory and is still found in most French regions
but particularly in the Dauphiné and the Périgord. It is very sensitive to spring frost and likes deep soil.

Pond Plants

Marshes, rivers and ponds are a particularly rich environment for flora. Some species will live around the edges and others will float, rootless, in the water. All will contribute to the eco-system either by providing oxygen to a pond or habitat for wildlife.

Broad-leaved Pondweed

Le potamot

(Potamogetum natans)

A floating plant with smooth, thick, oblong leaves, red stalks and spikes of purple flowers. It will grow in stagnant or slow moving waters at altitudes up to 2,000 m. Broad-leaved pondweed is slow to grow from seed but easily propagates from cuttings. It is a favourite of frogs and pond insects.

Bulrush, Great Reedmace

La massette

(Typha latifolia)

A common pond plant that can grow to 2.5 m, with tight, tufty, brown flowers forming striking cigar-shaped clumps. Like most reeds, it grows around the edges of the pond or in shallow waters and is a great habitat for marsh birds and insects. Used as a biological decontaminating agent in *lagunage*, it spreads quite rapidly and withstands cold weather.

Bur-reed

Le rubanier dressé
(Sparganium erectum)

A striking marginal pond plant growing to 1.5 m, with thick long leaves and globe-shaped flowers at the top of tall stems, which turn from green to white and light-brown between June and August. Much loved by marsh birds both for nesting and for its seeds.

Canadian Pondweed

L'élodée du Canada
(Elodea Canadensis)

Imported from Canada, this aquatic plant initially thrived in French ponds but is becoming rarer. It is a good oxygenator but once in place it spreads quickly.

Duckweed

Les lentilles d'eau
(Lemna)

Duckweed grows on the surface of stagnant or slow-moving waters. It reproduces by division and will very quickly spread across a whole pond if not kept under control, ducks being one possible method, as the English name suggests. Duckweed is also a good soil fertiliser, either straight from the pond or as part of the compost.

Flowering Rush

Le jonc fleuri
(Butomus umbellatus)

Despite its name (in both English and French) this tall attractive plant is not a member of the rush family. It is best planted at the edge of the pond or in shallow water. Tall stems (up to 1m) carry clusters of small pink, almond-scented flowers between June and August.

Hornwort
La cornifle (cératophylle)
(Ceratophyllum demersum and submersum)

A common perennial pond plant that can grow up to 3 m long, it provides an ideal habitat for pond insects and amphibians. It is also a very good oxygenating plant and propagates easily: simply take a cutting from a plant and throw it into your pond. The plant floats to the surface in summer and tends to sink towards the bottom of the pond in the winter.

Marsh Marigold
Le populage, souci d'eau
(Caltha palustris)

Another plant related to the buttercup family, with large heart-shaped golden flowers, the marsh marigold is one of the first pond plants to flower in the spring. It grows at altitudes up to 2,500 m and thrives in northern or colder parts of France. It prefers marshy grounds at the edge of the pond rather than deep water.

Purple Loosestrife
La salicaire
(Lythrum salicaria)

Another marginal plant at home in wetlands and ditches, the purple loosestrife grows to 1 m tall and has spikes of bright pink or purple flowers from June to September. The French name comes from the shape of the leaves, similar to those of the willow (*salix*). It has astringent properties and helps heal wounds.

Reed
Le roseau
(Phragmites communis)

A classic pond plant, the reed is another marginal plant – that is, typically found at the edges of the water. It grows to 3 m and produces purple-brown flowering plumes in the summer. The common reed is a fast grower and can be invasive, but it provides a perfect habitat for marsh birds and insects.

Rush
Le jonc commun
(Juncus)

The rush family numbers over 200 species, which range in height from 30 cm for the common rush, to 1.5 m for the taller varieties such as the *jonc des chaisiers*. Rush grows in wet ground or shallow water. The leaves wrap around the stem, with a small cluster of brown flowers towards the top of the stalk in July-August.

Sedge
La laîche, or carex
(Carex)

There are many members of the carex family of various heights, from dwarf varieties to specimens growing to 1.3 m. A thin grass-like plant, it tends to grow in clumps on wet ground near ponds and in marshes, and can be found at altitudes up to 1,500 m. Small spikes of white to purple flowers bloom between March and June.

Water Crowfoot
La renoncule aquatique
(Ranunculus aquatilis)

A member of the large buttercup family, the water-crowfoot floats on the surface. It oxygenates the pond and provides habitat for many pond creatures. It produces pert white flowers with five broad petals around a yellow centre between April and September.

Water Mint
La menthe aquatique
(Mentha aquatica)

Another classic of European wetlands, water mint grows in any wet soil, marshes, ditches, river banks and pond edges, at altitudes of up to 1,400 m. Spikes of small pale-pink flowers bloom in the summer. Its hairy brownish leaves have a strong flavour and, like garden mint, they are edible.

Trees & Shrubs

Tall trees should not be pruned, although they can be cut back, and they should be planted alone, in rows, groves, or possibly within a hedgerow. Other trees will react well to pruning and create the traditional French *cépée* (copse), clumps of shoots growing from a tree stump to create a hedge with a thick base.

Alder (Black, or Common)
L'aulne glutineux, commun ou noir, verne
(Alnus glutinosa)

This stately, fast-growing tree reaches heights of 25 to 30 m and is present throughout France along wate redges, where its roots stabilise the banks. The alder is endowed with many virtues, which made it indispensable to our forebears: its bark treats fevers and, in herbal teas, malaria. In concentrated form, its leaves were credited with curing ulcers, rheumatism and gout. It was also used as a black dye and for tanning leather. Its light, tender wood, similiar to precious wood, was used to make locks for canals, stakes, mill wheels and every utensil linked to water, as it does not rot easily.

Ash
Le frêne
(Fraxinus excelsior)

A large, hardy tree, which grows fast in cool soil and includes numerous species. It is often found on mountain plains and in valleys, where it was frequently planted as a wind-break hedge. Its pliable wood is used for staircases, tool handles, furniture and dishes, as well as in wood-burning stoves. Its leaves were used in herbal teas to make a refreshing and diuretic drink, due to their tonic and laxative properties. They were sometimes added to coffee and also used to make a fermented drink, the *frênette*. Ash bark, harvested in the spring, was considered an effective remedy for fever (antipyretic).

Aspen
Le tremble
(Populus tremula)

This Scandinavian native stands up particularly well to industrial pollution and grows in cities where a lot of other lobe-leafed trees would die. It grows quickly and produces frequent suckers. Be careful to keep it under control! Its white wood is used to make matches and paper pulp.

Bay
Le laurier
(Laurus nobilis)

Often found in kitchen gardens or along house facades, bay is commonly used in cooking. It can grow up to 10 m high, with evergreen foliage. It is indigenous to the woods of the Mediterranean and Corsica. Its leaves are used in herbal teas to encourage sweating (sudorific). Fat extracted from its berries, or bay butter, is used in veterinary medicine.

Beech
Le hêtre
(Fagus sylvatica)

This magnificent tree is found throughout France, often in forests, at altitudes of up to 1,700 m. It prefers loose, permeable, deep soil but does not mind chalky soil. A beech tree can live for several centuries, reach 40 m in height and grow to 6 m in circumference. Its wood is used to make furniture and paper and it makes particularly good fuel. The beechnut is appreciated by pigs and can be pressed to make a very delicate oil. Dried, beech leaves are very tough and were once used for making mattresses. The leaves from young shoots can be eaten in salads. Beech resin is used to treat respiratory troubles.

Berberis, Barberry
Epine-vinette, vinettier
(Berberis vulgaris)

Berberis grows up to 2 m, is melliferous and at home in clayish-chalky soil at altitudes of up to 1,900 m in the Alps. It has small, yellow flowers which attract bees, graceful foliage and red fruit. It has been cultivated in the Auvergne for a long time as hedging, as it is thorny and easily trimmed. Its roots and bark were once used in yellow dyes, as well as for their medicinal properties, such as a liver tonic. Jams, sweets and syrup were also made with its fruits. Berberis was systematically destroyed in the last century because it carried rust disease, which it transmitted to cereal crops. It is now quite rare in the wild.

Birch (White and Silver)
Le bouleau blanc ou pubescent
(Betula pubescens),
le bouleau verruqueux
(B. pendula, B. verrucosa):

Widespread throughout the northern hemisphere, the white birch grows in poor, moist, sunny soil. The silver birch does well in any soil, wet or dry, and is used to colonise difficult grounds like slag heaps (but generally not found in the south of France). It can be recognised by its drooping branches with greyish warts. Its leaves act as a diuretic and its abundant, sugary sap is used in fermented birch beer, as well as prescribed as a diuretic and against skin diseases. Birch twigs can be used to make brooms.

Blackberry, Bramble,
La ronce
(Rubus fructicosus)

There are numerous species of bramble. Generally, the bramble is a shrub with long, woody stems and sharp thorns. The young, bitter, astringent leaves were once dried and used in gargles for mouth ailments and sore throats. It flowers throughout the summer and the woodland variety produces delicious blackberries in August-September provided it is given enough light.

Blackthorn (Sloe)
Le prunellier, épine noire
(Prunus spinosa)

The black branches of this thorny, dense, melliferous bush produce white flowers which resemble those of the hawthorn. It grows to 5 m tall and is found throughout France and Corsica. Often used in hedging, it can grow at relatively high altitudes. The acidic fruit, sloes, are only edible after the first frosts and are used to make *eau-de-vie*. It is an astringent, sometimes prescribed for asthma. It is claimed that its bark reduces fevers and its leaves have diuretic properties.

Box
Le buis
(Buxus sempervirens)

Box grows in the wild and it was often used as hedging in rural gardens, because of its dense, evergreen foliage, although it was only rarely used as a formal, trimmed hedge or border. It was also planted singly at the entrance to houses or in kitchen gardens, sometimes clipped close into a ball, for blessing on Palm Sundays. People often hung a cross made of box branches at the head of their beds for good luck. Its extremely hard wood is used to make numerous objects: games, beads, flutes, etc. A native of the Mediterranean, it grows slowly, lives a long time, adapts to any, well-drained soil, and tolerates cold.

Broom
Genêt à balais
(Cytisus scoparius)

Broom thrives in chalky, siliceous terrain, from which it extracts nitrogen. Forming dense bushes with its stiff branches, dried broom makes good kindling. Its clumps of golden-yellow flowers, bear a wonderful almond perfume and are toxic, although they are used in small quantities in herbal tea recipes and in drugs for heart disease. One species is used in yellow dyes. The leaves of the rush-leaved broom, found in regions along the Mediterranean, are particularly toxic to humans.

Cherry and Wild Cherry

Le cerisier *(Cerasus = Prunus)* et le merisier, cerisier des oiseaux, cerisier des bois *(Prunus avium)*

Used in hedges around houses, the cherry tree is reasonably robust and grows at altitudes of up to 1,000 m in sunny spots protected from the wind. Like the wild cherry tree, its wood is used in sculpture, musical instruments and furniture. It does well in any soil providing it is not too wet or impermeable. It benefits from light pruning, just enough to remove dead wood. it is best to prune 'green' ('*en vert*'), that is, just after harvesting, before the tree is dormant.

The wild cherry tree is a handsome melliferous tree common everywhere in France except in the south, at altitudes of up to 1,300 m. Edible, though bitter, wild cherries are diuretic and used to make kirsch. The exceptional quality of the tree's wood makes it a favourite among cabinet- makers, turners, sculptors, game-makers, instrument makers and coopers. It grows fast, up to 30 m in height, and produces vigourous suckers, but has a short life span. It needs light, deep and cool soil. Wild cherry is becoming rare and is rarely re-planted. Many were lost when hedges were destroyed, or suffocated by other trees as a result of under-maintenance.

Chestnut

Le châtaignier
(Castanea sativa)

Found in nearly all parts of Europe, the sweet chestnut grows fast and is easily pruned, preferring healthy, acidic soils. It is used for beams, planks, furniture, fences, shingles, casks, in short, for almost everything, as it has two precious properties: it is rot-resistant and easy to split. Chestnuts can be eaten roasted or boiled and chestnut flour was used to make bread. The chestnut tree works well in hedging or in forests, as in the Cévennes and Corsica. The bark contains tannin, which serves as a black dye. Large areas of chestnut forests died from the 'ink disease' (*phytophtora fungus*), although the tree can live to over 1,000 years.

Cornelian Cherry

Le cornouiller mâle
(Cornus mas)

The cornelian cherry grows particularly well in chalky ground and can live for more than 300 years. Its early blooms bring bright yellow flowers followed by berries, cornelian cherries, which are delicious when they turn a deep red towards the end of August. When turning orange, jam or *eau-de-vie* can be made with them. Its hard wood is used in tool handles and in wood turning, and it provides a reliable fuel for burning. It propagates easily by transplanting its root suckers.

Dog or Wild Rose
Eglantier, rosier des chiens, rosier des champs
(Rosa canina)

This is the wild rose, indigenous to the French countryside where it grows freely. Its thin, thorny branches carry light, pale-pink or white flowers. Due to its vigour and hardiness, wild rose is often used as rootstock for many domestic roses. It is found both in acid and in chalky soils. Its fruit, rosehips, also called *gratte-cul* because of their scratchy seeds, are decorative in winter with their small, red globes rich in vitamin C. Rosehip jam is made from fruit harvested after the first frosts have softened them.

Dogwood
Le cornouiller sanguin *(Cornus sanguinea)*

Dogwood is common throughout France, even in Corsica. Its branches are used in basket-weaving and as stakes. It produces clumps of flowers (which are poisonous), black berries, and in winter, young, purplish-blue branches that are particularly decorative. It grows rapidly, up to 5 m tall, and lives around 30 years.

Elder and Red Elder
Le sureau noir *(Sambucus nigra)*
Sureau rouge ou à grappes *(Sambucus racemosa)*

More widespread than the red elder and with fruit which develops later in the season, the elder flourishes in fertile soil rich in nitrogen, and grows at altitudes of up to 1,200 m. Its fruit is delicious cooked, in jam or syrup. The elder has many medicinal properties, hence its nickname *'arbre aux fées'* (Fairy tree). Its flowers have for a long time been used in herbal teas to cure flu and heal conjunctivitis. Their sweet scent is used to flavour desserts. The flower heads are also eaten in fritters, used in vinegar or to make excellent aperitifs. Living up to 100 years, it should not to be confused with the dwarf elder, an unrelated toxic herbaceous plant that grows in ditches. The red elder grows no taller than 3 to 4 m high and is found mostly in the mountains. Its bright red berries, which attract birds, appear towards the end of August and are only edible cooked in compote, jam or syrup. The red elderberry is a diuretic and a tonic, rich in vitamin C and pectin. Depending on dose, the berries, leaves and bark, and even its roots, can also have a laxative, sudorific or even an analgesic effect.

Elm
L'orme
(*Ulmus minor*)

The exceptionally solid wood of elm trees was once used to make the cartshafts, wheel hubs, furniture, staircases and barn floors. In the Middle Ages, elms shaded the village squares, where judges would conduct hearings. Elms have been used since Francois I to line streets and avenues. Elm can be pruned into a dense hedge or pollarded. Trees live for 300 to 400 years. Currently threatened by Dutch elm disease (*la graphiose*), it is rapidly disappearing. It is now possible to find disease resistant hybrid imports. For seeds from old, resistant elms, contact Ponema (see Address Book p.217).

Fir
Le sapin
(*Abies*)

Fir offers good, light, solid wood for carpentry. The shoots of its young branches are said to be edible. It is the king of mountain forests, living up to 800 years. It is probably not a good idea to plant it, except in forest land or mountainous regions, as it grows fast and can become invasive, obstruct views or conceal a house. Nothing grows under its branches and, unless the lower branches are cut off, you will not be able to stand up under it.

Gorse
L'ajonc d'Europe
(*Ulex europaeus*)

The gorse is a shrub which grows 1 to 4 m tall with small, dense, spiny evergreen leaves and bright, nectar-filled yellow flowers loved by bees. It is found on moors and meadows, and in acid soil, as it has the particular ability of being able to fix nitrogen, which allows it to flourish in poor conditions. It can be shaped for hedging but be careful, however, as i ts seeds are poisonous.

Hawthorn
L'aubépine, épine blanche, épine de mai
(*Crataegus monogyna*)

The scented hawthorn grows all over France at altitudes as high as 1,600 m. Once widespread in hedging, it is vigorous, robust, requires little maintenance and tolerates heavy pruning. A thorny bush with small, incised leaves, it displays attractive white flowers in May and was linked to the Virgin Mary. It was also thought to bring good luck and keep lightning away from animal herds. It was planted in public squares to bring prosperity to villages. Its planting is strictly regulated in France, as it carries fire blight, a fungal disease that kills related species, including trees.

Hazel
Le noisetier
(Corylus avellana)

Hazel is common in thickets and hedges, because it grows quickly with a dense habit. It is found in nearly all parts of France, up to an altitude of 1,600 m. Hazelnuts are a treat and also make an exquisite oil. The bark of the hazel tree is a known astringent and good for fevers (antipyretic). The leaves, which have mild laxative properties, can be used in herbal teas. It also provides wood for poles, tool handles and wicker for basketry. The wood from its roots, beautifully veined, is used in marquetry. Divining rods are made of hazelwood.

Holly
Le houx
(Ilex aquifolium)

Holly can be found growing as a bush in hedging or free-standing as a large shrub. It prefers cool, shaded spots and can live up to 300 years. Its dense habit forms impenetrable hedging. Its branches were once used for tool handles and people used to make birdlime with its phloem (vegetable tissue) to catch small birds. Its red berries are poisonous; however, holly leaves have been used to cure rheumatism, and it was also claimed that they reduced fever.

Hornbeam
Le charme
(Carpinus betulus)

Hornbeam grows quickly in soils with little acidity. In winter its foliage is reddish-brown, as it does not shed its dead leaves (like the beech tree or certain oaks). It is easily pruned to form a hedge. An excellent wood for burning, it is also renowned for its toughness and strength. It was once used to make harnessing yokes.

Horse Chestnut
Le marronnier
(Aesculus hippocastanum)

The horse chestnut has been present in France since the Middle Ages. It probably originated in the Balkans but 'emigrated' towards the end of the 19th century, especially to cities. Its fruit, toxic if not cooked, was used to strengthen the veins while its astringent bark is said to be effective against haemorrhoids, varicose veins, obesity and diarrhoea. However, it is mostly used for decorative purposes, as its wood burns poorly and heats sparingly. As a tree, it provides dense shade and can grow to a height of up to 30 m over two or three centuries, with a canopy of up to 15 m.

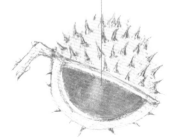

Juniper
Le genévrier
(Juniperus communis)

This small conifer is found throughout France on sunny, dry, rocky hillsides, at the edge of forests and in clearings. Its berries take two years to ripen, turning from green to black, and are used to flavour *sauerkraut* or gin after fermentation and maceration. Its wood adds a distinctive taste to smoked hams and prolongs their preservation. Juniper cinders were once used for washing clothes. In the Middle Ages, people credited the juniper with miraculous cures: essence of juniper was said to be blessed by the Virgin, giving it power against malevolent forces.

Lilac
Le lilas
(Syringa vulgaris)

Lilac is a native from central Europe and was introduced to western Europe in the Middle Ages as an ornamental variety, probably first in gardens owned by the clergy. It is particularly easy to grow and does well in any location. If you prune, do so after it has flowered by cutting only the wilted heads; lilac flowers on the previous year's growth so pruning any more would reduce the number of flowers. You might also choose to cut any dead branches in winter, which will help stimulate growth in the spring.

Lime Tree
Le tilleul *(Tilia platyphyllos [Large-leaved] or cordata [small-leaved])*

The graceful shape of the lime tree makes it a frequent choice for planting in lines along avenues or in the middle of a courtyard. Although considered poor wood, the lime is very tough and light. It is used to make bushels, musical instruments and ortho-paedic limbs. Its bark was used to make coarse fabric, paper, and ropes. Sometimes nicknamed 'Sully', after the French minister who ordered the planting of so many of them in village squares, it is the symbol of conjugal love. Its flowers make a calming infusion and the sap of the small-leaved lime helps clean the liver of bile.

Locust Tree,
or False Acacia
Le robinier faux acacia ou commun
(Robinia pseudoacacia)

The locust tree stabilises hillsides, prevents landslides, and often grows in ruins. It once served to make posts, as its wood keeps well in the open. Its beautiful white flowers can be eaten raw or cooked and are delicious in fritters, although its wood and seeds are toxic. The locust tree was introduced to France at the beginning of the 17th century. It lives up to 300 years.

Maple (Field Maple)
L'érable champêtre
(Acer campestre)

A melliferous nectar-producing tree that prefers cool soil. Its young leaves can be eaten in salad. Children enjoy spinning its fruits, samara, like helicopters. Its wood is dense and hard, excellent for fuel and used for tool handles and in cabinetmaking. It lives to between 120 and 150 years, reaches between 15 to 20 m in height and grows almost everywhere in France, except in acid soil and in the Mediterranean Basin. The sap of a related species, the Canadian maple, gives a delicious syrup.

Oak (Sessile Oak and Common or Pedunculate Oak)
Le chêne rouvre ou sessile *(Quercus petrae)*
et le chêne commun ou pédonculé *(Quercus robur)*

Common everywhere in France except the south, the sessile oak is well-adapted to the French climate. A slow grower, it prefers loose, siliceous and chalky soil and will live over 2,000 years. The acorn is a symbol of fecundity, and acorns have served as food for several thousand years. They were cooked for a long time to eliminate the tannins and then mashed, or they were crushed and turned into flour to make bread. During the war, toasted acorns were used as a coffee substitute. The acorn of the sessile oak grows directly on the stem, without stalk. The common oak, sometimes called 'pedunculate' because its acorns grow at the end of short stalks (peduncles). It prefers clayish, chalky and moist ground. Young trees can be coppiced or pollarded to make hedges. The tree itself is the symbol of strength and its wood is water-resistant. It has been used since Roman times, among others things to make watermill wheels, foundation posts for bridges, casks, and in shipbuilding, The association of oak and beech is common in French forests.

Pine (Scots Pine)
Le pin sylvestre
(Pinus sylvestris)

At the start of the 19th century the Scots pine decorated the grounds of chateaux, before large-scale plantations began to make use of it. The seeds contained in the cones, pine kernels, are edible, especially those of the parasol pine. Essence of turpentine can be extracted from its resin. Its wood is used in cabinetmaking, woodworking and paper milling.

Poplar (White or Black)
Le peuplier blanc ou noir
(Populus alba or nigra)

This fast-growing tree does best in cool, moist, deep soil, which explains why it grows on river-banks, canal banks and in the depths of damp valleys. Its light wood is used to make matches, trays and paper pulp. Its buds are sudorific, diuretic, antiseptic and tonic. The charcoal obtained from the poplar can be used as a deodoriser, an antiseptic and an absorbant.

Rowan or Mountain Ash
Le sorbier des oiseleurs, des oiseaux
(Sorbus aucuparia)

This is a very decorative tree with small white flowers. The clumps of red berries are much enjoyed by birds. They are rich in vitamin C and can be made into jelly. They also encourage menstruation. Weaving tools were once made from its fine, hard wood. Unlike the super-natural powers attributed to the holly, yew and oak, the rowan was thought to protect against magic. It does best on dry, non-chalky plateaux, as well as on ridges and hills in the north and east.

Sea Buckthorn
L'argousier, faux nerprun, saule épineux, griset
(Hippophae rhamnoides)

The sea buckthorn is indigenous to the coastal regions of the Channel (in the dunes), on the banks of the Rhine in the Alsace and beside mountain streams. Like the gorse, it is thorny and can grow in poor soil. It is very tough so is often used to rejuvenate damaged soils. Its berries, eaten in a fortifying syrup, are rich in vitamins (particularly vitamin C) and minerals.

Service Tree
Le cormier ou sorbier domestique
(Sorbus domestica)

The shape and fruite of the service tree are similar to the pear tree. It can reach 20 m in height and live 500 to 600 years. It is a low grower which prefers chalky ground at lower altitudes. Once highly valued, its pear-shaped fruits are edible when overripe. A drink can also be made from them, a reddish sorb wine or '*cormé*', which tastes like cider.

Spindle Tree
Fusain d'Europe,
bonnet carré
(*Evonymus europaeus*)

The spindle often gets
noticed because of its
strange, pink-coloured
fruit shaped liked bishops'
mitres, which reveal
orangey seeds inside.
Be careful, however,
because the seeds are
poisonous. The spindle
tree is found in most wild
hedges in France. Its
wood is especially
appreciated in marquetry
and as charcoal for drawing.
It grows quickly and does
best in cool, well-drained
soils rich in nitrogen.

Whitebeam
Le sorbier alisier blanc
(*Sorbus aria*)

The small, red berries of
the whitebeam used to be
cooked and eaten in the
Middle Ages. They are
reputed to have antidiabet-
ic properties. The tree is
also said to have magical
properties: in Germanic
countries, it was the tree
of Thor, god of thunder,
of blacksmiths and ore
diggers. It was used as a
talisman against lightning.
It was also claimed that a
spell cast on horses could
only be broken with a
whitebeam whip. Powder
from its leaves helps to
heal cuts. It can live for
over 100 years.

Willow (White and Velvet, Osier or Basket) and Goat Willow
Le saule blanc (*Salix alba*), le saule osier ou des
vannier (*Salix viminalis*) et le saule marsault (*Salix caprea*)

There are many different
species of willow, growing
in wetlands and on river-
banks throughout France.
Ranging from 15 to 25 m
tall, the white willow has
a delicate, grey-green
foliage. Like the smaller
basket willow (3-10 m),
it is often pollarded to
produce very decorative
yellow or orange shoots
used for basket-making
and to make ties for the
garden or posts for
woven fences. Charcoal
from willow wood is used
for pencils, and the bark
is said to have tonic,
antipyretic and antispas-
modic properties.
Goat willow can reach 10
m in height and displays
pointed, oval-shaped
leaves. It grows in wet

ground and is often found
in old villages near water
troughs, ponds or brooks
because it is fond of
nitrates. It can easily be
pruned to form hedging.
Its tender bark and young
shoots can be boiled and
eaten, or used in herbal
teas or as poultice to treat
body aches. It seldom
lives longer than 50 years.

Yew
L'if
(Taxus baccata)

The yew is regarded as a sacred tree and is often found in the old cemeteries of Normandy, Brittany and the south. This evergreen tree can live hundreds of years and is a symbol of eternity which has been venerated since the time of the Celts. Its trunk turns hollow as it expands and reaches magisterial proportions. The yew is toxic and this has given rise to many different superstitions: it was claimed that sleeping under a yew or in a bed made of yew wood could be deadly. In fact, the yew is used in the treatment of cancer and only its leaves and berries are extremely poisonous. Its wood is highly sought after for cabinetmaking.

Plants

English - French

A

Aaron's beard – see 'verbascum'
acacia [acacia]: acacia
alder [alnus]: aulne
amaranth [amaranthus gangeticus]: amarante à feuilles
anemone [anemone]: anémone; meadow anemone, or pasque flower [a. pulsatilla vulgaris]: anémone pulsatille, anémone des prés, coquerelle
angelica [angelica]: angélique
apple [malus pumila]: pommier (fruit: pomme)
apricot [prunus armeniaca]: abricotier (fruit: abricot)
artichoke, globe artichoke [cynara scolymus]: artichaut
ash [fraxinus excelsior]: frêne; mountain ash – see 'rowan'
asparagus [asparagus sp.]: asperge
aspen [populus tremula]: tremble
aster [aster sp.]: aster
aubergine, or eggplant (US) [solanum melongena]: aubergine
aubrietia [aubrieta]: aubriète
autumn crocus, or meadow saffron [colchicum]: colchique

B

basil [ocinum basilicum]: basilic
bay [laurus nobilis]: laurier, laurier sauce, laurier noble, laurier d'Apollon
bean [phaseolus vulgaris]: haricot; runner bean [p. coccinus]: haricot d'Espagne
beech [fagus sylvatica]: hêtre
beet [beta vulgaris esculenta]: betterave; decorative beet [beta vulgaris]: betterave décorative, poirée
bellflower [campanula]: campanule
berberis, or barberry [berberis vulgaris]: berbéris
bignonia, or trumpet vine [campsis]: bignone, jasmin de Virginie
bindweed [convolvulus]: liseron; field bindweed [c. arvensis]: liseron des champs; great bindweed
birch [betula]: bouleau; white birch [b. verrucosa]: bouleau verruqueux; silver birch [b. pendula]: bouleau blanc; downy birch [b. pubescens]: bouleau pubescent
blackberry, or bramble [rubus fructicosus]: ronce (fruit: mûre); dewberry [r. caesius]: ronce bleue
blackcurrant [ribes nigrum]: cassisier (fruit: cassis)
blackthorn, sloe [prunus spinoza]: prunellier, épine noire
bleeding heart – see 'dicentra'
blueberry [vaccinium myrtillus]: myrtille
borage [borago officinalis]: bourrache
box [buxus sempervirens]: buis
bramble – see 'blackberry'
broad bean [vicia faba]: fève
broad-leaved pondweed [potamogetum natans]: potamot

broccoli [brassica oleracea var. italica]: brocoli
broom [genista]: genêt; Scotch broom [cytisus scoparius]: genêt à balais
Brussel sprouts [b. oleracea var. gemmifera]: choux de Bruxelles
Bugleweed, or gipsywort [lycopus europaeus]: lycope d'Europe
Bulrush, or great reedmace [typha latifolia]: massette
burdock [lappa communis]: bardane
burnet [sanguisorba]: pimprenelle; great burnet [s. officinalis]: grande pimprenelle; small, or salad burnet [s. minor]: petite pimprenelle
bur-reed [sparganium]: rubanier; branched bur-reed [s. erectum]: rubanier dressé
buttercup [ranunculus]: bouton d'or; creeping buttercup, creeping crowfoot [r. repens]: renoncule rampante

C

cabbage [brassica oleracea]: chou; smooth cabbage (red, white and Savoy cabbage) [b. oleracea var. capitata]: chou cabus (blanc, rouge); cauliflower [b. oleracea var. botrytis]: chou-fleur.
camomile [anthemis nobilis]: camomille
Canadian pondweed [elodea Canadensis]: élodée du Canada
Cape gooseberry [physalis peruviana]: coqueret du Pérou (see also 'physalis')
carnation [dianthus]: oeillet; sweet William [d. barbatus]: œillet de poète. See also 'pink'.
carrot [daucus carota]: carotte
cauliflower – see 'cabbage'
celandine – see 'greater celandine' or 'lesser celandine'
celery (leaf), celeriac (root) [apium graveolens]: céleri, céleri-rave
chard, Swiss chard, or spinach beet [beta vulgaris cicla]: bette, blette, carde, poirée
charlock – see 'mustard'
cherry [prunus cerasus]: cerisier (fruit: cerise); wild cherry [prunus avium]: merisier, cerisier des oiseaux, cerisier des bois
cherry-laurel [prunus laurocerasus]: laurier-cerise
chervil [chaerophyllum cerefolium]: cerfeuil; turnip-rooted chervil [c. bulbosum]: cerfeuil tubéreux
chestnut, or Spanish chestnut [castanea sativa]: châtaigner (fruit: châtaigne, or marron); horse chestnut [aesculus hippocastanum]: marronier (fruit: marron)
chickweed [stellaria media]: stellaire
chicory [cichorium]: chicorée; wild chicory [c. intybus]: chicorée sauvage; broad-leaved and curled-leaved endive [c. endivia]: chicorée scarole and frisée; Witloof chicory, chicory [c. endivia]: endive
Chinese artichoke [stachys tuberifera]: crosne
chives [allium schoenoprasum]: ciboulette, civette

clary [salvia sclarea]: esclarée, sclarée, sauge toute-bonne
clematis [clematis]: clématite; wild clematis, traveller's-joy, old man's beard [c. vitalba]: clématite des haies, herbe aux gueux
clover [trifolium]: trèfle
columbine, or aquilegia [aquilegia]: ancolie
comfrey, or black wort, consound, assear [symphytum officinalis]: consoude, grande consoude, herbe à la coupure, oreille d'âne; Russian comfrey [s. peregrinum]: consoude de Russie
coriander [coriandrum sativum]: coriandre
cornflower [centaurea cyanus]: bleuet
cornelian cherry [cornus mas]: cornouiller male
couch grass [elymus repens]: chiendent
courgette [cucurbita pepo]: courgette
Coventry bells, or throatwort [campanula trachelium]: campanule gantelée
cowslip [p. veris]: primevère des marais, coucou
cranberry [vaccinium vitis-idaea]: airelle
cranesbill – see 'geranium'
cress, garden cress [lepidium sativum]: cresson alénois
crowfoot – see 'buttercup'
cuckoo flower, or lady's smock [cardamine pratensis]: cardamine
cucumber [cucumis sativus]: concombre
currant [ribes rubrum]: groseiller (fruit: groseille) (red/white: rouge/blanc); gooseberry [r. grossularia, or uva-crispa]: groseiller à maquereaux
cypress [cupressus]: cyprès

D

daffodil [narcissus]: jonquille
dahlia [dahlia]: dahlia
dandelion [taraxacum officinale]: pissenlit, dent de lion, laitue des chiens, salade de taupes
daylily [hemerocallis]: hémérocalle
daisy, or field daisy [bellis perennis]: pâquerette; ox-eye daisy, marguerite [chrysanthemum leucanthemum or maximum]: marguerite, marguerite des prairies
dewberry – see 'blackberry'
dicentra, or bleeding heart [dicentra]: dicentra, coeur de Marie
dill [anethum graveolens]: aneth
dock – see 'sorrel'
dog rose, or wild rose [rosa canina]: églantier, rosier des chiens, rosier des champs
dogwood [c. sanguinea]: cornouiller sanguin
duckweed [lemna]: lentilles d'eau

E

echinops [echinops]: chardon bleu
eggplant – see 'aubergine'
elder [sambucus]: sureau
elm [ulmus minor]: orme
endive – see 'chicory'
erigeron – see 'fleabane'

evening primrose [oenothera biennis]: onagre, aenothère

F

fennel [foeniculum vulgare]: fenouil
feverfew, German camomile [chrysanthemum parthenium]: matricaire
fig [ficus carica]: figuier (fruit: figue)
figwort [scrofularia]: scrofulaire; water figwort [scrofularia aquatica]: scrofulaire aquatique
fir [abies]: sapin
fleabane, erigeron [erigeron]: érigeron, vergerette
flowering rush [butomus umbellatus]: jonc fleuri, butome
forget-me-not [myosotis]: myosotis; water forget-me-not [m. palustris]: myosotis d'eau, mysosotis des marais
foxglove, or digitalis [digitalis]: digitale

G

garlic [allium sativum]: ail; bear's garlic, wood garlic, or ramson [allium ursinum]: ail des ours
geranium, or cranesbill [geranium]: géranium; herb Robert [g. robertianum]: herbe à Robert; marsh cranesbill [g. palustre]: géranium des marais; meadow geranium, meadow cranesbill [g. pratensis]: géranium des prés.
gerkhin [cucumis sativus]: cornichon
German camomile – see 'feverfew'
gipsywort – see 'bugleweed'
gladiolus [gladiolus]: glaieul
Good King Henry [chenopodium bonus-henricus]: chénopode bon-henri
gooseberry – see 'currant'
gorse [ulex europaeus]: ajonc, ajonc d'Europe
greater celandine [chelidonium majus]: chélidoine , grande éclaire, herbes aux verrues
Guelder rose [viburnum opulus]: viorne obier

H

hawthorn [crataegus monogyma]: aubépine, épine blanche, épine de mai
hazel [corylus avellana]: noisetier, coudrier (fruit: noisette)
heartsease – see 'pansy'
heather [erica]: bruyère
helianthus [helianthus]: hélianthe; tuberous helianthis [h. strumosus]: hélianthe scrofuleux. Helianthus are a large family including sunflower ('tournesol') and Jerusalem artichoke ('topinambour').
Hellebore, or Christmas rose [helleborus]: hellébore, rose de Noël; stinking hellebore [h. foetidus]: hellébore fétide
helychrysum [helychrysum]: immortelle
herb Robert – see 'geranium'
holly [ilex]: houx
hollyhock [alcea or althaea rosea]: rose trémière
honesty, moonwort, or moneywort [lunaria annua]: monnaie du Pape, herbe aux écus

honeysuckle [lonicera]: chèvrefeuille; woodland honeysuckle [l. periclymenum]: chèvrefeuille des bois
hop [humulus lupulus]: houblon
hornbeam [carpinus (betulus)]: charme
hornwort [ceratophyllum]: cératophylle; rigid horwort [c. demersum]: cornifle; softhornwort [c. submersum] cératophylle
horse chestnut – see 'chestnut'
horse-radish [cochlearia armoracia]: raifort
horsetail, common or field horsetail [equisetum arvense]: prêle, prêle des champs
houseleek [sempervivum tectorum]: joubarbe, joubarbe des toits, artichaut sauvage
hyacinth [hyacinthus]: jacinthe; water hyacinth [eichhornia]: jacinthe d'eau
hydrangea [hydrangea]: hortensia
hyssop [hyssopus officinalis]: hysope

I

ice plant [mesembryanthemum crystallinum]: ficoïde glaciale
iris [iris]: iris; yellow iris [i. pseudoacorus]: iris faux-acore, iris des marais
ivy [hedera helix]: lierre

J

Jerusalem artichoke [helianthus tuberosus]: topinambour
juniper [juniperus communis]: genévrier

K

kale [b. oleracea var. acephala]: chou frisé; fodder kale [b. oleracea var. convaracephala]: chou fourrager
knapweed, or black knapweed [centaurea nigra]: brown knapweed [centaurea jacea]: jacée
kohlrabi [Brassica oleracea gongylodes]: chou-rave

L

lady's smock – see 'cuckoo flower'
lamb's lettuce [valerianella locusta]: mâche
larch [larix dessidua]: mélèze
lauristinus [viburnum tinus]: laurier tin
lavender [lavendula]: lavande
leek [allium porrum]: poireau
lemon balm [melissa officinalis]: mélisse
lesser celandine [ranunculus ficaria]: ficaire, fausse renoncule
lettuce [lactuca sativa]: laitue
lilac [syringa vulgaris]: lilas
lilly [lilium]: lis; Madonna lily [l. candidum]: lis blanc
lily of the valley [convallaria]: muguet
lime tree [tilia]: tilleul
locust tree, or false acacia [robinia pseudoacacia]: robinier commun, robinier faux-acacia
loosestrife, yellow loosestrife [lysimachia vulgaris]: lysimaque, grande **lysimaque**; creeping yellow loosestrife, yellow pimpernel [l. nemorum]: lysimaque des bois; creeping jenny, monney wort, penny cress

[l. nummularia]: lysimaque nummulaire; purple loosestrife – see 'purple loosestrife'
lovage [levisticum officinale]: céleri vivace, livèche, ache de montagne
love-in-a-mist, or nigella [nigella]: nigelle
lucerne, or alfalfa [US] [medicago sativa]: luzerne
lupin [lupinus]: lupin

M

maiden's ruin – see 'southernwood'
Malabar spinach [basella rubra]: baselle
mallow [malva sylvestris]: mauve
maple [acer]: érable; field maple [a. campestre]: érable champêtre
marigold [tagetes]: souci, tagète; African or American marigold [tagetes erecta]: rose d'Inde; French marigold [tagetes patula]: oeillet d'Inde
marjoram [origanum majorana]: marjolaine
marrow [cucurbita pepo]: courge
marsh mallow [althaea officinalis]: guimauve
marsh marigold [caltha palustris]: populage, souci des marais
meadow saffron – see 'autumn crocus'
meadowsweet, or queen-of-the meadow [filipendula ulmaria]: reine-des-prés, ulmaire
medlar [mespilus germanica]: nêflier (fruit: nêfle)
melon [cucumis melo]: melon
mercury [mercurialis]: mercuriale
mimosa, or silver wattle [acacia]: mimosa
mint [mentha]: menthe; water mint [m. aquatica]: menthe aquatique; costmary, alecost [tanacetum balsamita]: menthecoq
moneywort – see 'honesty'
moonwort – see 'honesty'
mouse-ear [cerastium]: céraiste
mugwort, or motherwort [artemisia vulgaris]: armoise, absinthe sauvage, herbe de la Saint Jean
mulberry [morus]: mûrier (fruit: mûre - not to be confused with the fruit of the 'blackberry', also called 'mûre')
mustard [sinapis (alba)]: moutarde (blanche), sénévé; wild mustard, charlock [s. arvensis]: moutarde sauvage, or des champs

N

narcissus [narcissus]: narcisse
nasturtium [tropaelum majus]: capucine; tuberous nasturtium [tropaelum tuberosus]: capucine tubéreuse
nectarine [prunus persica laevis var. nectarina]: brugnon (Europe grown), nectarine (US grown)
nettle [urtica]: ortie; white dead-nettle [lamium album]: ortie blanche
New Zealand Spinach [tetragonia tetragonioides]: tétragone, épinard de Nouvelle Zélande
nigella – see 'love-in-a-mist'
nightshade [solanum]: morelle; bittersweet nightshade [solanum dulcamara]:

douce-amère; deadly nightshade [atropa belladona]: belladone
nutsedge [cyperus]: souchet; yellow nutsedge [cyperus esculentus]: souchet comestible

O

oak [quercus]: chêne (fruit: gland); pin oak [q. palustris]: chêne des marais; common, or pedunculate oak [q. robur]: chêne, chêne pédonculé; downy oak [q. pubescens]: chêne pubescent, blanc, or truffier; sessile oak [q. petrae]: chêne rouvre or sessile; holm oak, holly oak [q. ilex]: chêne vert
oca [oxalis crenata Jacq.]: oca du Pérou
old man – see 'southernwood'
oleander [nerium oleander]: laurier rose
olive [olea]: olivier (fruit: olive)
onion [allium cepa]: oignon; tree **onion** [allium cepa proliferum]: oignon rocambole, échalote d'Espagne
orach [atriplex]: arroche; garden **orach, mountain spinach [a. hortensis]:** arroche des jardins, bonne-dame
orchid [orchis]: orchidée; spotted **orchid [dactylorhiza]:** orchis tâchetée
oregano [origanum vulgare]: origan

P

pansy [viola]: pensée; wild pansy, heartsease [v. tricolor]: pensée sauvage
parsley [carum petroselinum]: persil
parsnip [pastinaca sativa]: panais, pastenade (South)
pasque flower – see 'anemone'
patience – see 'sorrel'
patipan [a variety of cucurbita pepo]: pâtisson
pea, garden pea [pisum sativum]: pois, petit pois
peach [prunus persica]: pêcher (fruit: pêche)
pear [pyrus communis]: poirier (fruit: poire); grape pear – see 'shadbush'
pearlwort [sagina]: sagine; procumbent pearlwort [sagina procumbens]: sagine couchée
pelargonium [pelargonium]: pélargonium (although often referred to erroneously as 'géranium')
penstemon [penstemon]: penstemon
pellitory [parietaria]: pariétaire
peony [paeonia officinalis]: pivoine
pepper [capsicum annuum]: poivron (sweet or bell pepper) or piment (chili or cayenne pepper)
periwinkle [vinca]: pervenche
petty spurge [euphorbia peplus]: euphorbe omblette
philadelphus [philadelphus]: seringat
phlox [phlox]: phlox
pimpernel – see 'loosestrife' and 'scarlet pimpernel'
pine [pinus]: pin; Douglas fir [pseudotsuga]: pin Douglas; maritime pine [p. pinaster]: pin maritime; Scots pine [p. sylvestris]: pin sylvestre
pink [d. plumarius]: œillet mignardise

plane tree [platanus]: platane
plantain [plantago]: plantain; narrowleaved plantain, rib-grass [p. lanceolata]: plantain lancéolé
plum [prunus domestica]: prunier (fruit: prune. The English 'prune' is 'pruneau')
poplar [populus]: peuplier
poppy [papaver]: pavot, coquelicot; field poppy [p. rheoas]: coquelicot
potato [solanum tuberosum]: pomme de terre
primrose [primula]: primevère; wild primrose (primula vulgaris]: primevère des jardins; evening primrose (not a 'primula') – see 'evening primrose'
privet [ligustrum]: troène
pumpkin [cucurbita maxima]: citrouille, potiron
purple loosestrife [lythrum salicaria]: salicaire, lysimaque rouge
purslane [portulaca oleracea]: pourpier
physalis (aka: alekenge, Chinese lantern, winter cherry, ground cherry) [physalis]: physalis, amour-en-cage, alkékenge, lanterne japonaise, alkekengi, Cape gooseberry (edible variety).
pyrethrum [tanacetum coccineum, or chrysanthemum coccineum]: pyrèthre

Q

queen-of-the meadow – see 'meadowsweet'
quince [cydonia vulgaris or oblonga]: cognassier (fruit: coing)

R

radish [raphanus sativus]: radis
ramson – see 'garlic'
raspberry [rubus idaeus, rubus strigosus]: framboisier (fruit: framboise)
reed [phragmites communis]: roseau reedmace – see 'bulrush'
rhubarb [rheum rhabarbarum]: rhubarbe; Chinese rhubarb [r. palmatum]: rhubarbe d'ornement
rib-grass – see 'plantain'
rocket [eruca sativa]: roquette
rose [rosa]: rose; dog rose, wild rose – see 'dog rose'
rose campion [lychnis coronaria]: coquelourde
rosemary [rosmarinus officinalis]: romarin
rowan, or mountain ash [sorbus aucuparia]: sorbier, sorbier des oiseleurs or des oiseaux
rush [juncus] jonc; compact rush [j. conglomeratus]: jonc aggloméré, or conglméré; common clubrush [scirpus lacustris]: jonc des tonneliers or des chaisiers, scirpe; soft rush [j. effusus]: jonc épars; flowering rush – see 'flowering rush'

S

scabious [scabiosa]: scabieuse
sage [salvia]: sauge; meadow clary [s. pratensis]: sauge des prés
sainfoin [onobrychis]: sainfoin

St-John's-Wort [hypericum perforatum]: millepertuis, herbe aux piqûres
salsify [tragopogon porrifolius]: salsifi; meadow salsify, showy goat's beard [t. pratensis]: salsifi des prés, barbe de bouc
sandwort [arenaria]: sabline; Corsican sandwort [a. Balearica]: sabline des Baléares
savory [satureia]: sariette
scarlet pimpernel [anagallis arvensis]: mouron rouge
scorzonera [scorzonera hispanica]: scorsonère
sea buckthorn [hippophae rhamnoides]: argousier, faux nerprun, saule épineux, griset
sedge [carex]: laîches, carex
serviceberry – see 'shadbush'
service tree [sorbus domestica]: cormier, sorbier domestique
shadbush ,shadberry, juneberry, grape pear, or serviceberry [amelanchier laevis or Canadensis]: amélanchier
shallot [allium cepa aggregatum]: échalotte
shepherd's purse [capsella bursa pastoris]: bourse-à-pasteur, capselle
showy goat's beard – see 'salsify'
silver wattle – see 'mimosa'
skirret [sium sisarum]: chervis
sloe – see 'backthorn'
snowdrop [galanthus]: perce-neige
soapwort, or bouncing-bet [saponaria officinalis]: saponaire, savonnière, herbe à foulon, herbe à savon
sorrel, dock [rumex acetosa]: oseille; patience dock, spinach sorrel [rumex patientia]: patience, épinard-oseille
southernwood, old man, or maiden's ruin [artemisia abrotanum]: aurone
spearwort (lesser) [ranunculus flammula]: petite douve, renoncule flammette; greater spearwort [ranunculus lingua]: grande douve
spinach [spinacia oleracea]: épinard; mountain spinach – see 'orach'; New Zealand spinach [tetragonia tetragonioides]: tétragone, épinard de Nouvelle Zélande
spinach beet – see 'chard'
spindle [euonymus europaeus]: fusain d'Europe, bonnet carré
spring cinquefoil [potentilla tabernaemontani]: potentille printanière
spruce [picea]: épicea
strawberry [fragaria]: fraisier (fruit: fraise); wild strawberry [f. vesca]: fraise des bois
sunflower [helianthus annuus]: tournesol
swede, rutabaga [brassica Napo-brassica]: rutabaga, chou-navet, chou de Suède, navet jaune
Swiss chard – see 'chard'

T

tansy [tanecetum vulgare]: tanaisie
tarragon [artemisia dracunculus]: estragon
teasel [dipsacus fullonum]: cardère, chardon à foulon

thistle [cirsium]: chardon
throatwort – see 'Coventry bell'
thuja [thuja]: thuya
thyme [thymus vulgaris]: thym, farigoule (south); creeping thyme [thymus serpyllum]: serpolet
tomato [lycopersicum esculentum]: tomate
tormentil [potentilla erecta]: potentille tormentille
tulip [tulipa]: tulipe
turnip [brassica rapa, or campestris]: navet

V

verbascum, or Aaron's beard [verbascum thapsus]: bouillon-blanc, molène commune
verbena [verbena]: verveine; lemon verbena [lippia citriodora]: verveine citronnelle
vetch [vicia sativa]: vesce
vine, grape vine [vitis vinifera]: vigne
violet [viola]: violette; field violet [v. arvensis]: violette des champs; marsh violet [v. palustris]: violette des marais
Virginia creeper [ampelopsis veitchii or parthenocissus]: vigne vierge

W

walnut [juglans regia]: noyer (fruit: noix)
water crowfoot [ranunculus aquatilis]: renoncule aquatique
water lily [nymphea]: nénuphar
water milfoil [myriophyllum]: myriophylle
water pennywort [hydrocotyle vulgaris]: écuelle d'eau
wayfaring tree [viburnum lantana]: viorne lantane
Welsh onion [allium fistulosum]: ciboule
whitebeam [sorbus aria]: sorbier alisier blanc
wild rose – see 'dog rose'
willow [salix]: saule; white willow [s. alba]: saule blanc; silver willow [s. cinerea]: saule cendré; basket willow, velvet osier [s. viminalis]: saule des vanniers, or saule osier; goat willow, pussy willow [s. caprea]: saule marsault
wisteria [wisteria]: glycine
woodruff [asperula odorata, or gallium odoratum]: aspérule odorante
wormwood [artemisia absinthium]: absinthe, armoise amère, herbe sainte, herbe aux vers génépi (in the Alps)

Y

Yarrow, milfoil, or achillea [achillea millefolium]: achillée millefeuille, mille feuilles, herbe aux coupures
yew [taxus baccata]: if

Z

zinnia [zinnia]: zinnia

Plants

French - English

A

abricotier (fruit: abricot) [prunus armenica]: apricot
absinthe, armoise amère, herbe sainte, herbe aux vers, or génépi (in the Alps) [artemisia absinthium]: wormwood
absinthe sauvage - see 'armoise'
acacia [acacia]: acacia
ache de montagne - see 'céleri vivace'
achillée millefeuille, mille feuilles, or herbe aux coupures [achillea millefolium]: yarrow, milfoil, achillea
aenothère - see 'onagre'
ail [allium sativum]: garlic; ail des ours [allium ursinum]: bear's garlic, wood garlic, ramson
airelle [vaccinium vitis-idaea]: cranberry
ajonc, ajonc d'Europe [ulex europaeus]: gorse
alisier - see 'sorbier'
alkékenge - see 'physalis'
amarante à feuilles [amaranthus gangeticus]: amaranth
amélanchier [amelanchier laevis or Canadensis]: juneberry, grape pear, alpine mespilus, service berry, shadbush, shadberry
amour-en-cage - see 'physalis'
ancolie [aquilegia]: columbine
anémone pulsatile, anémone des prés, or coquerelle [pulsatilla vulgaris]: pasque flower, meadow anemone
aneth [anethum graveolens]: dill
angélique [angelica]: angélica argousier, faux nerprun, saule épineux, or griset [hippophae rhamnoides]: sea buckthorn
armoise, absinthe sauvage, or herbe de la Saint Jean [artemisia vulgaris]: mugwort, motherwort
arroche [atriplex]: orach; arroche des jardins, or bonne-dame [a. hortensis]: garden orach, mountain spinach
artichaut [cynara scolymus]: globe artichoke; artichaut sauvage - see 'joubarbe'
asperge [asparagus]: asparagus
aspérule odorante [asperula odorata, or gallium odoratum]: woodruff
aster [aster]: aster
aubépine, épine blanche, or épine de mai [crataegus monogyma]: hawthorn
aubergine [solanum molengena]: aubergine, eggplant (US)
aubriète [aubrieta]: aubrietia
aulne [alnus]: alder
aurone [artemisia abrotanum]: southernwood, old man, maiden's ruin

B

barbe de bouc, or salsifi des prés [tragopogon pratensis]: showy goat's-beard, meadow salsify
bardane [lappa communis]: burdock
baselle [basella rubra]: Malabar spinach
basilic [ocinum basilicum]: basil
belladone [atropa belladona]: deadly nightshade
berbéris [berberis vulgaris]: berberis, barberry
bette, blette, carde, or poirée [beta vulgaris cicla]: chard, Swiss chard, spinach beet
betterave [beta vulgaris esculenta]: beet; betterave décorative, or poirée [b. vulgaris]: decorative beet
bignone, or jasmin de Virginie [campsis]: bignonia, trumpet vine
blette - see 'bette'
bleuet [centaurea cyanus]: cornflower
bonne-dame – see 'arroche'
bonnet carré - see 'fusain d'Europe'
bouillon-blanc, or molène commune [verbascum thapsus]: Aaron's beard, verbascum
bouleau [betula]: birch; bouleau verruqueux [b. verrucosa]: white birch; bouleau blanc [b. pendula]: silver birch; bouleau pubescent [b. pubescens]: downy birch
bourrache [borago officinalis]: borage
bourse-à-pasteur, capselle [capsella bursa pastoris]: shepherd's purse
bouton d'or – see 'renoncule'
brocoli [brassica oleracea var. italica]: broccoli
brugnon (Europe), nectarine (US) [prunus persica laevis var. nectarina]: nectarine
bruyère [erica]: heather
buis [buxus sempervirens]: box
butome – see 'jonc fleuri'

C

camomille [anthemis nobilis]: camomile, Roman chamomile
campanule [campanula]: bellflower; campanule gantelée [c. trachelium]: Coventry bells, throatwort
capselle - see 'bourse-à-pasteur'
capucine [tropaelum majus]: nasturtium; capucine tubéreuse [t. tuberosum]: tuberous
cardamine [cardamine pratensis]: cuckoo flower, lady's smock
carde - see 'bette'
cardère [dipsacus fullonum]: teasel
carotte [daucus carota]: carrot
cassisier (fruit: cassis) [ribes nigrum]: blackcurrant
céleri vivace, livèche, ache [levisticum officinale]: lovage
céleri, céleri-rave [apium graveolens]: celery (stalks), celeriac (tuber)
céraiste [cerastium]: mouse-ear
cératophylle [ceratophyllum submersum]: soft hornwort
cerfeuil [chaerophyllum cerefolium]: chervil; cerfeuil tubéreux [c. bulbosum]: turnip-rooted chervil
cerisier (fruit: cerise) [prunus cerasus]: cherry; cerisier des bois or des oiseaux - see 'merisier'
chardon [cirsium]: thistle; chardon à foulon [dipsacus fullonum]: teasel;
chardon bleu [echinops]: echinops
charme [carpinus (betulus)]: hornbeam

chasse-diable – see 'millepertuis'

châtaigner (fruit: châtaigne) [castanea sativa]: chestnut, Spanish chestnut

chélidoine, herbes aux verrues, or grande éclaire [chelidonium majus]: greater celandine

chêne (fruit: gland) [quercus]: oak; chêne des marais [q. palustris]: pin oak; chêne commun (sometimes called 'pédonculé') [q. robur]: common, or pedunculate oak; chêne vert [q. ilex]: holm oak, holly oak

chêne pubescent, blanc, or truffier) [q. pubescens]: downy oak; chêne rouvre or sessile [q. petrae]: sessile oak; chêne vert [q. ilex]: holm oak, holly oak

chénopode bon-henri [chenopodium bonus-henricus]: Good King Henry

chervis [sium sisarum]: skirret

chèvrefeuille [lonicera]: honeysuckle;

chèvrefeuille des bois [l. periclymenum]: woodland honeysuckle

chicorée [cichorium]: chicory; chicorée sauvage [c. intybus]: wild chicory; chicorée Witloof - see 'endive'

chiendent [elymus repens]: couch grass

chou [brassica oleracea]: cabbage; chou cabus (including 'chou rouge': red cabbage) [b. oleracea var. capitata]: cabbage (including white and Savoy cabbage); choux de Bruxelles [b. oleracea var. gemmifera]: Brussel sprouts; chou vert frisé [b. oleracea var. acephala]: kale; chou-fleur [b. oleracea var. botrytis]: cauliflower; chou fourrager [b. oleracea var. convaracephala]: fodder kale; chou-rave [b. oleracea gongylodes]: kohlrabi

ciboule [allium fistulosum]: Welsh onion

ciboulette, or civette [allium schoenoprasum]: chives

citrouille [cucurbita maxima]: pumpkin

civette - see 'ciboulette'

clématite [clematis]: clematis; clématite des haies, herbe aux gueux [c. vitalba]: traveller's-joy, old man's beard

cognassier (fruit: coing) [cydonia vulgaris or oblonga]: quince

colchique [colchicum]: Autumn crocus, meadow saffron

concombre [cucumis sativus]: cucumber

consoude, grande consoude, herbe à la coupure, or oreille d'âne [symphytum officinalis]: comfrey, black wort, consound, assear; consoude de Russie [s. peregrinum]: Russian comfrey

coquelicot [papaver rheoas]: field poppy

coquelourde [lychnis coronaria]: rose campion

coquerelle - see 'anémone des prés'

coqueret du Pérou (see also 'physalis') [physalis peruviana]: Cape gooseberry

coriandre [coriandrum sativum]: coriander

cormier, or sorbier domestique [sorbus domestica]: service tree

cornichon [cucumis sativus]: gerkhin

cornifle [ceratophyllum demersum]: rigid hornwort

cornouiller male [cornus mas]: cornelian cherry; cornouiller sanguin [c. sanguinea]: dogwood

coucou - see 'primevère'

coudrier - see 'noisetier'

courge [cucurbita pepo]: marrow

courgette [cucurbita pepo]: courgette

cresson alénois [lepidium sativum]: garden cress

crosne [stachys tuberifera]: Chinese artichoke

cyprès [cupressus]: cypress

D

dahlia [dahlia]: dahlia

dent-de-lion – see 'pissenlit'

dicentra, or coeur de Marie [dicentra]: bleeding heart, dicentra

digitale [digitalis]: digitalis, foxglove

douce-amère [solanum dulcamara]: bittersweet nightshade

E

échalotte [allium cepa aggregatum]: shallot

écuelle d'eau [hydrocotyle vulgaris]: common water pennywort

églantier, rosier des chiens or des champs [rosa canina]: dog rose, wild rose

élodée du Canada [elodea Canadensis]: Canadian pondweed

endive, chicorée witloof [cichorium endivia]: chicory

épicea [picea]: spruce

épinard [spinacia oleracea]: spinach; épinard de Nouvelle-Zélande – see 'tétragone'; épinard-oseille – see 'patience'

épine blanche - see 'aubépine'

épine de mai - see 'aubépine'

épine noire – see 'prunellier'

épine-vinette - see 'berbéris'

érable [acer]: maple; champêtre [a. campestre]: field maple

érigeron, or vergerette [erigeron]: fleabane, erigeron

esclarée, sclarée, or sauge toute-bonne [salvia sclarea]: clary, biennial clary

estragon [artemisia dracunculus]: tarragon

euphorbe omblette [euphorbia peplus]: petty spurge

F

farigoule - see 'thym'

faux nerprun - see 'argousier'

fenouil [foeniculum vulgare]: fennel

fève [vicia faba]: broad bean

ficaire, fausse renoncule [ranunculus ficaria]: lesser celandine

ficoïde glaciale [mesembryanthemum crystallinum]: ice plant

figuier (fruit: figue) [ficus carica]: fig

fraisier (fruit: fraise) [fragaria]: strawberry; fraise des bois [f. vesca]: wild strawberry

framboisier (fruit: framboise) [rubus idaeus, rubus strigosus]: raspberry

frêne [fraxinus excelsior]: ash

fusain d'Europe, bonnet carré [euonymus europaeus]: spindle

G

genêt [genista]: broom; genêt à balais [cytisus (scoparius)]: Scotch broom

genévrier [juniperus communis]: juniper

géranium [geranium]: geranium; géranium des marais [g. palustre]: marsh

cranesbill; géranium des prés [pratensis]: meadow geranium, meadow cranesbill (note: the term 'géranium' is often used to refer mistakenly to 'pelargonium')

glaieul [gladiolus]: gladiolus

glycine [wisteria]: wisteria

grande consoude - see 'consoude'

grande éclaire - see 'chélidoine'

griset - see 'argousier'

groseiller (fruit: groseille) (rouge/blanche) [ribes rubrum]: currant (red/white); groseiller à maquereaux [r. grossularia, or uva-crispa]: gooseberry

guimauve [althaea officinalis]: marsh mallow

H

haricot [phaseolus vulgaris]: bean; haricot d'Espagne [p. coccinus]: runner bean; haricot dolique [dolichos sesquipedalis]: yardlong bean

hélianthe [helianthus strumosus]: helianthus. Helianthus are a large family including sunflower ('tournesol') and Jerusalem artichoke ('topinambour').

hellébore, or rose de Noël [helleborus]: hellebore, Christmas rose; hellébore fétide [h. foetidus]: stinking hellebore

hémérocalle [hemerocallis]: daylily, hemerocallis

herbe à foulon - see 'saponnaire'

herbe à la coupure - see 'consoude'

herbe à Robert, bec-de-grue, or épingle de la Vierge [geranium robertianum]: herb Robert

herbe à savon - see 'saponaire'

herbe aux coupures - see 'achillée millefeuille'

herbe aux écus – see 'monnaie du Pape'

herbe aux gueux - see 'clématite des haies'

herbe aux piqûres - see 'millepertuis'

herbe aux verrues – see 'chélidoine'

herbe de la Saint-Jean - see 'millepertuis'

hêtre [fagus sylvatica]: beech

hortensia [hydrangea]: hydrangea

houblon [humulus lupulus]: hop

houx [ilex]: holly

hysope [hyssopus officinalis]: hyssop

I - J

if [taxus baccata]: yew

immortelle [helychrysum]: helychrysum

iris [iris]: iris; iris faux-acore, iris des marais [i. pseudoacorus]: yellow iris

jacée [centaurea jacea]: knapweed

jacinthe [hyacinthus]: hyacinth; jacinthe d'eau [eichhornia]: water hyacinth

jasmin de Virginie – see 'bignogne'

jonc [juncus]: rush; jonc agglomeré, or jonc congloméré [j. conglomeratus]: compact rush; jonc des tonneliers or des

chaisiers, scirpe [scirpus lacustris]: common clubrush; jonc épars [j. effusus]: soft rush

jonc fleuri, butome [butomus umbellatus]: flowering rush

jonquille [narcissus]: daffodil

joubarbe, joubarbe des toits, or artichaut sauvage [sempervivum tectorum]: houseleek

L

laîches, or carex [carex]: sedge

laitue [lactuca sativa]: lettuce

laitue des chiens - see 'pissenlit'

lanterne japonaise - see 'physalis'

laurier, laurier sauce, laurier noble, or laurier d'Apollon [laurus nobilis]: bay

laurier rose [nerium oleander]: oleander

laurier tin [viburnum tinus]: laurustinus

laurier-cerise [prunus laurocerasus]: cherry-laurel

lavande [lavendula]: lavender

lentilles d'eau [lemna]: duckweed

lierre [hedera helix]: ivy

lilas [syringa vulgaris]: lilac

lis [lilium]: lily; lis blanc [l. candidum]: Madonna lily

liseron [convolvulus]: bindweed; liseron des champs [c. arvensis]: field bindweed

livèche - see 'céleri vivace'

lunaire - see 'monnaie du Pape'

lupin [lupinus]: lupin

luzerne [medicago sativa]: lucerne, alfalfa (US)

lycope d'Europe [lycopus europaeus]: bugleweed, gipsywort

lysimaque, grande lysimaque [lysimachia vulgaris]: yellow loosestrife; lysimaque des bois [l. nemorum]: yellow pimpernel, creeping yellow loosestrife; lysimaque nummulaire [l. nummularia]: creeping jenny, monney wort, penny cress; lysimaque rouge – see 'salicaire'

M

mâche [valerianella locusta]: lamb's lettuce

marguerite, marguerite des prairies [chrysanthemum leucanthemum or maximum]: ox-eye daisy, marguerite

marjolaine [origanum majorana]: marjoram

marronnier (fruit: marron) [aesculus hippocastanum]: horse chestnut

massette [typha latifolia]: bulrush, great reedmace

matricaire [chrysantemum parthenium]: feverfew, German chamomile

mauve [malva sylvestris]: mallow

mélèze [larix dessidua]: larch

mélisse [melissa officinalis]: lemon balm

melon [cucumis melo]: melon

menthe [mentha]: mint; menthe aquatique [m. aquatica]: water mint; menthe-coq [tanacetum balsamita]: costmary, alecost

mercuriale [mercurialis]: mercury, merisier, cerisier des bois or des oiseaux [prunus avium]: wild cherry

mille feuilles - see 'achillée millefeuille'
millepertuis, herbe aux piqûres, herbe de la Saint-Jean, or chasse-diable [hypericum perforatum]: St-John's-Wort
mimosa [acacia]: mimosa, silver wattle
molène - see 'bouillon blanc'
monnaie du Pape, herbe aux écus [lunaria annua]: honesty, moonwort, moneywort
mouron rouge [anagallis arvensis]: scarlet pimpernel
moutarde, sénévé [sinapis (alba)]: mustard; moutarde sauvage, or des champs [s. arvensis]: wild mustard, charlock
muguet [convallaria]: lily of the valley
mûrier (fruit: mûre - not to be confused with the fruit of the 'blackberry', also called 'mûre') [morus]: mulberry bush
myosotis [myosotis]: forget-me-not; **myosotis d'eau, myosotis des marais [m. palustris]:** water forget-me-not
myriophylle [myriophyllum]: water milfoil
myrtille [vaccinium myrtillus]: blueberry

N

narcisse [narcissus]: narcissus
navet [brassica rapa or campestris]: turnip
néflier (fruit: nêfle) [mespilus germanica]: medlar
nénuphar [nymphea]: water lily
nigelle [nigella]: love-in-a-mist, nigella
noisetier, or coudrier (fruit: noisette) [corylus avellana]: hazel
noyer (fruit: noix) [juglans regia]: walnut

O

oca du Pérou [oxalis crenata Jacq.]: oca
oeillet [dianthus]: carnation; œillet de poète [d. barbatus]: sweet William; œillet mignardise [d. plumarius]: pink
oeillet d'Inde [tagetes patula]: French marigold
oignon [allium cepa]: onion
oignon rocambole, or échalote d'Espagne [allium cepa proliferum]: tree onion
olivier (fruit: olive) [olea]: olive
onagre, aenothère [oenothera biennis]: evening primrose
orchidée [orchis]: orchid
orchis tâchetée [dactylorhiza]: spotted orchid
oreille d'âne - see 'consoude'
origan [origanum vulgare]: oregano
orme [ulmus minor]: elm
ortie [urtica]: (stinging) nettle; ortie blanche [lamium album]: white dead-nettle
oseille [rumex acetosa]: sorrel

P

Panais, or pastenade (south) [pastinaca sativa]: parsnip
pâquerette [bellis perennis]: daisy, field daisy
pariétaire [parietaria]: pellitory
patience, or épinard-oseille [rumex patientia]: patience dock, spinach-dock

pâtisson [a variety of cucurbita pepo]: patipan
pavot [papaver]: poppy
pêcher (fruit: pêche) [prunus persica]: peach
pélargonium [pelargonium]: pelargonium
pensée [viola]: pansy; pensée sauvage [v. tricolor]: heartsease
penstemon [penstemon]: penstemon
perce-neige [galanthus]: snowdrop
persil [carum petroselinum]: parsley
pervenche [vinca]: periwinkle
petite douve, or renoncule flammette [ranunculus flammula]: lesser spearwort
peuplier [populus]: poplar
phlox [phlox]: phlox
physalis, amour-en-cage, alkékenge, or lanterne japonaise [physalis]: physalis, alkekengi, winter cherry, ground cherry. The edible variety ('variété comestible') is the Cape gooseberry [p. peruviana]: coqueret du Pérou
piment [capsicum annuum]: chili pepper
pimprenelle (grande / petite) [sanguisorba officinalis / minor]: great burnet / small, or salad burnet
pin [pinus]: pine, fir; pin Douglas [pseudotsuga]: Douglas fir; pin maritime [p. pinaster]: maritime pine; pin sylvestre [p. sylvestris]: Scots pine
pissenlit, dent de lion, laitue des chiens, or salade de taupes [taraxacum officinale]: dandelion
pivoine [paeonia officinalis]: peony
plantain [plantago]: plantain; plantain lancéolé [p. lanceolata]: narrow-leaved plantain, rib-grass
platane [platanus]: plane tree
poireau [allium porrum]: leek
poirée - see 'bette'
poirier (fruit: poire) [pyrus communis]: pear
pois, petit pois [pisum sativum]: pea, garden pea
poivron [capsicum annuum]: pepper, sweet pepper, bell pepper
pomme de terre [solanum tuberosum]: potato
pommier (fruit: pomme) [malus pumila]: apple
populage, or souci des marais [caltha palustris]: marsh marigold
potamot [potamogetan natans]: broad-leaved pondweed
potentille printanière [potentilla tabernaemontani]: Spring cinquefoil; potentille tormentille [p. erecta]: tormentil
potiron [cucurbita maxima]: pumpkin
pourpier [portulaca oleracea]: purslane
prêle, prêle des champs [equisetum arvense]: common horsetail, field horsetail
primevère [primula]: primrose; primevère des marais, coucou [p. veris]: cowslip; primevère des jardins [primula vulgaris]: wild primrose
prunellier, or épine noire [prunus spinoza]: blackthorn, sloe
prunier (fruit: prune) [prunus domestica]: plum

pyrèthre [tanacetum coccineum, or chrysanthemum coccineum]: pyrethrum

R

radis [raphanus sativus]: radish
raifort [cochlearia armoracia]: horse-radish
reine-des-prés, ulmaire [filipendula ulmaria]: meadowsweet, queen-of-the meadow
renoncule [ranunculus]: buttercup; **renoncule aquatique [r. aquatilis]:** water crowfoot; renoncule rampante [r. repens]: creeping buttercup, creeping crowfoot
rhubarbe [rheum rhabarbarum]: rhubarb; **rhubarbe d'ornement [r. palmatum]:** Chinese rhubarb
robinier commun, or robinier faux-acacia [robinia pseudoacacia]: locust tree, false acacia
romarin [rosmarinus officinalis]: rosemary
ronce (fruit: mûre) [rubus fructicosus]: blackberry, bramble; bleue [r. caesius]: dewberry
roquette [eruca sativa]: rocket
rose [rosa]: rose
rose d'Inde [tagetes erecta]: African or American marigold
rose trémière [alcea, or althaea rosea]: hollyhock
roseau [phragmites communis]: reed
rosier des champs or des chiens - see 'églantier'
rubanier [sparganium]: bur-reed; rubanier dressé [s. erectum]: branched bur-reed
rutabaga, chou-navet, chou de Suède, navet jaune [brassica Napo-brassica]: swede, rutabaga

S

sabline [arenaria]: sandwort; sabline des Baléares [a. Balearica]: Corsican sandwort
sagine couchée [sagina procumbens]: procumbent pearlwort
sainfoin [onobrychis]: sainfoin
salade de taupe – see 'pissenlit'
salicaire commune, or lysimaque rouge [lythrum salicaria]: purple loosestrife
salsifi [tragopogon porrifolius]: salsify; salsifi des prés, or barbe de bouc [t. pratensis]: meadow salsify, showy goat's-beard
sapin [abies]: fir
saponnaire, herbe à foulon, herbe à savon, or savonnière [saponaria officinalis]: soapwort, bouncing-Bet
sariette [satureia]: savory
sauge [salvia]: sage; sauge des prés [s. pratensis]: meadow clary
saule [salix]: willow; saule blanc [s. alba]: white willow; saule cendré [s. cinerea]: silver willow; saule des vanniers, or saule osier [s. viminalis]: basket willow, velvet osier; saule épineux - see 'argousier'; saule marsault [s. caprea]: goat willow, pussy willow

savonnière - see 'saponnaire'
scabieuse [scabiosa]: scabious
scirpe - see 'jonc des chaisiers'
sclarée - see 'esclarée'
scorsonère [scorzonera hispanica]: scorzonera
scrofulaire aquatique [scrofularia aquatica]: water figwort
sénévé - see 'moutarde'
seringat [philadelphus]: philadelphus
serpolet [thymus serpyllum]: creeping thyme
soleil – see 'tournesol'
sorbier [sorbus]: rowan: sorbier alisier blanc [s. aria]: whitebeam; sorbier des oiseleurs, or des oiseaux [s. aucuparia]: rowan, mountain ash; sorbier domestique, or cormier [s. domestica]: service tree
souchet comestible [cyperus esculentus]: yellow nutsedge
souci [calendula officinalis]: marigold
stellaire [stellaria media]: chickweed
sureau [sambucus]: elder

T

Tagète, or souci [tagetes]: marigold
tanaisie [tanecetum vulgare]: tansy
tétragone (aka: épinard de Nouvelle Zélande) [tetragonia tetragonioides]: New Zealand spinach
thuya [thuja]: thuja
thym, or farigoule (south-east) [thymus vulgaris]: thyme
tilleul [tilia]: lime tree
tomate [lycopersicum esculentum]: tomato
topinambour [helianthus tuberosus]: Jerusalem artichoke
tournesol, or soleil [helianthus annuus]: sunflower
trèfle [trifolium]: clover
tremble [populus tremula]: aspen
troène [ligustrum]: privet
tulipe [tulipa]: tulip

U - Z

ulmaire – see 'reine-des-prés'
vergerette – see 'érigeron'
verveine [verbena]: verbena; verveine citronnelle [lippia citriodora]: lemon verbena
vesce [vicia sativa]: vetch
vigne [vitis vinifera]: vine, grape vine
vigne vierge [ampelopsis veitchii or parthenocissus]: Virginia creeper
vinettier - see 'berbéris'
violette [viola]: violet; violette des champs [v. arvensis]: field violet; violette des marais [v. palustris]: marsh violet
viorne lantane [viburnum lantana]: wayfaring tree
viorne obier [viburnum opulus]: Guelder rose
zinnia [zinnia]: zinnia

Gardening Terms

English - French

A

Acidic: acide
Alkaline: alcalin
Algae: algues (f pl)
Annual (plant): (plante (f)) annuelle
Aphid: puceron (m)
Arbour: tonnelle (f)
Ash: cendre (f)

B

Bed: plate-bande (f); to bed out: repiquer
Biennial (plant): (plante (f)) bisannuelle
Biodiversity: biodiversité (f)
Blanch: forcer (v)
Bloom: fleur (f); in bloom: en fleurs; fleurir (v), bourgeonner (v)
Blossom: fleur (f); fleurir (v), s'épanouir (v)
Bog: marais (m), marécage (m); peat bog: tourbière (f)
Bone meal: poudre (f) d'os (m)
Bordeaux mixture: bouillie (f) bordelaise
Border: bordure (f)
Branch: branche (f)
Broadcast: à la volée (f); to sow broadcast: semer à la volée.
Bud: bourgeonner (v); bourgeon (m)
Bulb: bulbe (f), plante (f) à bulbe

C

Chalky: calcaire
Chop: couper (v), trancher (v), faucarder (v)
Clay: argile (f); clay soil: sol argileux
Clip: tailler (v)
Cob: bauge (f); cob wall: mur (m) en bauge
Cobble, cobblestone: pavé (m)
Cold-frame: chassis (m)
Compost: composte (m); ericaceous compost: terre (f) de bruyère (literally: 'soil for growing heather'); garden or potting compost: terreau (m)
Coppice: recéper (v), arbre (m) recépé; coppicing: recépage (m); copse: cépée (f)
Courtyard: cour (f)
Cow pat: bouse (f) de vache (f)
Crop: récolte (f), culture (f); crop rotation: assolement (m), rotation (f) des cultures; double-cropper (fruit shrub): (arbuste (m)) remontant
Crown: couronne (f); tree crown: couronne d'un arbre
Cut: couper (v); cutting: bouture (f); to take cuttings: bouturer (v), bouturage (m); cut back: rabattre, raccourcir; cut back to two buds (from the start of the stem): rabattre à 2 bourgeons; cut back hard: rabattre court

D

Damp: humide
Daub: pisé (m), torchis (m)
Deciduous: caduc (-uque); deciduous tree: arbre (m) à feuilles caduques:

Dig: bêcher, creuser; to dig the garden / the soil: bêcher le jardin / la terre; to dig a trench: creuser une tranchée
Disease: maladie (f); fungal disease: maladie cryptogamique
Dredge: curer (v)
Dress: top dress: pailler (v); top dressing: paillage (m)
Dry: sec (sèche)

E

Earth: terre (f)
Edge: bordure (f)
Espalier: espalier (m)
Evergreen (plant / tree): plante (f) / arbre (m) à feuilles persistentes
Excavate: creuser, faire des excavations

F

Fallow: friche (f): fallow land: terrain (m) en friche
Fan shape: en palmette, en éventail
Farm: ferme (f): on the farm: à la ferme; farmyard: cour (f) de ferme
Feed: engrais (m); liquid feed: purin (m) de plante (f)
Fence: clôture (f)
Fertiliser: engrais (m); chemical fertilisers: engrais minéraux or chimiques; natural or organic fertilisers: engrais organiques or biologiques
Flower: fleur (f), fleurir (v); repeat-flowering: remontant
Fly: green / black fly: puceron (m)
Force: forcer (v)
Fork: fourche (f)
Fruit (m): fruit; fruit tree: arbre fruitier, fruitier
Fungus: mildiou (m), champignon (m)

G

Garden: jardin (m), jardiner (v); garden centre: jardinerie (f)
Graft: greffer (v), greffe (f)
Grass: herbe (f); grasses: graminées
Gravel: gravier (m), gravillon (m)
Green house: serre (f)
Ground: sol (m), terre (f)
Grow: pousser, faire pousser; faire pousser des légumes: to grow vegetables; growth: pousse (f), croissance (f)
Guano: guano (m)

H

Hardy: rustique
Hedge: haie (f); dry / woven / mixed hedge: haie morte or sèche / plessée / mixte
Herb: herbe (f); kitchen herbs: herbes, herbes de cuisine, herbes aromatiques
Herbaceous (plant): (plante (f)) herbacée
Hoe: biner (v), sarcler (v); binette (f), houe (f)
Horn meal: corne (f) torréfiée

I

Improver (soil): amendement (m); mineral or stone based soil improver (typically crushed limestone, quick lime, slaked

lime) / humus-based soil improver: amendement calcique / humique

L

Land: terrain (m), terre (f)
Layer: 1) plants: marcotter (v), marcottage (m): layering; 2) hedge: plessage (m)
Lawn: pelouse (f), gazon (m)
Leaf: feuille (f); leafmould: terreau (m) de feuilles
Leguminous: légumineux (-euse)
Lime: chaux (f); lime-wash: badigeon (m) à la chaux; liming: chaulage (m)
Liner: bâche (f)
Lop: élaguer (v); lopping: élagage (f)
Lunar calendar: calendrier (m) lunaire

M

Manure: fumier; horse, cow, chicken manure: fumier de cheval, de vach, de poule; green manure: engrais vert; liquid manure: purin (m)
Marsh: marais (m)
Mildew: mildiou (m); powdery mildew: oïdium (m)
Moon: lune (f)
Mow: tondre (v), faucher (v); to mow the lawn: tondre la pelouse; (lawn) mower: tondeuse (f) (à gazon)
Mulch: pailler (v), paillage (m)

N

Neutral: neutre, basique
Nitrate: nitrate (f)
Nitrogen: azote (f)
Notch: entailler (v); entaille (f)
Nursery: pépinière (f)

O

Orchard: verger (m)
Organic: biologique; organic gardening / farming: jardinage (m) / agriculture (f) biologique

P

Palisade: palissade (f)
Paving: dallage (m); paving stone: dalle (f)
Peat: tourbe (f); peat bog: tourbière (f)
Pebble: caillou (m)
Pergola: pergola (f)
Perennial: vivace
Plant: plante (f); climbing plant, climber: plante grimpante
Plot: terrain (m)
Pollard: tailler (v) en têtard (m)
Pond: mare (f), étang (m)
Prune: tailler (v), émonder (v)
Pull out: arracher (v), arrachage (m)

R

Rake: ratisser (v), rateau (m); raking: ratissage (m)
Rambler: remontant (adj and m); rambling rose: rosier (m) remontant
Reap: faucher (v), récolter (v)
Root: racine (f); bare-rooted tree / plant: arbre (m) / plante (f) à racines nues; hair root: radicelle (f)
Rootstock: porte-greffe (m)

Runner: gourmand (m)

S

Sand: sable (m); sandy: sableux (-euse)
Scion: scion (m) (a one-year-old grafted tree)
Scrub: broussailles (f pl)
Seed: graine (f); seed supplier: grainetier (m)
Seedling: plant (m), jeune plant.
Shade: ombre (f); semi-shade: mi-ombre
Shovel: pelle (f)
Skim: écrémer (v)
Slope: pente (f)
Soil: sol (m), terre (f); soil balance: pH (m); soil structure: structure (f) du sol
Sow: semer (v); to sow broadcast / in drills: semer à la volée / en lignes
Spade: bêche (f)
Stake: tuteurer (v), tuteur (m)
Stockade fencing: palissade (f)
Stone: pierre (f); paving stone: dallage (m)
Stump: souche (f)
Sucker: drageonner (v), drageon (m), rejet (m)
Sun: soleil (m); sunny: ensoleillée
Swamp: marécage (m); swampy: marécageux (-euse)

T

Thin out: éclaircir (v)
Train: palisser (v); training: palissage (m)
Tree: arbre (m)
Trench: tranchée (f)
Trim: tailler (v), couper (v)
Trunk: tronc (m)
Tuber: racine (f)
Twig: brindille (f)

V

Vegetable: légume (m); vegetable garden: potager (m)

W

Wall: mur (m); retaining / cob wall: mur de soutènement / en terre; low wall: muret (m)
Water: arroser (v), eau (f); watering: arrosage (m); watering can: arrosoir (m)
Weave: tresser (v), plesser (v); plessis (m); woven panel: claie (f)
Weed: désherber (v); mauvaise herbe (f); weedkiller: désherbant (m)

Gardening Terms

French - English

A

Acide: acidic
Alcalin: alkaline
Algues (f pl): algae
Amendement (m): soil improver; amendement calcique / humique mineral or stone based soil improver (typically crushed limestone, quick lime, slaked lime) / humus-based soil improver
Annuelle (f)(plante): annual (plant)
Arbre (m): tree
Argile (f): clay; argileux (-euse): clay, clayish, clayey
Arracher: to pull out
Arroser: to water, watering; arrosage: watering
Arrosoir (m): watering can
Assolement (m): crop rotation
Azote (f): nitrogen

B

Bâche (f): liner
Badine (f): pleacher (the long, flexible shoots of coppiced trees that are woven through upright stems or stakes)
Basique: neutral
Bauge (f): cob; mur (m) en bauge: cob wall
Bêcher: to dig; bêche (f) spade
Biner: to hoe; binette (f): hoe
Biodiversité (f): biodiversity
Biologique: organic; jardinage (m) / agriculture (f) biologique: organic gardening / farming
Bisannuelle (f)(plante): biennial (plant)
Bordure (f): border, edge
Borner (une plante): to firm the earth around a newly bedded plant
Bouillie (f) bordelaise: Bordeaux mixture
Bourgeon (m): bud; bourgeonner (v): to bud
Bouse (f) de vache (f): cow pat
Bouturer: to take cuttings; bouturage (m): taking cuttings; bouture (m): cutting
Branche (f): branch
Brindille (f): twig
Rroussailles (f pl): scrub
Bulbe (m): bulb; plante à bulbe: bulb
Buttage (m), butter une plante (f): to mound earth over the base of a plant (for protection against the cold in winter, especially rose bushes)

C

Caduc (-uque): deciduous; arbre (m) à feuilles caduques: deciduous tree
Calcaire: chalky
Calendrier (m) lunaire: lunar calendar
Caillou (m): pebble
Cendre (f): ash
Cépée (f): copse
Champignon (m): mushroom, fungus
Chassis (m): cold-frame
Chaulage (m): liming
Chaux (f): lime; badigeon (m) à la chaux: lime-wash
Claie (f): woven panel

Clôture (f): fence
Composte (m): compost
Corne (f) torréfiée: horn meal
Couper: to cut
Cour (f): yard, courtyard; cour de ferme (f): farmyard
Couronne (f)(d'un arbre): crown, tree crown
Creuser: to dig, to excavate
Croissance (f): growth; croitre: to grow
Culture (f): culture, cultivation; cultiver: to cultivate, to grow
Curer: to dredge

D

Dalle (f): paving stone; dallage: paving
Désherber: to weed; désherbant: weed-killer
Drageon (m): sucker; drageonner: to develop through suckers or suckering

E

Eau (f): water
Éclaircir: to thin out
Écrémer: to skim
Élaguer: to lop; élagage (m): lopping
Émonder: to prune; émondage (m): pruning
Engrais (m): fertiliser, feed; engrais minéraux or chimiques: chemical fertilisers; engrais organiques ou biologiques: natural or organic fertilisers; engrais vert: green manure
Entailler: to notch; entaille (f): a notch
Espalier (m): espalier
Étang (m): pond

F

Faucarder: to chop
Faucher: to mow, to reap
Ferme (f): farm
Feuille (f): leaf; plante (f) à feuilles caduques / persistentes: deciduous / evergreen plant
Fleur (f): flower, bloom, blossom; en fleurs: in bloom; fleurir: to flower, to bloom, to blossom
Forcer: to blanch, to force
Fourche (f): fork
Friche (f): fallow land; terrain (m) en friche: fallow or derelict land.
Fruit (m): fruit.
Fruitier (m): fruit tree
Fumier (m)(de cheval, de vache, de poule): manure (horse, cow, chicken)

G

Gazon (m): lawn
Gourmand (m): runner
Graine (f): seed; grainetier (m): seed supplier
Graminée (f): grass
Gravier (m), gravillon (m): gravel
Greffer: to graft; greffe (f): graft; porte-greffe (m): rootstock
Guano (m): guano

H

Habiller les racines: to tidy and trim the roots of a bare-rooted plant for planting.
Haie (f): hedge; haie morte or sèche / plessée / mixte: dry / woven / mixed hedge

Herbacée (f): herbaceous
Herbe (f): grass; mauvaise herbe: weed; herbes de cuisine, herbes aromatiques: kitchen herbs
Houe (f): hoe
Humide: damp

J

Jardin (m): garden; jardinier (-ière): gardener
Jardinerie (f): garden centre

L

Légume (m): vegetable
Légumineuse: leguminous
Lune (f): moon; calendrier (m) lunaire: lunar calendar

M

Maladie (f): disease; maladie cryptogamique: fungal disease
Marais (m): marsh
Marcotter: to layer (a plant for propagation); marcottage (m): layering
Mare (f): pond
Marécage (m): swamp, bog; marécageux (-euse): boggy, swampy
Mildiou (m): mildew
Mur (m): wall; mur de soutènement / en terre: retaining / cob wall
Muret (m): low wall

N

Neutre: neutral
Nitrate (f): nitrate

O

Oïdium (m): powdery mildew
Ombre (f): shade, shadow; mi-ombre: semi-shade
Or (m) brun: fertiliser made of manure mixed with seaweed

P

Pailler: to mulch or top dress the soil with straw or other dry material such as dried grass cuttings, bark, or dried leaves; paillage (m): mulching
Palissade (f): stockade fencing, palisade
Palisser: to train a plant against a trellis.
Palmette (f): fan shape
Pavé (m): cobble, cobblestone
Pelle (f): shovel
Pelouse (f): lawn
Pente (f): slope
Pépinière (f): nursery
Pergola (f): pergola
pH (m): soil balance
Pierre (f): stone
Pisé (m): daub
Plant (m): seedling
Plante (f): plante; plante grimpante: climber, climbing plant
Plate-bande (f): (flower) bed
Plessage (m): hedge laying; plesse (f): woven hedge; plessis (m): weave
Potager (m): vegetable garden
Poudre (f) d'os (m): bone meal
Pousser: to grow; faire pousser: to grow (transitive: to grow vegetables: faire pousser des légumes)

Pralinage (m), praliner les racines: soaking roots in a manure slurry before planting.
Puceron (m): aphid, green or black fly
Purin (m): liquid manure; purin de plante (f): liquid feed, plant concoction

R

Rabattre: to cut back; rabattre à 2 bourgeons: cut back to two buds (from the start of the stem); rabattre court: cut back hard
Racine (f): root, tuber; arbre (m) / plante (f) à racines nues: bare-rooted tree / plant
Radicelle (f): hair root
Racourcir: to cut back; raccourcir les pousses de l'année: to cut back this year's growth
Ratisser: to rake; rateau (m): rake
Recéper: to coppice; arbre (m) recépé: a coppice
Récolte (f): crop
Rejet (m): sucker
Remontant: rambler, repeat-flowering (for flowers), double-cropper (for fruit)
Repiquer: to bed out; repiquer des plants: to bed out seedlings
Rustique: hardy

S

Sableux: sandy
Sarcler: to hoe
Scion (m): scion (one-year-old grafted tree)
Sec: dry
Semer: to sow; semer à la volée / en lignes: to sow broadcast / in drills
Serre (f): green house
Soleil (m): sun; au soleil: in the sun; ensoleillé(e): sunny
Souche (f): stump
Structure (f): structure; structure du sol: soil structure
Sol (m): soil, ground

T

Tailler: to prune, to trim, to clip; taille (f): pruning
Talus (m): raised earthbank
Terrain (m): plot, land, soil
Terrasse (f): terrace
Terre (f): earth, soil; terre de bruyère (f): ericaceous compost
Terreau (m): garden or potting compost; terreau de feuilles: leafmould
Têtard (m): tadpole; tailler en têtard: to pollard a tree
Tondre: to mow; tondeuse (f)(à gazon): (lawn) mower
Torchis (m): daub
Tourbe (f): peat; tourbière (f): peat bog
Tranchée (f): trench
Tronc (m): trunk
Tuteur (m): stake; tuteurer une plante: to stake a plant

V

Verger (m): orchard
Vivace: perennial
Volée (f): semer à la volée: to sow broadcast

Beaulieu F., "Refaire ou recréer des talus, c'est restaurer son paysage", Maison Paysannes de France, no.110.

Bertrand B., "Les secrets de l'ortie", Editions de Terran. By the same author, a series of short books on plants: "Pour l'amour d'une ronce", "La consoude, trésor du jardin", "Le coquelicot, poète des champs", "Le pissenlit, l'or du pré", etc.

Beucher P., "Le Beau jardin du paresseux", Eugen Ulmer, 2000. The author, who has created a 3,000 sq m garden with a vegetable plot and an orchard, discloses his secrets for a low maintenance, low budget garden.

Blamey M. and Grey-Wilson C., "La Flore continentale d'Europe occidentale", Paris, Arthaud, 1991.

Bresson A. et Capitani J.-P. (eds), "L'encyclopédie du potager", Editions Actes Sud, 2003.

Brunet P. (ed.), "L'Atlas des paysages ruraux de France", éditions Jean-Pierre de Monza, 1992.

Clément G., "Le Jardin planétaire", catalogue de l'exposition, Paris, Albin Michel, 2000; "Le Jardin en mouvement", Paris, Sens et Tonka, 1998; "Thomas et le voyageur", Paris, Albin Michel, 1997. Some of the most interesting discussions on gardening and the garden advocating a return to a gardening approach which is more respectful of biological cycles, without excluding creativity.

Coffe J.-P., "Le Potager plaisir", Paris, Plon, 1998. A good practical book on the vegetable garden.

Collectif, "Guide pratique des haies dans le Perche", Parc régional naturel du Perche, 2001.

Couderc R. and Vexiau C., "Créer une mare ou l'art de faire son trou", Maisons Paysannes de France, No. 132.

Couplan F., "L'Hernier des montagnes", Lausanne, Favre, 2000; "Guide des plantes sauvages comestibles et toxiques", Lausannes-Paris, Delachaux et Nieslé, 1995; "Retrouvez les légumes oubliés", Paris, La Maison Rustique/Flammarion, 1986 (nomenclature des légumes anciens).

Cruse E., "L'homme, la pierre et la rose", Maisons Paysannes de France, no. 120.

Dumont E., "Vergers à l'ancienne", Paris, La Maison Rustique/Flammarion, 2000. Advice by a specialist and passionate gardener.

Fitter R., Fitter A. and Blamey M., "Guide des fleurs sauvages", Lausanne-Paris, Delachaux et Nieslé, 1993.

Groupe de recherches historiques et archéologiques de la vallée de la Sumène, "Arbres en Haute-Auvergne, Homme et Nature", 1993; "Plantes alimentaires du jardin ethnobotanique d'Antignac (Cantal)", Centre AVENA à Antignac.

Haudebourg M.-T., "Au bonheur des jardins d'autrefois: jardins de curé, jardins de grand-mère", Paris, Hachette, 1998. Good illustrations and solid historical perspective on traditional rural gardens.

Lapeyre Q., "Les plantes anciennes de nos jardins", Maisons Paysannes de France, no. 112.

Lavogez G., "Les paysages ruraux et les abords des maisons", Maisons Paysannes de France, nos. 122-123; "Clôtures et barrières paysannes en bois", Maisons Paysannes de France, no. 128 and 130; "Clôtures et barrières rurales", Maisons Paysannes de France, nos. 129 and 131.

Lespinasse J.-M. and Leterme E. (eds), "De la taille à la conduite des arbres fruitiers", Editions du Rouergue, 2005.

Leterme E., "Les Fruits retrouvés", Rodez, Editions du Rouergue, 1998; "Le greffage et la plantation des arbres fruitiers", Rodez, Editions du Rouergue, 1998.

Lieutaghi P., "La plante compagne: Pratique et imaginaire de la flore sauvage en Europe occidentale", Arles, Actes Sud, 1998; "Jardins des savoirs, jardins d'histoire", Les Alpes de Lumière, nos. 110-111.

Pelt J.-M., "Des légumes", Paris, Fayard, 1993. A historical and sociological study.

Soltner D., "Planter des haies", 9th ed., Editions Sciences et Techniques Agricoles (Le Clos Lorelle, 49130 Saintes-Gemmes-sur-Loire, 0241 66 38 26), 1999. A reference work on hedge planting.

Terrasson F., "La peur de la nature", Editions Sang de la terre, 1997.

Thorez J.-P., "Le Guide du jardinage biologique", Terre Vivante. One of many title published by Terre Vivante, which include, among other: Baines C., "Créer un jardin sauvage"; Stickland S., "Le Compost au jardin", "Variétés d'hier, légumes d'aujourd'hui"; and the almost indispensable magazine "Les quatre saisons du jardin", full of practical tips.

Vivier M., "Jardins ruraux en Basse-Normandie", in the series "Les Carnets d'ici", CRECET, 1998. An ethno-historical study on rural gardens and gardeners, but very readable and interesting.

NURSERIES

(Check opening times before visiting nurseries as some may not be open to the public all year round or throughout the day)

Les roseraies de Berty
Traditional rose varieties grown without chemical pesticide or fertiliser. Wonderful garden with more than 500 specimens against the backdrop of the wild Roubreau valley in the Ardèche. No charge. Dogs not allowed. Closed in the summer and on Sundays. (Ardèche, south of Aubenas)
Address : 07110 Largentière
Te : 04 75 88 30 56
Fax : 04 75 88 36 93
Web : http://site.voila.fr/roseraiedeberty/accueil.html

Roses d'antan
(Sylvie and Philippe Viton)
(Côtes d'Armor, Brittany)
Hundreds of old roses and some modern varieties; some clematis too.
Address : EARL Pépinères de Kermunut, 222000 Grâces
Tel : 02 96 44 41 10 / 0681 98 31 40
Fax : 02 96 21 35 41
Web : http://rosesdantan.com
Email : contact@rosesdantan.com

Joël Rouille ('Osez l'osier')
Willow grower and weaver who also sells live willows. Seminars and training sessions on willow- weaving. (Indre-et-Loire, between Tours and Chinon)
Tel : 02 47 45 33 14
Fax : 02 47 45 91 74
Web : http://www.joel-rouille-osier.com/
Email : jrouille@club-internet.fr

Aquatique de la Moine
All sorts of pond plants (marginal, floating, oxygenating, etc.) (Loire Atlantique)
Address : La Sutellerie, 44190 Gétigne
Tel/fax : 02 40 547465

Christophe Delay
Traditional fruit trees (Isère, near Villard-de-Lans)
Address : Les Combes, 38780 Estrablin
Tel : 0474 57 14 42

Eric Dumont
Traditional fruit trees and old varieties. Growing fruit trees has been in the family for 13 generations. (Aube, south of Troyes)
Address : 42 avenue des martyrs de la Résistance, 10800 Buchères
Tel : 03 25 41 84 87
Fax : 03 25 41 96 59
Web : http://perso.wanadoo.fr/pepinieresdumont/
Email : ERDUMONT@wanadoo.fr

Jardins de la Brande (Philippe Burey)
A gardener specialising in old varieties of shrubs (and with a secret passion for treehouses)
(Dordogne, between Bergerac and Périgueux)
Address : La Brande, 24380 Fouleix
Tel : 05 53 07 47 85

Jardin concept (Jean-Bernard Daniel)
Something for southern gardens: olive trees, figs, grape vine and other Mediterranean plants (Gard, Uzès)
Address : 1 rue du Serre Bonnet, 30703 Uzès Cedex
Tel/fax : 04 66 03 16 62

Pépinière Le jardin de campagne
Old and rare roses, and perennials. Good garden around a 17th c. farmhouse, open on Saturdays (Near Pontoise, 30 km from Paris)
Address : 13 rue de Butel, 95810 Grisy les Plâtres
Tel : 01 34 66 62 87
Web : http://www.jardindecampagne.com/
Email : jardindecampagne@wanadoo.fr

Jardivigne
A nursery specialising in old and new varieties of vine since 1927. Online ordering facility. (Lot, between Villeneuve-sur-Lot and Agen)
Address: 47110 Sainte Livrade sur Lot
Tel : 05 53 01 30 80
Fax : 05 53 01 25 05
Web : http://www.jardivigne.com/
Email : contact@jardivigne.com

Pépinières Brochet-Lanvin
Perennials, grasses, shrubs, old roses. The garden (open all year round) also has a collection of willows, elders, honeysuckle. (Marne, between Reims and Epernay)
Address : Lieu-dit "La Presle", Route de Reims, 51480 Matigny la Forêt
Tel : 03 26 59 43 39
Fax : 03 26 59 42 20
Email : jbpresle-brochetlanvin@club-internet.fr
Web : http://jbpresle-brochetlanvin.club.fr/nouveau_fichier1.html

Plantagenêt Plantes
Perennials and rustic plants, in particular a good selection of plants for dry and chalky soil, and for shaded or damp ground. (Maine-et-Loire, between Angers and Saumur)
Address : Argentay, 7 rue des figuiers, 49700 Les Verchers sur Layon
Tel : 0241 3814 62
Fax : 02 41 38 59 49

Pépinière des Farguettes
Roses and clematis (Dordogne, 8 km south-east of Bergerac)
Address : Les Farguettes, 24520 Saint Nexans
Tel : 05 53 24 37 54,
Fax : 05 53 24 37 54

Pépinière Jouve-Racamond
Large stock of traditional fruit trees (old stock) and ornamental plants. (Bouches-du-Rhône, between Avignon and Cavaillon)
Address : RN7, 13670 Saint Andiol

Tel : 04 90 95 00 07
Fax : 04 90 95 11 43

SEED SUPPLIERS

Graines Baumaux
A seed producer offering a good selection of organic seeds. Online catalogue and ordering facility (Meurthe-et-Moselle, Nancy).
Address : BP 100, 54062 Nancy Cedex
Web : http://www.graines-baumaux.fr/
Email : contact@graines-baumaux.fr

Fabres Graines
Established in 1860 in Metz (but the seeds are produced in the seed production facility near Angers established in 1839), offers a good selection of old vegetables. Online ordering facility (Moselle, Metz)
Address : 21 rue des Drapiers, 57083 Metz Cedex 3
Tel : 03 87 74 07 65
Web : http://www.fabre-graines.com
Email : fabre.graines@wanadoo.fr

Le Potager d'un Curieux
Small organic seed producer offering old varieties of vegetables, flowers and medicinal plants.
Address : La Molière, 84400 Saignon (Vaucluse, near Apt)
Tel : 04 90 74 44 68
Web : http://lepotager.com
Email : lepotager@wanadoo.fr

Graines Grelin
300 vegetable seed varieties and 260 flower seeds including many rare ones.
Address : 95, Impasse du Manoir, 73800 Arbin (Savoie, near Montmélian)
Tel : 04 79 84 14 53

Association Ponema – see 'Associations'

Le Jardin du Naturaliste (Olivier Tranchard)
A catalogue of 650 varieties specialising in native plants.
Address : 36bis rue Dufour-Lebrun, 60590 Talmontiers (Oise, between Gournay and Gisors).
Tel : 03 44 84 92 96

Phytosem
A seed producer specialising in traditional vegetable varieties and wild flowers and plants, using organic processes in the South of France (Hautes Alpes and Mediterranean region).
Address : Z.I. La Plaine de Lachaup, Châteauvieux, 05000 Gap (Hautes Alpes, just south of Gap)
Tél : 04 92 53 94 37
Fax : 04 92 53 33 93
Web : http://www.phytosem.com
E-mail : info@phytosem.com

La Ferme de Sainte Marthe
Old varieties of vegetables, flowers, and trees; green manures and other organic products.

Address : BP 10, 41700 Cour Cheverny
(Loir-et-Cher,south of Blois)
Tel : 02 54 44 20 03
(catalogue orders: 0820 203 868)
Web : http://www.fermedesaintemarthe.com

G.I.E. Le biau germe
A group of organic seed producers offering a
range of traditional varieties and promoting
biodiversity.
Address : 47360 Montpezat (Lot-et-Garonne, 15
km north of Agen)
Tél : 05 53 95 95 04
Fax : 05 53 95 96 08
Web : http://www.biaugerme.com/index.html
Email : service@biaugerme.com

Association Kokopelli
An association promoting sustainable
development and working for the preservation
of old varieties.
Address : 131 Impasse des Palmiers, 30100 Alès
(Gard, Alès)
Tel : 04 66 30 64 91 ou 04 66 30 00 55
Fax : 04 66 30 61 21
Web : http://www.kokopelli.asso.fr/
Email : kokopelli.semences@wanadoo.fr

Germinance
Old and rare varieties grown organically.
Address : Les Rétifs, 49150 Saint Martin d'Acé
(Maine-et-Loire, just north of Baugé)
Tel : 02 41 82 73 23
Fax : 02 41 82 86 48

Le jardin de Sauveterre
Wild flower seeds and seedlings for all
conditions, bare-rooted plants. Garden open to
visitors by prior appointment between 1 June
and 15 August.
Address : Jacques et Collette Girardeau,
Laboutant, 23320 Moutier-Malcard (Creuse,
between Guéret and La Châtre)
Tel : 05 55 80 60 24
Web : http://www.chez.com/sauveterre/
Email : Jacques.GIRARDEAU@wanadoo.fr

Les Semailles
Seeds and plants for the vegetable garden; green
manures; herbs; other organic products. Online
ordering facility.
Address : 20 rue du Sabotier, 5340
Faulx-les-Tomdes, Belgium (south-east of Namur)
Tel : 081 75 02 97
Web : http://semaille.com
Email : semaille@semaille.com

ORGANIC FERTILISERS AND REMEDIES

Hector SARL Produits Naturels
Organic soil improvers, bentonite, fungicides,
pest control, gardening tools.
Address : 22a rue Claire-Oster, 57200
Sarreguemines
(Moselle, Sarreguemines, by the German border)

Tel : 03 87 95 33 20

Victor le Jardinier
Manure, compost, green manure, liquid feed,
roténone, anti-insect wraps, pheromone traps,
Bordeaux mixture, bird houses, useful
nematodes, etc.
Address : Protertyl, BP 204, 14209 Hérouville-
Saint-Clair (Calvados, just north of Caen)
Tel : 02 31 47 15 90
Web : http://www.jardinage-bio.com
Email : contact@jardinage-bio.com

Jardiniers de France – see "Associations"

Biopin
Ecological varnishes and coatings for wood,
based on natural products (natural oils, bee's
wax, etc.). Distributed by Domus, a manufacturer
and distributor of eco-friendly products.
Address : Domus Matériaux Ecologiques, 1 rue
Dewoitine 31700 Cornebarrieu (Houte Garonne)
Tel : 05 61 85 43 06
Fax : 05 61 85 48 93
Email : info@domus-materiaux.fr
Web : http://www.domus-construction.fr

ASSOCIATIONS

Connaître et Protéger la Nature (CPN)
For adults and children interested in learning
more on wildlife, fauna and flora. Contact the
main office or log onto their website to find your
nearest 'club'.
Address : Fédération des CPN, Maison des CPN,
80240 Boult-au-Bois
Tel : 03 24 30 21 90
Web : http://www.fcpn.org

Croqueurs de Pommes
An association (accredited by law as an organisation for the protection of the environment) that
will be of interest to those wanting to learn about
and plant old apple varieties. Contact the main
office for your local branch or log onto their
website (full of tips on caring for apple trees).
Address (Paris section) : 24 rue Emile Zola, 9500
Eaubonne (just north of Paris)
Tel : 01 39 59 14 28
Web : www.croqueurs-de-pommes.asso.fr

La Garance Voyageuse
An association and a magazine on plants and
trees, in particular wild plants.
Address : 48370 Saint Germain-de-Calberte
(Lozère, nearest large town is Alès, 35 km
south-east)
Tel : 04 66 45 94 10
Fax : 04 66 45 91 84
Web : http://www.garancevoyageuse.org/
Email : garance@wanadoo.fr

Intelligence Verte (La Ferme de Sainte Marthe)
An association created by a group of
environmentally-minded French personalities

(including Michel Lis, a well known gardener
and author). The association produces old
varieties of seeds and plants, and promotes ecological principles through seminars and training
days for amateur gardeners and professional
growers. Order the catalogue by phone (0820 2
03 868) or by email (info@intelligenceverte.org)
Address : 41200 Millancay (Loir-et-Cher,
between Blois and Vierzon)
Tel : 02 54 95 45 04
Fax : 02 54 95 45 01
Web : http://www.intelligenceverte.org
Email : info@IntelligenceVerte.org

Jardiniers de France
An association created in Valenciennes in 1876
and one of the largest gardeners' associations in
France, which is recognised by the Agriculture
Minister, Home Office and Ministry of Culture as
'd'utilité publique'. They sell a selection of
organic seeds and materials (online ordering
facility) and they have a magazine. There are
local associations throughout France so there is
probably one near you.
Address : 40, route d'Aulnoy - BP 559, 59308
Valenciennes, Cedex
Tel : 03 27 46 37 50 or 0826 020 313 (0,15 euro
/ min.)
Fax : 03 27 29 08 12
Web : http://www.jardiniersdefrance.com
E-mail : contacts@jardiniersdefrance.com

Association des Murs à Pêches de Montreuil
An association created in 1994 to protect the
traditional the old walled peach orchards in
Montreuil.
Address : 15 rue du Général Gallieni, 93100
Montreuil-sous-Bois (just outside Paris)
Tel : 01 48 70 23 80
Web : www.mursapeches.org
Email : infos@mursapeches.org

Ponema
A volunteer association promoting wild and
natural gardens. Members can use the 'seed
exchange bank' of old varieties of wild plants.
Address : Annepont, 17350 Saint-Savinien
Web : www.ponema.org

Renova
An association of nurseries, fruit growers and
canners in the Ariège and Haute-Garonne working for the protection and promotion of orchards
and old fruit tree varieties. Seminars and workshops on growing fruit trees, regeneration of old
orchards, mobile press to produce apple juice
and cider.
Address : 12 place du Champs-de-Mars, 09350
Daumazan
Tel/fax : 05 61 60 27 71

Société Nationale d'Horticulture de France
The equivalent of the Royal Horticultural Society,
it has an extensive library with a large selection of
old gardening manuals, and a magazine, 'Jardins

de France'.
Address : 84 rue de Grenelle, 75007 Paris
Tel : 01 44 39 78 78
Fax : 01 45 44 96 57
Web : www.snhf.org

Savoirs de Terroirs
Workshops on traditional crafts, including gardening skills and plants. Resource centre and magazine. Active mostly in the Ardèche area.
Address : Le Miolaure, 07200 Saint-Julien-du-Serre
Tel/fax : 04 75 35 88 50
Web : http://savoirsdeterroirs.free.fr/
Email : http://savoirsdeterroirs.free.fr/

Terre Vivante
An organisation that has been promoting eco-friendly gardening, and eco-friendly living, for over 20 years. Workshops, resource centre and magazine. Every May, a seeds and plants fair.
Address : Domaine de Raud, 38710 Mens
Te l : 04 76 34 80 80
Fax : 04 76 34 84 02
Web : http://www.terrevivante.org
Email : infos@terrevivante.org

GARDENS OPEN TO THE PUBLIC

Les Conservatoires et les jardins botaniques
Their purpose is to promote the conservation, study, and understanding of botanical species through educational projects. To find out about 'conservatoires' and 'jardins' in your area, contact:
- Association des jardins botaniques de France et des pays francophones:
Address : 7 rue Victor-Considérant, 25000 Besançon.
Tel/fax : 03 81 88 16 65
Web : http://perso.club-internet.fr/jbfpf
- Fédération des conservatoires botaniques nationaux (9 in metropolitan France):
Address : 9 allée du Bot, 29200 Brest
Tel: 02 98 41 88 95

Oh Légumes Oubliés
A farm growing and selling old or rare varieties of plants and vegetables and a selection of seeds. Guided tours.
Address : Château de Belloc, 33670 Sadirac (Gironde, south-east of Bordeaux)
Tel : 05 56 30 61 00 / 62 00
Fax : 05 56 30 60 30
Web : http://www.ohlegumesoublies.com/
Email : contact@ohlegumesoublies.com

Potager et verger conservatoire du musée du Revermont
Old and local vegetables, medicinal plants, old apples and pears, and roses. "Discovery" tour of landscaped garden. Open between 1 April and 1 November. Guided group tour on request.
Address : Cuisat, 01370 Treffort (Ain)
Tel : 04 74 51 32 42

Fax : 04 74 51 30 93
Email : musees.paysdelain@cg01.fr

Ecomusée d'Alsace
Model heritage village with traditional gardens and crafts.
Address : 68190 Ungersheim
Tel : 03 89 74 44 74
Fax : 03 89 74 44 65
Web : www.ecomusee-alsace.com

Les jardins du prieuré de Notre-Dame d'Orsan
Gardens in the medieval tradition with interesting examples of plessage amidst 16th and 17th century buildings. Workshops on hedge weaving, hedges and roses. Open 30 March – 1 November.
Address : lieu-dit Orsan, 18170 Maisonnais (Cher, south-west of Bourges)
Tel : 02 48 56 27 50
Fax : 02 48 56 39 64
Web : www.prieuredorsan.com

Le jardin textile de Bassignac
A theme garden on plants used for weaving textiles and as dyes (over 150 plants). Weaving workshops. Open 15 June – 15 September.
Address : Parensol, 15240 Brassignac
Tel/fax : 04 71 67 32 50
Web : http://www.tissage-jardin.ht.st/

Jardin ethnobotanique d'Antignac
Small but very pleasant garden in the Sumène valley in the Cantal with old wild and cultivated varieties from the region. Folk museum attached. Guided tours.
Address : 15240 Antignac
Tel : 04 71 40 23 76

Jardin ethnobotanique d'Arvières
A garden about man's relationship with plants from the Neolithic to the discovery of the Americas. Aromatic, sacred, medicinal and other plants, in the stunning surroundings of an old chartreuse (charterhouse). Guided tours (15 May – 15 October) and gardening days.
Address: Association Les Amis du jardin d'Arvières, La Fruitière, 01260 Virieux-le-Petit
Tel/fax : 04 79 87 02 06
Web : http://membres.lycos.fr/arvieres
Email : jardin-darvieres@wanadoo.fr

Jardins ethnobotaniques de la Gardie
Eight separate gardens in one site, including a conservation orchard, Mediterranean rock garden, beekeeping garden, medieval vegetable garden, old cereals and cornfield flowers, and an old mining site with plants able to grow on heavy metals and slag heaps. Open april-September. Guided tours on request.
Address : Arc'Avène, 30340 Rousson (Gard)
Tel/fax : 04 66 85 66 90
Email : jardins.ethno@wanadoo.fr

Salagon – jardins ethnobotaniques du musée conservatoire de Haute-Provence

Several gardens: medieval, fragrant, modern, exotic, and a willow grove, on the grounds of a Romanesque church and medieval priory. Open 1 May – 30 September, weekends and school holidays. Closed January. Guided tours, workshops, ethnobotany seminars.
Address : Prieuré de Salagon, 04300 Mane
Tel : 04 92 75 70 50
Fax : 04 92 75 70 58
Email : musee.salagon@wanadoo.fr

Jardin du musée des pays de Seine-et-Marne
Old varieties of willow and wild plants. Preservation of rural and folk traditions.
Address : 77750 Saint-Cyr-sur-Morin (Seine-et-Marne, south of la Ferté-sous-Jouarre)
Tel : 01 60 24 46 00

La prairie Saint-Gildas
An area of natural wetlands on the banks of the river Indre in Châteauroux. Guided tours.
Address : 36000 Châteauroux
Tel : 02 54 08 33 05
Fax : 02 54 07 03 11
Web : www.ville-chateauroux.fr
Email : espaces-verts@ville-chateauroux.fr

Les Jardins du Marais
A private 2.5 acre organic garden with an ornamental garden, a vegetable plot and an 'experimental' garden, all with no chemicals, no watering, no digging or other mechanical assistance.
Address : Yves Gillen and Annick Bertrand, Herbignac, 44410 Hoscas (Loire Atlantique, north of La Baule)
Tel : 02 40 91 47 44

Les Jardins de l'Albarède
A beautiful private garden combining old buildings, flowers and smells. Wild flowers and old roses, orchard with local apple varieties and topiary. Open morning 15 June – 15 September. Guided tours by prior appointment.
Address : 24250 Saint Cybranet
Tel:fax : 05 53 28 38 91
Email: lalbarede@editionsuniverselles.net

La Roseraie de Berty - see Nurseries

Le jardin de Sauveterre – see Seed Suppliers

PLANT FESTIVALS AND FAIRS

The list below is a selection of the most important gardening events in France. There are also numerous regional events which local gardeners and nurseries will know about.

Festival des jardins de Chaumont-sur-Loire
This is the official conservation institute for parks, gardens and French landscapes (Conservatoire national des parcs et jardin et du paysage). The festival takes place every year between April and

October.
Address : Ferme du Château, 41150 Chaumont-sur-Loire (Loir-et-Cher, half-way between Blois and Amboise)
Tel : 02 54 20 99 22
Fax : 02 54 20 99 24
Web : http://www.chaumont-jardin.com/
Email : cipjp.chaumont@wanadoo.fr

Les journées des plantes de Courson
The vast grounds of the chateau are open to the public all year round and a plant festival is held twice a year in the spring (May) and in the autumn (October). The chateau is open 15 March – 15 November.
Address : Domaine de Courson, 91680 Courson Monteloup (Essonne, south of Versailles)
Tel : 01 64 58 90 12
Fax : 01 64 58 97 00
Web : http://www.coursondom.com/
Email : courson@coursondom.com

Domaine de Saint-Jean de Beauregard
Fête des plantes vivaces in April and fête des fruits et légumes d'hier et d'aujourd'hui (November) are two well-known events in the gardener's calendar. Gardens, including a superb 17th c. vegetable garden, open to the public 15 March – 15 November.
Address : 91940 Saint-Jean de Beauregard (Essonne, 30 km south-west of Paris)
Tel : 01 60 12 00 01
Fax : 01 60 12 56 31
Web : www.domsaintjeanbeauregard.com
Email : info@ domsaintjeanbeauregard.com

Château de Villandry
A wonderful late renaissance garden mixing flowers and vegetables. "Journées du potager" held throughout September, with workshops and discussion groups run by the chateau's gardeners. Gardens open all year round.
Address : 37510 Villandry (Indre-et-Loire, 15 km west of Tours)
Tel : 02 47 50 02 09
Fax : 02 47 50 12 85
Web : http://www.chateauvillandry.com
Email : info@chateauvillandry.com

Foire aux potirons et aux légumes rares
The annual meeting of all cucurbitae lovers with hundreds of varieties of marrows, pumpkins, etc. and cabbages (mid-October)
Address : Club des Jardins d'Antan, 36230 Tranzault (Indre, between Chateauroux and La Châtre)
Tel : 02.54.30.81.80

Les journées des pommes et des fruits de pays
An event organised by the Société pomologique du Berry taking place the first Sunday in October. The Société is an association promoting traditional varieties of apple and fruit trees, with several orchards (conservation orchard, educational orchard, etc.) and workshops

(including making apple juice).
Address : Mairie, 36230 Neuvy-Saint-Sépulchre (Indre, between Chateauroux and Guéret)
Tél : 02 54 30 94 35
Web : http://perso.wanadoo.fr/societe.pomologique.berry/
Email : societe.pomologique.berry@wanadoo.fr

La foire aux plants bios au centre Terre Vivante – see Associations.

GARDEN EQUIPMENT AND FURNITURE

Etablissements Leneindre
Woven timber fences, trellis, numerous styles of palisades in chestnut wood, etc.
Address : 31 rue de Petit-Vaux, 91360 Epinay-sur-Orge
Tel : 01 69 09 20 24
Fax : 01 69 34 78 23
Web : http://www.clotures-leneindre.com
Email : contact@clotures-leneindre.com

Gartool
Compost bins in recycled material and shredders.
Address : Gartool SA, 431 avenbue Blaise Pascal, 77555 Moissy Craymayel
Tel : 01 64 13 33 33
Fax : 01 64 88 07 55

Les Grès de l'Ile de France – Cossutta SA
Paving, borders, carved stones.
Address : 16 rue du Moulin, 02810 Gandelu
Tel : 03 23 71 42 20
Fax : 02 23 71 44 79

Olivier Grelin
Inventor of the "grelinette", a two-handle fork for easy digging.
See Seed Suppliers, Graines Grelin.

WATER TREATMENT AND 'LAGUNAGE'

Philippe Rousille
Piscines naturelles, water gardens.
Address : 23 rude des Palombes, 31270 Villeneuve-Tolosane (Haute-Garonne)
Tel : 05 62 87 23 55

Atelier Reeb
Water features, fountains, drainage, lagunage.
Address : 13 quai des Bateliers, 67000 Strasbourg (Alsace)
Tel : 03 88 36 07 54

Eau Vivante
Lagunage for private individuals.
Address : 32220 Saint-Lizier-du-Plante (Gers)
Tel : 05 62 62 05 52

Calips'Eau
Water purification using reeds.

Address : 6 rue des Fusains, 38200 Villette d'Anthon (Isère)
Tel : 04 72 88 08 04
Fax : 04 78 55 68 96

Neutra SARL
Water cisterns for the recycling of rain water
Address : 50 Grand'Rue, 67110 Grundershoffen (Alsace)
Tel : 03 88 72 99 27
Fax : 03 88 72 99 36

Celloplast
A range of biological products for the treatment of garden ponds and lakes containing micro-organisms which eliminate toxic substances.
Address : 13 route des Préaux, BP 26, 53340 Ballee
Tel : 02 43 64 14 14
Fax : 02 43 98 49 97

Société française des bentonites et dérivés
Construction and insulation material for ponds.
Address : Quai Sud, 76470 Le Tréport
Tel : 02 35 50 57 70
Fax : 02 35 50 14 13

TRAINING, INFORMATION AND FUNDING

Conseils d'Aménagement, d'Architecture et d'Urbanisme (CAUE)
With branches in most départements these centres provide information and training on traditional building and gardening techniques. Contact your local authority for details of your nearest branch.

Centre Pilote Européen d'Agriculture Biologique
Start-up training for those interested in going into organic farming provided by Ferme de Saint Marthe (see Seed Suppliers).

Savoirs de Terroirs – see Associations.

Ecole de Breuil
Classes and diplomas in horticulture and courses for amateur gardeners.
Address : Bois de Vincennes, Route de la Ferme, 75012 Paris.
Tel : 01 43 28 28 94
Fax : 01 43 65 34 59

National and Regional Parks
Many national and regional parks have conservation programmes in place, some of which include financial support to farmers and private individuals for the planting and maintenance of trees and hedges and the conservation of natural habitats. Get in touch with your mairie or regional authority.

Index

Websites, books and magazines from the publishers of *How to create a* JARDIN PAYSAN

ALSO IN THIS SERIES:
HOW TO RENOVATE A HOUSE IN FRANCE (ISBN 0-9544669-5-0)
The essential guide to creating your dream home in France

Whether you are buying an old house, worrying about damp stone walls, struggling to understand lime render, shopping for partition walls, hunting for builders, trying to get planning permission, or are in any way involved with a renovation project in France: this book is for you.

Aimed at anyone renovating or thinking of renovating property in France, 'How to Renovate a House in France' is packed with ideas, inspiration and know-how. Whether you intend to do most of the work yourself or hand the job over to a builder, this book will show you what it entails and how to achieve it: from the initial project planning through to choosing the right materials and completing the project.

With a mix of great photography designed to inspire you, illustrated 'how to' tables and a detailed 'Basics' section packed full of useful information, this book will take the worry out of renovating in France and put the enjoyment back in.

TWO GREAT WEBSITES FOR ANYONE BUYING & RENOVATING IN FRANCE!

www.PropertyFinderFrance.net

PropertyFinderFrance is designed for anyone thinking of buying a place in France. Working with more than 100 estate agents across all the most popular and beautiful regions of France, the site has well over 2,000 properties (including building plots) for sale on its listings, all of which are selected with UK or international buyers in mind. Prices start from as little as €20,000, making this the ideal place to start your search for that dream home in France. With so many properties on offer, you can manage your own selections with a favourites file, which you can return to each time you come back to the site. PropertyFinderFrance gives you direct links to the estate agents, making your house-hunting as effective as possible.

www.RenovationFrance.net

A sister-site to PropertyFinderFrance, RenovationFrance is an online magazine for people renovating properties in France, and is the ideal place to share experiences and information. The 'Project Diaries' section gives you a chance to post pictures and updates about your own project on the site, while there is a growing collection of features on completed home renovations too. The site also has a range of advice and information on many different aspects of renovating in France, as well as a directory of products and services, including English-speaking builders, and a lively discussion forum.

WE ALSO HAVE A RANGE OF TITLES FOR THOSE PLANNING RENOVATION AND SELF-BUILD PROJECTS IN BRITAIN:

Homebuilding & Renovating magazine
Britain's best selling self-build and home renovation magazine is a must for anyone planning, just starting or in the middle of a self-build, renovation or conversion. Full of inspirational readers' homes, houseplan ideas, practical guides, expert advice and a complete Beginner's Guide section.

www.homebuilding.co.uk
Access vast amounts of self-build and home renovation information, including a huge directory of supplier contacts and hundreds of case history examples complete with pictures and costings. If you're new to self-build, start by taking a look at our Beginners Guide section.

www.plotfinder.net

Find your perfect plot of land with www.plotfinder.net. This site is a database which holds details on over 5,000 building plots and properties for renovation currently for sale in the UK.

The Homebuilder's Handbook (ISBN 0-9544669 6-9)

Featuring thousands of contact details, this is the ultimate sourcebook for anyone planning to renovate, convert, or build their own home. It contains great solutions to make your build happen faster and cheaper, and essential leads to choosing and buying materials.

Homebuilding & Renovating Shows
Whatever stage you are at in creating your perfect home, from planning to building, converting, extending or renovating; the Homebuilding and Renovating Show can provide you with the inspiration, solutions, products and services you need to help you achieve your dream.

Book of Great Value Self-Build Homes (ISBN 0-9544669-0-X)

A collection of 24 inspiring high quality, low budget self-built homes from £32,000 up to £150,000. They all show how it is possible for you to achieve a spacious family home in any style on a budget. How to maximise usable floorspace, and at the same time create a unique family home.

Book of Contemporary Homes (ISBN 0-9544669-2-6)

Nineteen unique contemporary style homes in full colour. An invaluable source of inspiration for anyone planning to build. Remarkable projects built from £60,000 to over £1m. If you dream of designing and building a contemporary style home, this book is for you.

Barn Conversions
A collection of 22 inspiring conversions. from low budget DIY projects to majestic and awar-winning rural gems. In this book, you will discover ingenious ways to create practical living spaces without losing the excitment and charm of the original structure, and follow the stories of people who have achieved this with success and style.

TO ORDER ANY OF OUR BOOKS, CALL US ON: 01527 834435